The Quran With Tafsir Ibn Kathir
Part 16 of 30: Al Kahf 075 To Ta Ha 135

The Quran With Tafsir Ibn Kathir
Part 16 of 30:
Al Kahf 075 To
Ta Ha 135

With
Arabic Script, Transliteration of Arabic, Meaning in English
and Ibn Kathir's Abridged Tafsir (Explanation)

Muhammad Saed Abdul-Rahman
BSc, DipHE

© Muhammad Saed Abdul-Rahman,2012
ISBN 978-1-86179-873-2

All Rights reserved

British Library Cataloguing in Publication Data. A Catalogue record for this book is available from the British Library

Designed, Typeset and produced by:
MSA Publication Limited, 4 Bello Close, Herne Hill,
London SE24 9BW
United Kingdom

Cover design: Houriyah Abdul-Rahman

TABLE OF CONTENTS

TABLE OF CONTENTS V

PRELUDE XIII

    OPENING SERMAN XIII
    OUR MISSION XIV
    BIOGRAPHY OF HAFIZ IBN KATHIR (701 H - 774 H) XIV
        Ibn Kathir's Teachers xiv
        Ibn Kathir's Students xv
        Ibn Kathir's Books xv
        Ibn Kathir's Death xvi

PREFACE XVII

    ABOUT THIS BOOK XVII
    PERFORMING PROSTRATION WHILE READING THE QUR'AN XVII

PART 16 FULL ARABIC TEXT 1

INTRODUCTION TO CHAPTER (SURAH) 18: AL-KAHF (THE CAVE) 12

    IBN KATHIR'S INTRODUCTION 12
        What has been mentioned about the Virtues of this Surah and the first and last ten Ayat, which provide protection from the Dajjal 12

CHAPTER (SURAH) 18: AL-KAHF (THE CAVE), VERSES 075 – 110 14

    Surah: 18 Ayah: 74 (end of Part 15, included here for completing the tafsir that follows), Ayah: 75 (beginning of Part 16) & Ayah: 76 14
        Tafsir Ibn Kathir 14
        The Story of killing the Boy 14
    Surah: 18 Ayah: 77 & Ayah: 78 15
        Tafsir Ibn Kathir 16
        The Story of repairing the Wall Allah tells us that 16
    Surah: 18 Ayah: 79 16
        Tafsir Ibn Kathir 17
        Interpretations of why the Ship was damaged 17
    Surah: 18 Ayah: 80 & Ayah: 81 17
        Tafsir Ibn Kathir 17
        Interpretation of why the Boy was killed 17
    Surah: 18 Ayah: 82 18
        Tafsir Ibn Kathir 18
        Interpretation of why the Wall was repaired for no Charge 18
        Was Al-Khidr a Prophet 19
        Why he was called Al-Khidr 19
    Surah: 18 Ayah: 83 & Ayah: 84 20
        Tafsir Ibn Kathir 21

The Story of Dhul-Qarnayn Allah says to His Prophet , ... 21
Surah: 18 Ayah: 85, Ayah: 86, Ayah: 87 & Ayah: 88.. 21
    Tafsir Ibn Kathir 22
        His traveling and reaching the Place where the Sun sets (the West) 22
Surah: 18 Ayah: 89, Ayah: 90 & Ayah: 91... 23
    Tafsir Ibn Kathir 24
        His Journey East.. 24
Surah: 18 Ayah: 92, Ayah: 93, Ayah: 94, Ayah: 95 & Ayah: 96.. 24
    Tafsir Ibn Kathir 25
        His Journey to the Land of Ya'juj and Ma'juj, and building the Barrier............................ 25
Surah: 18 Ayah: 97, Ayah: 98 & Ayah: 99... 27
    Tafsir Ibn Kathir 27
        The Barrier restrains Them, but It will be breached when the Hour draws nigh.............. 27
Surah: 18 Ayah: 100, Ayah: 101 & Ayah: 102 29
    Tafsir Ibn Kathir 30
        Hell will be displayed before the Disbelievers on the Day of Resurrection 30
Surah: 18 Ayah: 103, Ayah: 104, Ayah: 105 & Ayah: 106 30
    Tafsir Ibn Kathir 31
        The Greatest Losers in respect of (Their) Deeds.. 31
Surah: 18 Ayah: 107 & Ayah: 108.. 33
    Tafsir Ibn Kathir 33
        The Reward of the Righteous Believers... 33
Surah: 18 Ayah: 109.. 34
    Tafsir Ibn Kathir 34
        The Words of the Lord can never be finished 34
Surah: 18 Ayah: 110.. 35
    Tafsir Ibn Kathir 35
        Muhammad is a Human Being and a Messenger, and the God is One............................ 35

INTRODUCTION TO CHAPTER (SURAH) 19: MARYAM (MARY).. **36**
    IBN KATHIR'S INTRODUCTION 36

CHAPTER (SURAH) 19: MARYAM (MARY), VERSES 001 – 098 .... **36**
Surah: 19 Ayah: 1, Ayah: 2, Ayah: 3, Ayah: 4, Ayah: 5 & Ayah: 6..................................... 36
    Tafsir Ibn Kathir 37
        The Story of Zakariyya and His Supplication for a Son The discussion about the separate
        letters has already preceded at the beginning of Surat Al-Baqarah................................. 37
Surah: 19 Ayah: 7 39
    Tafsir Ibn Kathir 40
        The acceptance of His Supplication 40
Surah: 19 Ayah: 8 & Ayah: 9... 40
    Tafsir Ibn Kathir 41
        His amazement after the acceptance of His Supplication 41
Surah: 19 Ayah: 10 & Ayah: 11... 41

Table of Contents

Tafsir Ibn Kathir 42
 The Sign of the Pregnancy 42
Surah: 19 Ayah: 12, Ayah: 13, Ayah: 14 & Ayah: 15 43
 Tafsir Ibn Kathir 43
 The Birth of the Boy and His Characteristics 43
Surah: 19 Ayah: 16, Ayah: 17, Ayah: 18, Ayah: 19, Ayah: 20 & Ayah: 21 45
 Tafsir Ibn Kathir 46
 The Story of Maryam and Al-Masih (`Isa) 46
Surah: 19 Ayah: 22 & Ayah: 23 48
 Tafsir Ibn Kathir 48
 The Conception and the Birth 48
Surah: 19 Ayah: 24, Ayah: 25 & Ayah: 26 49
 Tafsir Ibn Kathir 50
 What was said to Her after the Birth Some reciters read the Ayah as, (Who was below her) 50
Surah: 19 Ayah: 27, Ayah: 28, Ayah: 29, Ayah: 30, Ayah: 31, Ayah: 32 & Ayah: 33 51
 Tafsir Ibn Kathir 52
 Maryam with Al-Masih before the People, Their Rejection of Her and His Reply to Them 52
Surah: 19 Ayah: 34, Ayah: 35, Ayah: 36 & Ayah: 37 55
 Tafsir Ibn Kathir 56
 `Isa is the Servant of Allah and not His Son 56
 `Isa commanded the Worship of Allah Alone, then the People differed after Him 56
Surah: 19 Ayah: 38, Ayah: 39 & Ayah: 40 58
 Tafsir Ibn Kathir 59
 The Disbeliever's warning of the Day of Distress 59
Surah: 19 Ayah: 41, Ayah: 42, Ayah: 43, Ayah: 44 & Ayah: 45 61
 Tafsir Ibn Kathir 61
 Ibrahim's Admonition of His Father 61
Surah: 19 Ayah: 46, Ayah: 47 & Ayah: 48 62
 Tafsir Ibn Kathir 63
 The Reply of Ibrahim's Father 63
 The Reply of Allah's Friend (Khalil) 63
Surah: 19 Ayah: 49 & Ayah: 50 65
 Tafsir Ibn Kathir 65
 Allah gave Ibrahim Ishaq and Ya`qub 65
Surah: 19 Ayah: 51, Ayah: 52 & Ayah: 53 66
 Tafsir Ibn Kathir 67
 Mentioning Musa and Harun 67
Surah: 19 Ayah: 54 & Ayah: 55 68
 Tafsir Ibn Kathir 68
 Mentioning Isma`il 68
Surah: 19 Ayah: 56 & Ayah: 57 70
 Tafsir Ibn Kathir 70

Mentioning Idris 70
Surah: 19 Ayah: 58 71
   Tafsir Ibn Kathir 71
      These Prophets are the Chosen Ones 71
Surah: 19 Ayah: 59 & Ayah: 60 72
   Tafsir Ibn Kathir 73
      They were succeeded by Wicked People and Good People 73
Surah: 19 Ayah: 61 & Ayah: 62 & Ayah: 63 74
   Tafsir Ibn Kathir 75
      The Description of the Gardens of the Truthful and Those Who repent 75
Surah: 19 Ayah: 64 & Ayah: 65 77
   Tafsir Ibn Kathir 77
      The Angels do not descend, except by Allah's Command 77
Surah: 19 Ayah: 66, Ayah: 67, Ayah: 68, Ayah: 69 & Ayah: 70 78
   Tafsir Ibn Kathir 79
      Man's Amazement about Life after Death and the Refutation against this Amazement .. 79
Surah: 19 Ayah: 71 & Ayah: 72 81
   Tafsir Ibn Kathir 81
      Everyone will be brought to Hell, then the Righteous will be saved 81
Surah: 19 Ayah: 73 & Ayah: 74 82
   Tafsir Ibn Kathir 83
      The Disbelievers boast over Their good Fortune in the World 83
Surah: 19 Ayah: 75 84
   Tafsir Ibn Kathir 84
      The Rebellious Person is given Respite but He is not forgotten 84
Surah: 19 Ayah: 76 85
   Tafsir Ibn Kathir 85
      Increasing Guidance of Those Who are guided 85
Surah: 19 Ayah: 77, Ayah: 78, Ayah: 79 & Ayah: 80 86
   Tafsir Ibn Kathir 86
      Refuting the Disbelievers Who claim that They will be given Wealth and Children in the Hereafter 86
Surah: 19 Ayah: 81, Ayah: 82, Ayah: 83 & Ayah: 84 87
   Tafsir Ibn Kathir 88
      The Idols of the Polytheists will deny Their Worship 88
      The Power of the Devils over the Disbelievers 89
Surah: 19 Ayah: 85, Ayah: 86 & Ayah: 87 89
   Tafsir Ibn Kathir 90
      The Condition of the Righteous and the Criminals on the Day of Resurrection 90
Surah: 19 Ayah: 88, Ayah: 89, Ayah: 90, Ayah: 91, Ayah: 92, Ayah: 93, Ayah: 94 & Ayah: 95 91
   Tafsir Ibn Kathir 92
      The Stern Rejection of attributing a Son to Allah 92
Surah: 19 Ayah: 96, Ayah: 97 & Ayah: 98 94

Table of Contents

Tafsir Ibn Kathir 95
   Allah places Love of the Righteous People in the Hearts 95
   The Qur'an descended to give Glad Tidings and to warn 96

CHAPTER (SURAH) 20: TA-HA (TA-HA), VERSES 001–135 97

Surah: 20 Ayah: 1, Ayah: 2, Ayah: 3, Ayah: 4, Ayah: 5, Ayah: 6, Ayah: 7 & Ayah: 8 97
  Tafsir Ibn Kathir 98
   The Qur'an is a Reminder and a Revelation from Allah 98
Surah: 20 Ayah: 9 & Ayah: 10 100
  Tafsir Ibn Kathir 100
   A Discussion of the Message of Musa 100
Surah: 20 Ayah: 11, Ayah: 12, Ayah: 13, Ayah: 14, Ayah: 15 & Ayah: 16 101
  Tafsir Ibn Kathir 102
   The First Revelation to Musa 102
Surah: 20 Ayah: 17, Ayah: 18, Ayah: 19, Ayah: 20 & Ayah: 21 104
  Tafsir Ibn Kathir 105
   The Stick of Musa turned into a Snake 105
Surah: 20 Ayah: 22, Ayah: 23, Ayah: 24, Ayah: 25, Ayah: 26, Ayah: 27, Ayah: 28, Ayah: 29, Ayah: 30, Ayah: 31, Ayah: 32, Ayah: 33, Ayah: 34 & Ayah: 35 106
  Tafsir Ibn Kathir 107
   The Hand of Musa turning White without any Disease 107
   Allah commanded Musa to go to Fir`awn to convey the Message. Allah said, ... 108
   The Supplication of Musa 108
Surah: 20 Ayah: 36, Ayah: 37, Ayah: 38, Ayah: 39 & Ayah: 40 109
  Tafsir Ibn Kathir 110
   Glad Tidings of the acceptance of Musa's Supplication and the Reminder of the Previous Blessings 110
Surah: 20 Ayah: 40, Ayah: 41, Ayah: 42, Ayah: 43 & Ayah: 44 111
  Tafsir Ibn Kathir 112
   Choosing Musa to go to Fir`awn and to be Soft and Gentle in His Invitation 112
Surah: 20 Ayah: 45, Ayah: 46, Ayah: 47 & Ayah: 48 114
  Tafsir Ibn Kathir 114
   Musa's fear of Fir`awn and Allah's strengthening Him 114
   Musa admonishes Fir`awn 115
Surah: 20 Ayah: 49, Ayah: 50, Ayah: 51 & Ayah: 52 116
  Tafsir Ibn Kathir 116
   The Conversation between Musa and Fir`awn 116
Surah: 20 Ayah: 53, Ayah: 54, Ayah: 55 & Ayah: 56 117
  Tafsir Ibn Kathir 118
   The Completion of Musa's Reply to Fir`awn 118
   Musa showed Fir`awn all of the Signs but He did not believe Concerning Allah's statement, ... 119
Surah: 20 Ayah: 57, Ayah: 58 & Ayah: 59 119
  Tafsir Ibn Kathir 120

Fir`awn describes Musa's Proofs as being Magic and Their Agreement to hold a Contest 120
Surah: 20 Ayah: 60, Ayah: 61, Ayah: 62, Ayah: 63 & Ayah: 64 121
Tafsir Ibn Kathir 121
The Meeting of the Two Parties, Musa's Propagation of the Message and the Magicians 121
Surah: 20 Ayah: 65, Ayah: 66, Ayah: 67, Ayah: 68, Ayah: 69 & Ayah: 70 123
Tafsir Ibn Kathir 124
The Competition, Musa's Victory, and the Magician's Faith 124
The Number of Magicians 125
Surah: 20 Ayah: 71, Ayah: 72 & Ayah: 73 125
Tafsir Ibn Kathir 126
Fir`awn's turning against the Magicians, His threatening Them and Their Reply 126
Surah: 20 Ayah: 74, Ayah: 75 & Ayah: 76 127
Tafsir Ibn Kathir 128
The Magicians admonish Fir`awn 128
Surah: 20 Ayah: 77, Ayah: 78 & Ayah: 79 130
Tafsir Ibn Kathir 131
The Children of Israel leave Egypt 131
Surah: 20 Ayah: 80, Ayah: 81 & Ayah: 82 132
Tafsir Ibn Kathir 132
A Reminder for the Children of Israel of 132
Surah: 20 Ayah: 83, Ayah: 84, Ayah: 85, Ayah: 86, Ayah: 87, Ayah: 88 & Ayah: 89 134
Tafsir Ibn Kathir 135
Musa goes to the Appointment with Allah and the Children of Israel succumb to worship the Calf 135
Surah: 20 Ayah: 90 & Ayah: 91 137
Tafsir Ibn Kathir 138
Harun prohibits them from worship of Calf and the Persistence of the Children of Israel in doing so 138
Surah: 20 Ayah: 92, Ayah: 93 & Ayah: 94 138
Tafsir Ibn Kathir 139
What happened between Musa and Harun after Musa returned 139
Surah: 20 Ayah: 95, Ayah: 96, Ayah: 97 & Ayah: 98 139
Tafsir Ibn Kathir 140
How As-Samiri made the Calf 140
The Punishment of As-Samiri and the burning of the Calf Thereupon, ... 141
Surah: 20 Ayah: 99, Ayah: 100 & Ayah: 101 142
Tafsir Ibn Kathir 142
The Entire Qur'an is the Remembrance of Allah and mentioning the Punishment of Those Who turn away from It 142
Surah: 20 Ayah: 102, Ayah: 103 & Ayah: 104 143
Tafsir Ibn Kathir 144
The Blowing of the Sur and the Day of Resurrection 144

Table of Contents

Surah: 20 Ayah: 105, Ayah: 106, Ayah: 107 & Ayah: 108 .... *145*
    Tafsir Ibn Kathir 146
        The destruction of the Mountains, and the Earth becomes a Smooth Plain 146
        The People will rush towards the Voice of the Caller 146
Surah: 20 Ayah: 109, Ayah: 110, Ayah: 111 & Ayah: 112 .... *147*
    Tafsir Ibn Kathir 147
        The Intercession and the Recompense 147
Surah: 20 Ayah: 113 & Ayah: 114 .... *150*
    Tafsir Ibn Kathir 150
        The Qur'an was revealed so that the People would have Taqwa and reflect 150
        The Command to the Prophet to listen to the Qur'an when it is revealed without making haste to recite it 151
Surah: 20 Ayah: 115, Ayah: 116, Ayah: 117, Ayah: 118, Ayah: 119, Ayah: 120, Ayah: 121 & Ayah: 122 .... *151*
    Tafsir Ibn Kathir 153
        The Story of Adam and Iblis 153
Surah: 20 Ayah: 123, Ayah: 124, Ayah: 125 & Ayah: 126 .... *155*
    Tafsir Ibn Kathir 156
        The Descent of Adam to the Earth and the Promise of Good for the Guided and Evil for the Transgressors 156
Surah: 20 Ayah: 127 .... *157*
    Tafsir Ibn Kathir 157
        Severe Torment for Him Who transgresses beyond bounds 157
Surah: 20 Ayah: 128, Ayah: 129 & Ayah: 130 .... *158*
    Tafsir Ibn Kathir 159
        Many Nations were destroyed and in Them is a Lesson 159
        The Command to be patient and perform the Five daily Prayers 159
Surah: 20 Ayah: 131 & Ayah: 132, Ayah: 133, Ayah: 134 & Ayah: 135 .... *161*
    Tafsir Ibn Kathir 162
        Do not look at the Enjoyment of the Wealthy, be patient in the worship of Allah 162
        The Request of the Polytheists for Proofs while the Qur'an is itself a Proof 165

PRELUDE

Opening Serman

Indeed, all praise is due to Allah. We praise Him and seek His help and forgiveness. We seek refuge with Allah from our soul's evil and our wrong doings. He whom Allah guides, no one can misguide; and he whom He misguides, no one can guide

I bear witness that there is no (true) god except Allah – alone without a partner, and I bear witness that Muhammad (peace and blessings of Allah be upon him) is His 'abd (servant) and messenger.

$$\text{يَٰٓأَيُّهَا ٱلَّذِينَ ءَامَنُوا۟ ٱتَّقُوا۟ ٱللَّهَ حَقَّ تُقَاتِهِۦ وَلَا تَمُوتُنَّ إِلَّا وَأَنتُم مُّسْلِمُونَ}$$

O you who believe! Fear Allâh (by doing all that He has ordered and by abstaining from all that He has forbidden) as He should be feared. (Obey Him, be thankful to Him, and remember Him always), and die not except in a state of Islâm (as Muslims with complete submission to Allâh)).

$$\text{يَٰٓأَيُّهَا ٱلنَّاسُ ٱتَّقُوا۟ رَبَّكُمُ ٱلَّذِى خَلَقَكُم مِّن نَّفْسٍ وَٰحِدَةٍ وَخَلَقَ مِنْهَا زَوْجَهَا وَبَثَّ مِنْهُمَا رِجَالًا كَثِيرًا وَنِسَآءً وَٱتَّقُوا۟ ٱللَّهَ ٱلَّذِى تَسَآءَلُونَ بِهِۦ وَٱلْأَرْحَامَ إِنَّ ٱللَّهَ كَانَ عَلَيْكُمْ رَقِيبًا}$$

O mankind! Be dutiful to your Lord, Who created you from a single person (Adam), and from him (Adam) He created his wife (Hawwâ (Eve)) and from them both He created many men and women; and fear Allâh through Whom you demand (your mutual rights), and (do not cut the relations of) the wombs (kinship). Surely, Allâh is Ever an All-Watcher over you.

$$\text{يُصْلِحْ لَكُمْ أَعْمَٰلَكُمْ وَيَغْفِرْ لَكُمْ ذُنُوبَكُمْ وَمَن يُطِعِ ٱللَّهَ وَرَسُولَهُۥ فَقَدْ فَازَ فَوْزًا عَظِيمًا}$$

He will direct you to do righteous good deeds and will forgive you your sins. And whosoever obeys Allâh and His Messenger (peace be upon him), he has indeed achieved a great achievement (i.e. he will be saved from the Hell-fire and will be admitted to Paradise).

Indeed, the best speech is Allah's Book and the best guidance is Muhammad's () guidance. The worst affairs (of religion) are those innovated (by people), for every such innovation is an act of misguidance leading to the Fire

Our Mission

Our mission is to gather in one place, for the English-speaking public, all relevant information needed to make the Qur'an more understandable and easier to study. This book tries to do this by providing the following:

1. The Arabic Text for those who are able to read Arabic
2. Transliteration of the Arabic text for those who are unable to read the Arabic script. This will give them a sample of the sound of the Qur'an, which they could not otherwise comprehend from reading the English meaning.
3. The meaning of the qur'an (translated by Dr. Muhammad Taqi-ud-Din Al-Hilali, Ph.D. and Dr. Muhammad Muhsin Khan)
4. Explanation (abridged Tafsir) by Ibn Kathir (translated by Safi-ur-Rahman al-Mubarakpuri)

We hope that by doing this an ordinary English-speaker will be able to pick up a copy of this book and study and comprehend The Glorious Qur'an in a way that is acceptable to the understanding of the Rightly-guided Muslim Ummah (Community).

Biography of Hafiz Ibn Kathir (701 H - 774 H)

By the Honored Shaykh `Abdul-Qadir Al-Arna'ut, may Allah protect him.

He is the respected Imam, Abu Al-Fida', `Imad Ad-Din Isma il bin 'Umar bin Kathir Al-Qurashi Al-Busrawi - Busraian in origin; Dimashqi in training, learning and residence.

Ibn Kathir was born in the city of Busra in 701 H. His father was the Friday speaker of the village, but he died while Ibn Kathir was only four years old. Ibn Kathir's brother, Shaykh Abdul-Wahhab, reared him and taught him until he moved to Damascus in 706 H., when he was five years old.

Ibn Kathir's Teachers

Ibn Kathir studied Fiqh - Islamic jurisprudence - with Burhan Ad-Din, Ibrahim bin `Abdur-Rahman Al-Fizari, known as Ibn Al-Firkah (who died in 729 H). Ibn Kathir heard Hadiths from `Isa bin Al-Mutim, Ahmad bin Abi Talib, (Ibn Ash-Shahnah) (who died in 730 H), Ibn Al-Hajjar, (who died in 730 H), and the Hadith narrator of Ash-Sham (modern day Syria and surrounding areas); Baha Ad-Din Al-Qasim bin Muzaffar bin `Asakir (who died in 723 H), and Ibn Ash-Shirdzi, Ishaq bin Yahya Al-Ammuddi, also known as `Afif Ad-Din, the Zahiriyyah Shaykh who died in 725 H, and Muhammad bin Zarrad. He remained with Jamal Ad-Din, Yusuf bin Az-Zaki AlMizzi who died in 724 H, he benefited from his knowledge and also married his daughter. He also read with Shaykh Al-Islam, Taqi Ad-Din Ahmad bin `Abdul-Halim bin `Abdus-Salam bin Taymiyyah who died in 728 H. He also read with the Imam Hafiz and historian Shams Ad-Din, Muhammad bin Ahmad bin Uthman bin Qaymaz Adh-Dhahabi, who died in 748 H. Also, Abu Musa Al-Qarafai, Abu Al-Fath Ad-Dabbusi and

'Ali bin `Umar As-Suwani and others who gave him permission to transmit the knowledge he learned with them in Egypt.

In his book, Al-Mu jam Al-Mukhtas, Al-Hafiz Adh-Dhaliabi wrote that Ibn Kathir was, "The Imam, scholar of jurisprudence, skillful scholar of Hadith, renowned Faqih and scholar of Tafsir who wrote several beneficial books."

Further, in Ad-Durar Al-Kdminah, Al-Hafiz Ibn Hajar AlAsqalani said, "Ibn Kathir worked on the subject of the Hadith in the areas of texts and chains of narrators. He had a good memory, his books became popular during his lifetime, and people benefited from them after his death."

Also, the renowned historian Abu Al-Mahasin, Jamal Ad-Din Yusuf bin Sayf Ad-Din (Ibn Taghri Bardi), said in his book, AlManhal As-Safi, "He is the Shaykh, the Imam, the great scholar `Imad Ad-Din Abu Al-Fida'. He learned extensively and was very active in collecting knowledge and writing. He was excellent in the areas of Fiqh, Tafsfr and Hadith. He collected knowledge, authored (books), taught, narrated Hadith and wrote. He had immense knowledge in the fields of Hadith, Tafsir, Fiqh, the Arabic language, and so forth. He gave Fatawa (religious verdicts) and taught until he died, may Allah grant him mercy. He was known for his precision and vast knowledge, and as a scholar of history, Hadith and Tafsir."

Ibn Kathir's Students

Ibn Hajji was one of Ibn Kathir's students, and he described Ibn Kathir: "He had the best memory of the Hadith texts. He also had the most knowledge concerning the narrators and authenticity, his contemporaries and teachers admitted to these qualities. Every time I met him I gained some benefit from him."

Also, Ibn Al-`Imad Al-Hanbali said in his book, Shadhardt Adh-Dhahab, "He is the renowned Hafiz `Imad Ad-Din, whose memory was excellent, whose forgetfulness was miniscule, whose understanding was adequate, and who had good knowledge in the Arabic language." Also, Ibn Habib said about Ibn Kathir, "He heard knowledge and collected it and wrote various books. He brought comfort to the ears with his Fatwas and narrated Hadith and brought benefit to other people. The papers that contained his Fatwas were transmitted to the various (Islamic) provinces. Further, he was known for his precision and encompassing knowledge."

Ibn Kathir's Books

1 - One of the greatest books that Ibn Kathir wrote was his Tafsir of the Noble Qur'an, which is one of the best Tafsir that rely on narrations [of Ahadith, the Tafsir of the Companions, etc.]. The Tafsir by Ibn Kathir was printed many times and several scholars have summarized it.

2- The History Collection known as Al-Biddyah, which was printed in 14 volumes under the name Al-Bidayah wanNihdyah, and contained the stories of the Prophets and previous nations, the Prophet's Seerah (life story) and Islamic history until his time. He also added a book Al-Fitan, about the Signs of the Last Hour.

3- At-Takmil ft Ma`rifat Ath-Thiqat wa Ad-Du'afa wal Majdhil which Ibn Kathir collected from the books of his two Shaykhs Al-Mizzi and Adh-Dhahabi; Al-Kdmal and Mizan Al-Ftiddl. He added several benefits regarding the subject of Al-Jarh and AtT'adil.

4- Al-Hadi was-Sunan ft Ahadith Al-Masdnfd was-Sunan which is also known by, Jami` Al-Masdnfd. In this book, Ibn Kathir collected the narrations of Imams Ahmad bin Hanbal, Al-Bazzar, Abu Ya`la Al-Mawsili, Ibn Abi Shaybah and from the six collections of Hadith: the Two Sahihs [Al-Bukhari and Muslim] and the Four Sunan [Abu Dawud, At-Tirmidhi, AnNasa and Ibn Majah]. Ibn Kathir divided this book according to areas of Fiqh.

5-Tabaqat Ash-Shaf iyah which also contains the virtues of Imam Ash-Shafi.

6- Ibn Kathir wrote references for the Ahadith of Adillat AtTanbfh, from the Shafi school of Fiqh.

7- Ibn Kathir began an explanation of Sahih Al-Bukhari, but he did not finish it.

8- He started writing a large volume on the Ahkam (Laws), but finished only up to the Hajj rituals.

9- He summarized Al-Bayhaqi's 'Al-Madkhal. Many of these books were not printed.

10- He summarized `Ulum Al-Hadith, by Abu `Amr bin AsSalah and called it Mukhtasar `Ulum Al-Hadith. Shaykh Ahmad Shakir, the Egyptian Muhaddith, printed this book along with his commentary on it and called it Al-Ba'th Al-Hathfth fi Sharh Mukhtasar `Ulum Al-Hadith.

11- As-Sfrah An-Nabawiyyah, which is contained in his book Al-Biddyah, and both of these books are in print.

12- A research on Jihad called Al-Ijtihad ft Talabi Al-Jihad, which was printed several times.

Ibn Kathir's Death

Al-Hafiz Ibn Hajar Al-Asgalani said, "Ibn Kathir lost his sight just before his life ended. He died in Damascus in 774 H." May Allah grant mercy upon Ibn Kathir and make him among the residents of His Paradise.

PREFACE

In the name of Allah, Most Gracious, Most Merciful.

About this book

The previous publication of this book included some background information to the chapters of the Qur'an by an Islamic scholar known as Abul Ala Maududi. This information was used to shed more light on the chapters by giving a summery of why each chapter was given its name, It's period of revelation and the circumstances surrounding its revelatiom. However, some Muslims objected to the inclusion of the contributions of Maududi.

In this new publication of Tafsir Ibn Kathir, we have removed all traces of the contribution of Abul Ala Maududi. Personally, I do not know the reasons for the objections to Maududi, but this work concerns only the tafsir of Ibn Kathir, so we have not included anything from Maududi in it. We have also corrected all the typing and formatting errors found in the previous publication. We have not alter the structure of the book. The reader is still able to read the full Arabic Text of the thirty Parts of the Qur'an and follow its meanings in the English language. The transliteration of the Arabic text should also give the reader a taste of the sound of the original Arabic.

May Almighty Allah accept this effort from us, and make it a source of blessings for us in this world and in the next. I bear witness that there is none worthy of worship but Allah and I bear witness that Muhammad (may the peace and blessings of Allah be upon him) is the slave and messenger of Allah.

Performing Prostration While Reading the Qur'an

Question:

Could you please give a list of the Qur'anic verses when a prostration is recommended? What happens if we read these verses and not perform a prostration?

A. Jalil

Answer:

There are 15 verses in the Qur'an that mention prostration before God Almighty as a good action by God-fearing believers. Therefore, it is strongly recommended to perform such a prostration when we read or listen to any of these verses, whether during prayer or in any situation.

Some scholars are of the view that even if one has not performed ablution, one should prostrate oneself. These verses are given here, starting with the Arabic title of the surah which is followed by two numbers, the first indicating the surah, and the second indicating the verse,: Al-Araf 7: 206; Al-Raad 13: 15; Al-Nahl 16: 50; Al-Isra 17: 109; Maryam 19: 58; Al-Hajj 22: 18 & 22: 77; Al-Furqan 25: 60; Al-Naml 27: 26;

Al-Sajdah 32: 15; Saad 38: 25; Fussilat 41: 38; Al-Najm 53: 62; Al-Inshiqaq 84: 21 and Al-Alaq 96: 19.

If you do not perform a prostration when you read or listen to any of these verses, you have done badly because you miss out on the reward of performing a prostration for God. You incur no sin and violate no divine order.

Reference:
http://archive.arabnews.com/?page=5&section=0&article=97811&d=1&m=7&y=2007

The Glorious Qur'an Juz' 16 (Part 16): Chapter (Surah) 18: Al-Kahf (The Cave) 075 To Chapter (Surah) 20: Ta-Ha (Ta-Ha) 135

PART 16 FULL ARABIC TEXT

Chapter (Surah) 18: Al-Kahf 075-110

۞ قَالَ أَلَمْ أَقُل لَّكَ إِنَّكَ لَن تَسْتَطِيعَ مَعِىَ صَبْرًا ۝ قَالَ إِن سَأَلْتُكَ عَن شَىْءٍۭ بَعْدَهَا فَلَا تُصَٰحِبْنِى ۖ قَدْ بَلَغْتَ مِن لَّدُنِّى عُذْرًا ۝ فَٱنطَلَقَا حَتَّىٰٓ إِذَآ أَتَيَآ أَهْلَ قَرْيَةٍ ٱسْتَطْعَمَآ أَهْلَهَا فَأَبَوْا أَن يُضَيِّفُوهُمَا فَوَجَدَا فِيهَا جِدَارًا يُرِيدُ أَن يَنقَضَّ فَأَقَامَهُۥ ۖ قَالَ لَوْ شِئْتَ لَتَّخَذْتَ عَلَيْهِ أَجْرًا ۝ قَالَ هَٰذَا فِرَاقُ بَيْنِى وَبَيْنِكَ ۚ سَأُنَبِّئُكَ بِتَأْوِيلِ مَا لَمْ تَسْتَطِع عَّلَيْهِ صَبْرًا ۝ أَمَّا ٱلسَّفِينَةُ فَكَانَتْ لِمَسَٰكِينَ يَعْمَلُونَ فِى ٱلْبَحْرِ فَأَرَدتُّ أَنْ أَعِيبَهَا وَكَانَ وَرَآءَهُم مَّلِكٌ يَأْخُذُ كُلَّ سَفِينَةٍ غَصْبًا ۝ وَأَمَّا ٱلْغُلَٰمُ فَكَانَ أَبَوَاهُ مُؤْمِنَيْنِ فَخَشِينَآ أَن يُرْهِقَهُمَا طُغْيَٰنًا وَكُفْرًا ۝ فَأَرَدْنَآ أَن يُبْدِلَهُمَا رَبُّهُمَا خَيْرًا مِّنْهُ زَكَوٰةً وَأَقْرَبَ رُحْمًا ۝ وَأَمَّا ٱلْجِدَارُ فَكَانَ لِغُلَٰمَيْنِ يَتِيمَيْنِ فِى ٱلْمَدِينَةِ وَكَانَ تَحْتَهُۥ كَنزٌ لَّهُمَا وَكَانَ أَبُوهُمَا صَٰلِحًا فَأَرَادَ رَبُّكَ أَن يَبْلُغَآ أَشُدَّهُمَا وَيَسْتَخْرِجَا كَنزَهُمَا رَحْمَةً مِّن رَّبِّكَ ۚ وَمَا فَعَلْتُهُۥ عَنْ أَمْرِى ۚ ذَٰلِكَ تَأْوِيلُ مَا لَمْ تَسْطِع عَّلَيْهِ صَبْرًا ۝ وَيَسْـَٔلُونَكَ عَن ذِى ٱلْقَرْنَيْنِ ۖ قُلْ سَأَتْلُوا۟ عَلَيْكُم مِّنْهُ ذِكْرًا ۝ إِنَّا مَكَّنَّا لَهُۥ فِى ٱلْأَرْضِ وَءَاتَيْنَٰهُ مِن كُلِّ شَىْءٍ سَبَبًا ۝ فَأَتْبَعَ سَبَبًا ۝ حَتَّىٰٓ إِذَا بَلَغَ مَغْرِبَ ٱلشَّمْسِ وَجَدَهَا تَغْرُبُ فِى عَيْنٍ حَمِئَةٍ وَوَجَدَ عِندَهَا قَوْمًا ۗ قُلْنَا يَٰذَا ٱلْقَرْنَيْنِ إِمَّآ أَن تُعَذِّبَ وَإِمَّآ أَن تَتَّخِذَ فِيهِمْ حُسْنًا ۝ قَالَ أَمَّا مَن ظَلَمَ فَسَوْفَ نُعَذِّبُهُۥ ثُمَّ يُرَدُّ إِلَىٰ رَبِّهِۦ فَيُعَذِّبُهُۥ عَذَابًا نُّكْرًا ۝ وَأَمَّا مَنْ ءَامَنَ وَعَمِلَ صَٰلِحًا فَلَهُۥ جَزَآءً ٱلْحُسْنَىٰ ۖ وَسَنَقُولُ

لَهُۥ مِنْ أَمْرِنَا يُسْرًا ۝ ثُمَّ أَتْبَعَ سَبَبًا ۝ حَتَّىٰٓ إِذَا بَلَغَ مَطْلِعَ ٱلشَّمْسِ وَجَدَهَا تَطْلُعُ عَلَىٰ قَوْمٍ لَّمْ نَجْعَل لَّهُم مِّن دُونِهَا سِتْرًا ۝ كَذَٰلِكَ وَقَدْ أَحَطْنَا بِمَا لَدَيْهِ خُبْرًا ۝ ثُمَّ أَتْبَعَ سَبَبًا ۝ حَتَّىٰٓ إِذَا بَلَغَ بَيْنَ ٱلسَّدَّيْنِ وَجَدَ مِن دُونِهِمَا قَوْمًا لَّا يَكَادُونَ يَفْقَهُونَ قَوْلًا ۝ قَالُوا۟ يَٰذَا ٱلْقَرْنَيْنِ إِنَّ يَأْجُوجَ وَمَأْجُوجَ مُفْسِدُونَ فِى ٱلْأَرْضِ فَهَلْ نَجْعَلُ لَكَ خَرْجًا عَلَىٰٓ أَن تَجْعَلَ بَيْنَنَا وَبَيْنَهُمْ سَدًّا ۝ قَالَ مَا مَكَّنِّى فِيهِ رَبِّى خَيْرٌ فَأَعِينُونِى بِقُوَّةٍ أَجْعَلْ بَيْنَكُمْ وَبَيْنَهُمْ رَدْمًا ۝ ءَاتُونِى زُبَرَ ٱلْحَدِيدِ ۖ حَتَّىٰٓ إِذَا سَاوَىٰ بَيْنَ ٱلصَّدَفَيْنِ قَالَ ٱنفُخُوا۟ ۖ حَتَّىٰٓ إِذَا جَعَلَهُۥ نَارًا قَالَ ءَاتُونِىٓ أُفْرِغْ عَلَيْهِ قِطْرًا ۝ فَمَا ٱسْطَٰعُوٓا۟ أَن يَظْهَرُوهُ وَمَا ٱسْتَطَٰعُوا۟ لَهُۥ نَقْبًا ۝ قَالَ هَٰذَا رَحْمَةٌ مِّن رَّبِّى ۖ فَإِذَا جَآءَ وَعْدُ رَبِّى جَعَلَهُۥ دَكَّآءَ ۖ وَكَانَ وَعْدُ رَبِّى حَقًّا ۝ ۞ وَتَرَكْنَا بَعْضَهُمْ يَوْمَئِذٍ يَمُوجُ فِى بَعْضٍ ۖ وَنُفِخَ فِى ٱلصُّورِ فَجَمَعْنَٰهُمْ جَمْعًا ۝ وَعَرَضْنَا جَهَنَّمَ يَوْمَئِذٍ لِّلْكَٰفِرِينَ عَرْضًا ۝ ٱلَّذِينَ كَانَتْ أَعْيُنُهُمْ فِى غِطَآءٍ عَن ذِكْرِى وَكَانُوا۟ لَا يَسْتَطِيعُونَ سَمْعًا ۝ أَفَحَسِبَ ٱلَّذِينَ كَفَرُوٓا۟ أَن يَتَّخِذُوا۟ عِبَادِى مِن دُونِىٓ أَوْلِيَآءَ ۚ إِنَّآ أَعْتَدْنَا جَهَنَّمَ لِلْكَٰفِرِينَ نُزُلًا ۝ قُلْ هَلْ نُنَبِّئُكُم بِٱلْأَخْسَرِينَ أَعْمَٰلًا ۝ ٱلَّذِينَ ضَلَّ سَعْيُهُمْ فِى ٱلْحَيَوٰةِ ٱلدُّنْيَا وَهُمْ يَحْسَبُونَ أَنَّهُمْ يُحْسِنُونَ صُنْعًا ۝ أُو۟لَٰٓئِكَ ٱلَّذِينَ كَفَرُوا۟ بِـَٔايَٰتِ رَبِّهِمْ وَلِقَآئِهِۦ فَحَبِطَتْ أَعْمَٰلُهُمْ فَلَا نُقِيمُ لَهُمْ يَوْمَ ٱلْقِيَٰمَةِ وَزْنًا ۝ ذَٰلِكَ جَزَآؤُهُمْ جَهَنَّمُ بِمَا كَفَرُوا۟ وَٱتَّخَذُوٓا۟ ءَايَٰتِى وَرُسُلِى هُزُوًا ۝ إِنَّ ٱلَّذِينَ ءَامَنُوا۟ وَعَمِلُوا۟ ٱلصَّٰلِحَٰتِ كَانَتْ لَهُمْ جَنَّٰتُ ٱلْفِرْدَوْسِ نُزُلًا ۝ خَٰلِدِينَ فِيهَا لَا يَبْغُونَ عَنْهَا حِوَلًا ۝ قُل لَّوْ كَانَ ٱلْبَحْرُ مِدَادًا لِّكَلِمَٰتِ رَبِّى لَنَفِدَ ٱلْبَحْرُ قَبْلَ أَن تَنفَدَ كَلِمَٰتُ رَبِّى وَلَوْ جِئْنَا بِمِثْلِهِۦ مَدَدًا ۝ قُلْ إِنَّمَآ أَنَا۠ بَشَرٌ مِّثْلُكُمْ يُوحَىٰٓ

إِلَىٰٓ أَنَّمَآ إِلَٰهُكُمْ إِلَٰهٌ وَٰحِدٌ ۖ فَمَن كَانَ يَرْجُوا۟ لِقَآءَ رَبِّهِۦ فَلْيَعْمَلْ عَمَلًا صَٰلِحًا وَلَا يُشْرِكْ بِعِبَادَةِ رَبِّهِۦٓ أَحَدًۢا ۝

(Al-Kahf 075-110)

Chapter (Surah) 19: Maryam 001-098

بِسْمِ ٱللَّهِ ٱلرَّحْمَٰنِ ٱلرَّحِيمِ

كٓهيعٓصٓ ۝ ذِكْرُ رَحْمَتِ رَبِّكَ عَبْدَهُۥ زَكَرِيَّآ ۝ إِذْ نَادَىٰ رَبَّهُۥ نِدَآءً خَفِيًّا ۝ قَالَ رَبِّ إِنِّى وَهَنَ ٱلْعَظْمُ مِنِّى وَٱشْتَعَلَ ٱلرَّأْسُ شَيْبًا وَلَمْ أَكُنۢ بِدُعَآئِكَ رَبِّ شَقِيًّا ۝ وَإِنِّى خِفْتُ ٱلْمَوَٰلِىَ مِن وَرَآءِى وَكَانَتِ ٱمْرَأَتِى عَاقِرًا فَهَبْ لِى مِن لَّدُنكَ وَلِيًّا ۝ يَرِثُنِى وَيَرِثُ مِنْ ءَالِ يَعْقُوبَ ۖ وَٱجْعَلْهُ رَبِّ رَضِيًّا ۝ يَٰزَكَرِيَّآ إِنَّا نُبَشِّرُكَ بِغُلَٰمٍ ٱسْمُهُۥ يَحْيَىٰ لَمْ نَجْعَل لَّهُۥ مِن قَبْلُ سَمِيًّا ۝ قَالَ رَبِّ أَنَّىٰ يَكُونُ لِى غُلَٰمٌ وَكَانَتِ ٱمْرَأَتِى عَاقِرًا وَقَدْ بَلَغْتُ مِنَ ٱلْكِبَرِ عِتِيًّا ۝ قَالَ كَذَٰلِكَ قَالَ رَبُّكَ هُوَ عَلَىَّ هَيِّنٌ وَقَدْ خَلَقْتُكَ مِن قَبْلُ وَلَمْ تَكُ شَيْـًٔا ۝ قَالَ رَبِّ ٱجْعَل لِّىٓ ءَايَةً ۚ قَالَ ءَايَتُكَ أَلَّا تُكَلِّمَ ٱلنَّاسَ ثَلَٰثَ لَيَالٍ سَوِيًّا ۝ فَخَرَجَ عَلَىٰ قَوْمِهِۦ مِنَ ٱلْمِحْرَابِ فَأَوْحَىٰٓ إِلَيْهِمْ أَن سَبِّحُوا۟ بُكْرَةً وَعَشِيًّا ۝ يَٰيَحْيَىٰ خُذِ ٱلْكِتَٰبَ بِقُوَّةٍ ۖ وَءَاتَيْنَٰهُ ٱلْحُكْمَ صَبِيًّا ۝ وَحَنَانًا مِّن لَّدُنَّا وَزَكَوٰةً ۖ وَكَانَ تَقِيًّا ۝ وَبَرًّۢا بِوَٰلِدَيْهِ وَلَمْ يَكُن جَبَّارًا عَصِيًّا ۝ وَسَلَٰمٌ عَلَيْهِ يَوْمَ وُلِدَ وَيَوْمَ يَمُوتُ وَيَوْمَ يُبْعَثُ حَيًّا ۝ وَٱذْكُرْ فِى ٱلْكِتَٰبِ مَرْيَمَ إِذِ ٱنتَبَذَتْ مِنْ أَهْلِهَا مَكَانًا شَرْقِيًّا ۝ فَٱتَّخَذَتْ مِن دُونِهِمْ حِجَابًا فَأَرْسَلْنَآ إِلَيْهَا رُوحَنَا فَتَمَثَّلَ لَهَا بَشَرًا سَوِيًّا ۝ قَالَتْ إِنِّىٓ أَعُوذُ بِٱلرَّحْمَٰنِ مِنكَ إِن كُنتَ تَقِيًّا ۝ قَالَ إِنَّمَآ أَنَا۠ رَسُولُ رَبِّكِ لِأَهَبَ لَكِ غُلَٰمًا زَكِيًّا ۝ قَالَتْ أَنَّىٰ يَكُونُ لِى غُلَٰمٌ وَلَمْ يَمْسَسْنِى بَشَرٌ وَلَمْ أَكُ بَغِيًّا ۝ قَالَ كَذَٰلِكِ قَالَ رَبُّكِ هُوَ عَلَىَّ هَيِّنٌ ۖ وَلِنَجْعَلَهُۥٓ ءَايَةً لِّلنَّاسِ وَرَحْمَةً مِّنَّا ۚ وَكَانَ أَمْرًا

مَقْضِيًّا ۝ ‌۞ فَحَمَلَتْهُ فَٱنتَبَذَتْ بِهِۦ مَكَانًا قَصِيًّا ۝ فَأَجَآءَهَا ٱلْمَخَاضُ إِلَىٰ جِذْعِ ٱلنَّخْلَةِ قَالَتْ يَـٰلَيْتَنِى مِتُّ قَبْلَ هَـٰذَا وَكُنتُ نَسْيًا مَّنسِيًّا ۝ فَنَادَىٰهَا مِن تَحْتِهَآ أَلَّا تَحْزَنِى قَدْ جَعَلَ رَبُّكِ تَحْتَكِ سَرِيًّا ۝ وَهُزِّىٓ إِلَيْكِ بِجِذْعِ ٱلنَّخْلَةِ تُسَـٰقِطْ عَلَيْكِ رُطَبًا جَنِيًّا ۝ فَكُلِى وَٱشْرَبِى وَقَرِّى عَيْنًا ۖ فَإِمَّا تَرَيِنَّ مِنَ ٱلْبَشَرِ أَحَدًا فَقُولِىٓ إِنِّى نَذَرْتُ لِلرَّحْمَـٰنِ صَوْمًا فَلَنْ أُكَلِّمَ ٱلْيَوْمَ إِنسِيًّا ۝ فَأَتَتْ بِهِۦ قَوْمَهَا تَحْمِلُهُۥ ۖ قَالُوا۟ يَـٰمَرْيَمُ لَقَدْ جِئْتِ شَيْـًٔا فَرِيًّا ۝ يَـٰٓأُخْتَ هَـٰرُونَ مَا كَانَ أَبُوكِ ٱمْرَأَ سَوْءٍ وَمَا كَانَتْ أُمُّكِ بَغِيًّا ۝ فَأَشَارَتْ إِلَيْهِ ۖ قَالُوا۟ كَيْفَ نُكَلِّمُ مَن كَانَ فِى ٱلْمَهْدِ صَبِيًّا ۝ قَالَ إِنِّى عَبْدُ ٱللَّهِ ءَاتَىٰنِىَ ٱلْكِتَـٰبَ وَجَعَلَنِى نَبِيًّا ۝ وَجَعَلَنِى مُبَارَكًا أَيْنَ مَا كُنتُ وَأَوْصَـٰنِى بِٱلصَّلَوٰةِ وَٱلزَّكَوٰةِ مَا دُمْتُ حَيًّا ۝ وَبَرًّۢا بِوَٰلِدَتِى وَلَمْ يَجْعَلْنِى جَبَّارًا شَقِيًّا ۝ وَٱلسَّلَـٰمُ عَلَىَّ يَوْمَ وُلِدتُّ وَيَوْمَ أَمُوتُ وَيَوْمَ أُبْعَثُ حَيًّا ۝ ذَٰلِكَ عِيسَى ٱبْنُ مَرْيَمَ ۚ قَوْلَ ٱلْحَقِّ ٱلَّذِى فِيهِ يَمْتَرُونَ ۝ مَا كَانَ لِلَّهِ أَن يَتَّخِذَ مِن وَلَدٍ ۖ سُبْحَـٰنَهُۥٓ ۚ إِذَا قَضَىٰٓ أَمْرًا فَإِنَّمَا يَقُولُ لَهُۥ كُن فَيَكُونُ ۝ وَإِنَّ ٱللَّهَ رَبِّى وَرَبُّكُمْ فَٱعْبُدُوهُ ۚ هَـٰذَا صِرَٰطٌ مُّسْتَقِيمٌ ۝ فَٱخْتَلَفَ ٱلْأَحْزَابُ مِنۢ بَيْنِهِمْ ۖ فَوَيْلٌ لِّلَّذِينَ كَفَرُوا۟ مِن مَّشْهَدِ يَوْمٍ عَظِيمٍ ۝ أَسْمِعْ بِهِمْ وَأَبْصِرْ يَوْمَ يَأْتُونَنَا ۖ لَـٰكِنِ ٱلظَّـٰلِمُونَ ٱلْيَوْمَ فِى ضَلَـٰلٍ مُّبِينٍ ۝ وَأَنذِرْهُمْ يَوْمَ ٱلْحَسْرَةِ إِذْ قُضِىَ ٱلْأَمْرُ وَهُمْ فِى غَفْلَةٍ وَهُمْ لَا يُؤْمِنُونَ ۝ إِنَّا نَحْنُ نَرِثُ ٱلْأَرْضَ وَمَنْ عَلَيْهَا وَإِلَيْنَا يُرْجَعُونَ ۝ وَٱذْكُرْ فِى ٱلْكِتَـٰبِ إِبْرَٰهِيمَ ۚ إِنَّهُۥ كَانَ صِدِّيقًا نَّبِيًّا ۝ إِذْ قَالَ لِأَبِيهِ يَـٰٓأَبَتِ لِمَ تَعْبُدُ مَا لَا يَسْمَعُ وَلَا يُبْصِرُ وَلَا يُغْنِى عَنكَ شَيْـًٔا ۝ يَـٰٓأَبَتِ إِنِّى قَدْ جَآءَنِى مِنَ ٱلْعِلْمِ مَا لَمْ يَأْتِكَ فَٱتَّبِعْنِىٓ أَهْدِكَ صِرَٰطًا سَوِيًّا ۝ يَـٰٓأَبَتِ لَا تَعْبُدِ ٱلشَّيْطَـٰنَ ۖ إِنَّ ٱلشَّيْطَـٰنَ كَانَ لِلرَّحْمَـٰنِ عَصِيًّا ۝ يَـٰٓأَبَتِ إِنِّىٓ أَخَافُ أَن يَمَسَّكَ عَذَابٌ مِّنَ ٱلرَّحْمَـٰنِ فَتَكُونَ

لِلشَّيْطَٰنِ وَلِيًّا ۝ قَالَ أَرَاغِبٌ أَنتَ عَنْ ءَالِهَتِى يَٰٓإِبْرَٰهِيمُ ۖ لَئِن لَّمْ تَنتَهِ لَأَرْجُمَنَّكَ ۖ وَٱهْجُرْنِى مَلِيًّا ۝ قَالَ سَلَٰمٌ عَلَيْكَ ۖ سَأَسْتَغْفِرُ لَكَ رَبِّىٓ ۖ إِنَّهُۥ كَانَ بِى حَفِيًّا ۝ وَأَعْتَزِلُكُمْ وَمَا تَدْعُونَ مِن دُونِ ٱللَّهِ وَأَدْعُوا۟ رَبِّى عَسَىٰٓ أَلَّآ أَكُونَ بِدُعَآءِ رَبِّى شَقِيًّا ۝ فَلَمَّا ٱعْتَزَلَهُمْ وَمَا يَعْبُدُونَ مِن دُونِ ٱللَّهِ وَهَبْنَا لَهُۥٓ إِسْحَٰقَ وَيَعْقُوبَ ۖ وَكُلًّا جَعَلْنَا نَبِيًّا ۝ وَوَهَبْنَا لَهُم مِّن رَّحْمَتِنَا وَجَعَلْنَا لَهُمْ لِسَانَ صِدْقٍ عَلِيًّا ۝ وَٱذْكُرْ فِى ٱلْكِتَٰبِ مُوسَىٰٓ ۚ إِنَّهُۥ كَانَ مُخْلَصًا وَكَانَ رَسُولًا نَّبِيًّا ۝ وَنَٰدَيْنَٰهُ مِن جَانِبِ ٱلطُّورِ ٱلْأَيْمَنِ وَقَرَّبْنَٰهُ نَجِيًّا ۝ وَوَهَبْنَا لَهُۥ مِن رَّحْمَتِنَآ أَخَاهُ هَٰرُونَ نَبِيًّا ۝ وَٱذْكُرْ فِى ٱلْكِتَٰبِ إِسْمَٰعِيلَ ۚ إِنَّهُۥ كَانَ صَادِقَ ٱلْوَعْدِ وَكَانَ رَسُولًا نَّبِيًّا ۝ وَكَانَ يَأْمُرُ أَهْلَهُۥ بِٱلصَّلَوٰةِ وَٱلزَّكَوٰةِ وَكَانَ عِندَ رَبِّهِۦ مَرْضِيًّا ۝ وَٱذْكُرْ فِى ٱلْكِتَٰبِ إِدْرِيسَ ۚ إِنَّهُۥ كَانَ صِدِّيقًا نَّبِيًّا ۝ وَرَفَعْنَٰهُ مَكَانًا عَلِيًّا ۝ أُو۟لَٰٓئِكَ ٱلَّذِينَ أَنْعَمَ ٱللَّهُ عَلَيْهِم مِّنَ ٱلنَّبِيِّـۧنَ مِن ذُرِّيَّةِ ءَادَمَ وَمِمَّنْ حَمَلْنَا مَعَ نُوحٍ وَمِن ذُرِّيَّةِ إِبْرَٰهِيمَ وَإِسْرَٰٓءِيلَ وَمِمَّنْ هَدَيْنَا وَٱجْتَبَيْنَآ ۚ إِذَا تُتْلَىٰ عَلَيْهِمْ ءَايَٰتُ ٱلرَّحْمَٰنِ خَرُّوا۟ سُجَّدًا وَبُكِيًّا ۩ ۝ ۞ فَخَلَفَ مِنۢ بَعْدِهِمْ خَلْفٌ أَضَاعُوا۟ ٱلصَّلَوٰةَ وَٱتَّبَعُوا۟ ٱلشَّهَوَٰتِ ۖ فَسَوْفَ يَلْقَوْنَ غَيًّا ۝ إِلَّا مَن تَابَ وَءَامَنَ وَعَمِلَ صَٰلِحًا فَأُو۟لَٰٓئِكَ يَدْخُلُونَ ٱلْجَنَّةَ وَلَا يُظْلَمُونَ شَيْـًٔا ۝ جَنَّٰتِ عَدْنٍ ٱلَّتِى وَعَدَ ٱلرَّحْمَٰنُ عِبَادَهُۥ بِٱلْغَيْبِ ۚ إِنَّهُۥ كَانَ وَعْدُهُۥ مَأْتِيًّا ۝ لَّا يَسْمَعُونَ فِيهَا لَغْوًا إِلَّا سَلَٰمًا ۖ وَلَهُمْ رِزْقُهُمْ فِيهَا بُكْرَةً وَعَشِيًّا ۝ تِلْكَ ٱلْجَنَّةُ ٱلَّتِى نُورِثُ مِنْ عِبَادِنَا مَن كَانَ تَقِيًّا ۝ وَمَا نَتَنَزَّلُ إِلَّا بِأَمْرِ رَبِّكَ ۖ لَهُۥ مَا بَيْنَ أَيْدِينَا وَمَا خَلْفَنَا وَمَا بَيْنَ ذَٰلِكَ ۚ وَمَا كَانَ رَبُّكَ نَسِيًّا ۝ رَّبُّ ٱلسَّمَٰوَٰتِ وَٱلْأَرْضِ وَمَا بَيْنَهُمَا فَٱعْبُدْهُ وَٱصْطَبِرْ لِعِبَٰدَتِهِۦ ۚ هَلْ تَعْلَمُ لَهُۥ سَمِيًّا ۝ وَيَقُولُ ٱلْإِنسَٰنُ أَءِذَا مَا مِتُّ لَسَوْفَ أُخْرَجُ حَيًّا ۝ أَوَلَا يَذْكُرُ ٱلْإِنسَٰنُ أَنَّا خَلَقْنَٰهُ مِن قَبْلُ

وَلَمْ يَكُ شَيْئًا ۞ فَوَرَبِّكَ لَنَحْشُرَنَّهُمْ وَٱلشَّيَـٰطِينَ ثُمَّ لَنُحْضِرَنَّهُمْ حَوْلَ جَهَنَّمَ جِثِيًّا ۞ ثُمَّ لَنَنزِعَنَّ مِن كُلِّ شِيعَةٍ أَيُّهُمْ أَشَدُّ عَلَى ٱلرَّحْمَـٰنِ عِتِيًّا ۞ ثُمَّ لَنَحْنُ أَعْلَمُ بِٱلَّذِينَ هُمْ أَوْلَىٰ بِهَا صِلِيًّا ۞ وَإِن مِّنكُمْ إِلَّا وَارِدُهَا ۚ كَانَ عَلَىٰ رَبِّكَ حَتْمًا مَّقْضِيًّا ۞ ثُمَّ نُنَجِّى ٱلَّذِينَ ٱتَّقَواْ وَّنَذَرُ ٱلظَّـٰلِمِينَ فِيهَا جِثِيًّا ۞ وَإِذَا تُتْلَىٰ عَلَيْهِمْ ءَايَـٰتُنَا بَيِّنَـٰتٍ قَالَ ٱلَّذِينَ كَفَرُواْ لِلَّذِينَ ءَامَنُوٓاْ أَىُّ ٱلْفَرِيقَيْنِ خَيْرٌ مَّقَامًا وَأَحْسَنُ نَدِيًّا ۞ وَكَمْ أَهْلَكْنَا قَبْلَهُم مِّن قَرْنٍ هُمْ أَحْسَنُ أَثَـٰثًا وَرِءْيًا ۞ قُلْ مَن كَانَ فِى ٱلضَّلَـٰلَةِ فَلْيَمْدُدْ لَهُ ٱلرَّحْمَـٰنُ مَدًّا ۚ حَتَّىٰٓ إِذَا رَأَوْاْ مَا يُوعَدُونَ إِمَّا ٱلْعَذَابَ وَإِمَّا ٱلسَّاعَةَ فَسَيَعْلَمُونَ مَنْ هُوَ شَرٌّ مَّكَانًا وَأَضْعَفُ جُندًا ۞ وَيَزِيدُ ٱللَّهُ ٱلَّذِينَ ٱهْتَدَوْاْ هُدًى ۗ وَٱلْبَـٰقِيَـٰتُ ٱلصَّـٰلِحَـٰتُ خَيْرٌ عِندَ رَبِّكَ ثَوَابًا وَخَيْرٌ مَّرَدًّا ۞ أَفَرَءَيْتَ ٱلَّذِى كَفَرَ بِـَٔايَـٰتِنَا وَقَالَ لَأُوتَيَنَّ مَالًا وَوَلَدًا ۞ أَطَّلَعَ ٱلْغَيْبَ أَمِ ٱتَّخَذَ عِندَ ٱلرَّحْمَـٰنِ عَهْدًا ۞ كَلَّا ۚ سَنَكْتُبُ مَا يَقُولُ وَنَمُدُّ لَهُۥ مِنَ ٱلْعَذَابِ مَدًّا ۞ وَنَرِثُهُۥ مَا يَقُولُ وَيَأْتِينَا فَرْدًا ۞ وَٱتَّخَذُواْ مِن دُونِ ٱللَّهِ ءَالِهَةً لِّيَكُونُواْ لَهُمْ عِزًّا ۞ كَلَّا ۚ سَيَكْفُرُونَ بِعِبَادَتِهِمْ وَيَكُونُونَ عَلَيْهِمْ ضِدًّا ۞ أَلَمْ تَرَ أَنَّآ أَرْسَلْنَا ٱلشَّيَـٰطِينَ عَلَى ٱلْكَـٰفِرِينَ تَؤُزُّهُمْ أَزًّا ۞ فَلَا تَعْجَلْ عَلَيْهِمْ ۖ إِنَّمَا نَعُدُّ لَهُمْ عَدًّا ۞ يَوْمَ نَحْشُرُ ٱلْمُتَّقِينَ إِلَى ٱلرَّحْمَـٰنِ وَفْدًا ۞ وَنَسُوقُ ٱلْمُجْرِمِينَ إِلَىٰ جَهَنَّمَ وِرْدًا ۞ لَّا يَمْلِكُونَ ٱلشَّفَـٰعَةَ إِلَّا مَنِ ٱتَّخَذَ عِندَ ٱلرَّحْمَـٰنِ عَهْدًا ۞ وَقَالُواْ ٱتَّخَذَ ٱلرَّحْمَـٰنُ وَلَدًا ۞ لَّقَدْ جِئْتُمْ شَيْـًٔا إِدًّا ۞ تَكَادُ ٱلسَّمَـٰوَاتُ يَتَفَطَّرْنَ مِنْهُ وَتَنشَقُّ ٱلْأَرْضُ وَتَخِرُّ ٱلْجِبَالُ هَدًّا ۞ أَن دَعَوْاْ لِلرَّحْمَـٰنِ وَلَدًا ۞ وَمَا يَنۢبَغِى لِلرَّحْمَـٰنِ أَن يَتَّخِذَ وَلَدًا ۞ إِن كُلُّ مَن فِى ٱلسَّمَـٰوَاتِ وَٱلْأَرْضِ إِلَّآ ءَاتِى ٱلرَّحْمَـٰنِ عَبْدًا ۞ لَّقَدْ أَحْصَىٰهُمْ وَعَدَّهُمْ عَدًّا ۞ وَكُلُّهُمْ ءَاتِيهِ يَوْمَ ٱلْقِيَـٰمَةِ فَرْدًا ۞ إِنَّ

ٱلَّذِينَ ءَامَنُوا۟ وَعَمِلُوا۟ ٱلصَّٰلِحَٰتِ سَيَجْعَلُ لَهُمُ ٱلرَّحْمَٰنُ وُدًّا ۝ فَإِنَّمَا يَسَّرْنَٰهُ بِلِسَانِكَ لِتُبَشِّرَ بِهِ ٱلْمُتَّقِينَ وَتُنذِرَ بِهِۦ قَوْمًا لُّدًّا ۝ وَكَمْ أَهْلَكْنَا قَبْلَهُم مِّن قَرْنٍ هَلْ تُحِسُّ مِنْهُم مِّنْ أَحَدٍ أَوْ تَسْمَعُ لَهُمْ رِكْزًۢا ۝

(Maryam 001-098)

Chapter (Surah) 20: Ta-Ha 001-135

بِسْمِ ٱللَّهِ ٱلرَّحْمَٰنِ ٱلرَّحِيمِ

﴿ طه ۝ مَآ أَنزَلْنَا عَلَيْكَ ٱلْقُرْءَانَ لِتَشْقَىٰٓ ۝ إِلَّا تَذْكِرَةً لِّمَن يَخْشَىٰ ۝ تَنزِيلًا مِّمَّنْ خَلَقَ ٱلْأَرْضَ وَٱلسَّمَٰوَٰتِ ٱلْعُلَى ۝ ٱلرَّحْمَٰنُ عَلَى ٱلْعَرْشِ ٱسْتَوَىٰ ۝ لَهُۥ مَا فِى ٱلسَّمَٰوَٰتِ وَمَا فِى ٱلْأَرْضِ وَمَا بَيْنَهُمَا وَمَا تَحْتَ ٱلثَّرَىٰ ۝ وَإِن تَجْهَرْ بِٱلْقَوْلِ فَإِنَّهُۥ يَعْلَمُ ٱلسِّرَّ وَأَخْفَى ۝ ٱللَّهُ لَآ إِلَٰهَ إِلَّا هُوَ لَهُ ٱلْأَسْمَآءُ ٱلْحُسْنَىٰ ۝ وَهَلْ أَتَىٰكَ حَدِيثُ مُوسَىٰٓ ۝ إِذْ رَءَا نَارًا فَقَالَ لِأَهْلِهِ ٱمْكُثُوٓا۟ إِنِّىٓ ءَانَسْتُ نَارًا لَّعَلِّىٓ ءَاتِيكُم مِّنْهَا بِقَبَسٍ أَوْ أَجِدُ عَلَى ٱلنَّارِ هُدًى ۝ فَلَمَّآ أَتَىٰهَا نُودِىَ يَٰمُوسَىٰٓ ۝ إِنِّىٓ أَنَا۠ رَبُّكَ فَٱخْلَعْ نَعْلَيْكَ إِنَّكَ بِٱلْوَادِ ٱلْمُقَدَّسِ طُوًى ۝ وَأَنَا ٱخْتَرْتُكَ فَٱسْتَمِعْ لِمَا يُوحَىٰٓ ۝ إِنَّنِىٓ أَنَا ٱللَّهُ لَآ إِلَٰهَ إِلَّآ أَنَا۠ فَٱعْبُدْنِى وَأَقِمِ ٱلصَّلَوٰةَ لِذِكْرِىٓ ۝ إِنَّ ٱلسَّاعَةَ ءَاتِيَةٌ أَكَادُ أُخْفِيهَا لِتُجْزَىٰ كُلُّ نَفْسٍۭ بِمَا تَسْعَىٰ ۝ فَلَا يَصُدَّنَّكَ عَنْهَا مَن لَّا يُؤْمِنُ بِهَا وَٱتَّبَعَ هَوَىٰهُ فَتَرْدَىٰ ۝ وَمَا تِلْكَ بِيَمِينِكَ يَٰمُوسَىٰ ۝ قَالَ هِىَ عَصَاىَ أَتَوَكَّؤُا۟ عَلَيْهَا وَأَهُشُّ بِهَا عَلَىٰ غَنَمِى وَلِىَ فِيهَا مَـَٔارِبُ أُخْرَىٰ ۝ قَالَ أَلْقِهَا يَٰمُوسَىٰ ۝ فَأَلْقَىٰهَا فَإِذَا هِىَ حَيَّةٌ تَسْعَىٰ ۝ قَالَ خُذْهَا وَلَا تَخَفْ سَنُعِيدُهَا سِيرَتَهَا ٱلْأُولَىٰ ۝ وَٱضْمُمْ يَدَكَ إِلَىٰ جَنَاحِكَ تَخْرُجْ بَيْضَآءَ مِنْ غَيْرِ سُوٓءٍ ءَايَةً أُخْرَىٰ ۝ لِنُرِيَكَ مِنْ ءَايَٰتِنَا ٱلْكُبْرَى ۝ ٱذْهَبْ إِلَىٰ فِرْعَوْنَ إِنَّهُۥ طَغَىٰ ۝ قَالَ رَبِّ ٱشْرَحْ لِى صَدْرِى ۝ وَيَسِّرْ لِىٓ أَمْرِى ۝ وَٱحْلُلْ عُقْدَةً مِّن لِّسَانِى ۝ يَفْقَهُوا۟ قَوْلِى

۝ وَٱجْعَل لِّى وَزِيرًا مِّنْ أَهْلِى ۝ هَـٰرُونَ أَخِى ۝ ٱشْدُدْ بِهِۦٓ أَزْرِى ۝ وَأَشْرِكْهُ فِىٓ أَمْرِى ۝ كَىْ نُسَبِّحَكَ كَثِيرًا ۝ وَنَذْكُرَكَ كَثِيرًا ۝ إِنَّكَ كُنتَ بِنَا بَصِيرًا ۝ قَالَ قَدْ أُوتِيتَ سُؤْلَكَ يَـٰمُوسَىٰ ۝ وَلَقَدْ مَنَنَّا عَلَيْكَ مَرَّةً أُخْرَىٰٓ ۝ إِذْ أَوْحَيْنَآ إِلَىٰٓ أُمِّكَ مَا يُوحَىٰٓ ۝ أَنِ ٱقْذِفِيهِ فِى ٱلتَّابُوتِ فَٱقْذِفِيهِ فِى ٱلْيَمِّ فَلْيُلْقِهِ ٱلْيَمُّ بِٱلسَّاحِلِ يَأْخُذْهُ عَدُوٌّ لِّى وَعَدُوٌّ لَّهُۥ ۚ وَأَلْقَيْتُ عَلَيْكَ مَحَبَّةً مِّنِّى وَلِتُصْنَعَ عَلَىٰ عَيْنِىٓ ۝ إِذْ تَمْشِىٓ أُخْتُكَ فَتَقُولُ هَلْ أَدُلُّكُمْ عَلَىٰ مَن يَكْفُلُهُۥ ۖ فَرَجَعْنَـٰكَ إِلَىٰٓ أُمِّكَ كَىْ تَقَرَّ عَيْنُهَا وَلَا تَحْزَنَ ۚ وَقَتَلْتَ نَفْسًا فَنَجَّيْنَـٰكَ مِنَ ٱلْغَمِّ وَفَتَنَّـٰكَ فُتُونًا ۚ فَلَبِثْتَ سِنِينَ فِىٓ أَهْلِ مَدْيَنَ ثُمَّ جِئْتَ عَلَىٰ قَدَرٍ يَـٰمُوسَىٰ ۝ وَٱصْطَنَعْتُكَ لِنَفْسِى ۝ ٱذْهَبْ أَنتَ وَأَخُوكَ بِـَٔايَـٰتِى وَلَا تَنِيَا فِى ذِكْرِى ۝ ٱذْهَبَآ إِلَىٰ فِرْعَوْنَ إِنَّهُۥ طَغَىٰ ۝ فَقُولَا لَهُۥ قَوْلًا لَّيِّنًا لَّعَلَّهُۥ يَتَذَكَّرُ أَوْ يَخْشَىٰ ۝ قَالَا رَبَّنَآ إِنَّنَا نَخَافُ أَن يَفْرُطَ عَلَيْنَآ أَوْ أَن يَطْغَىٰ ۝ قَالَ لَا تَخَافَآ ۖ إِنَّنِى مَعَكُمَآ أَسْمَعُ وَأَرَىٰ ۝ فَأْتِيَاهُ فَقُولَآ إِنَّا رَسُولَا رَبِّكَ فَأَرْسِلْ مَعَنَا بَنِىٓ إِسْرَٰٓءِيلَ وَلَا تُعَذِّبْهُمْ ۖ قَدْ جِئْنَـٰكَ بِـَٔايَةٍ مِّن رَّبِّكَ ۖ وَٱلسَّلَـٰمُ عَلَىٰ مَنِ ٱتَّبَعَ ٱلْهُدَىٰٓ ۝ إِنَّا قَدْ أُوحِىَ إِلَيْنَآ أَنَّ ٱلْعَذَابَ عَلَىٰ مَن كَذَّبَ وَتَوَلَّىٰ ۝ قَالَ فَمَن رَّبُّكُمَا يَـٰمُوسَىٰ ۝ قَالَ رَبُّنَا ٱلَّذِىٓ أَعْطَىٰ كُلَّ شَىْءٍ خَلْقَهُۥ ثُمَّ هَدَىٰ ۝ قَالَ فَمَا بَالُ ٱلْقُرُونِ ٱلْأُولَىٰ ۝ قَالَ عِلْمُهَا عِندَ رَبِّى فِى كِتَـٰبٍ ۖ لَّا يَضِلُّ رَبِّى وَلَا يَنسَى ۝ ٱلَّذِى جَعَلَ لَكُمُ ٱلْأَرْضَ مَهْدًا وَسَلَكَ لَكُمْ فِيهَا سُبُلًا وَأَنزَلَ مِنَ ٱلسَّمَآءِ مَآءً فَأَخْرَجْنَا بِهِۦٓ أَزْوَٰجًا مِّن نَّبَاتٍ شَتَّىٰ ۝ كُلُوا۟ وَٱرْعَوْا۟ أَنْعَـٰمَكُمْ ۗ إِنَّ فِى ذَٰلِكَ لَـَٔايَـٰتٍ لِّأُو۟لِى ٱلنُّهَىٰ ۝ مِنْهَا خَلَقْنَـٰكُمْ وَفِيهَا نُعِيدُكُمْ وَمِنْهَا نُخْرِجُكُمْ تَارَةً أُخْرَىٰ ۝ وَلَقَدْ أَرَيْنَـٰهُ ءَايَـٰتِنَا كُلَّهَا فَكَذَّبَ وَأَبَىٰ ۝ قَالَ أَجِئْتَنَا لِتُخْرِجَنَا مِنْ أَرْضِنَا بِسِحْرِكَ يَـٰمُوسَىٰ ۝ فَلَنَأْتِيَنَّكَ بِسِحْرٍ مِّثْلِهِۦ

فَٱجْعَلْ بَيْنَنَا وَبَيْنَكَ مَوْعِدًا لَّا نُخْلِفُهُۥ نَحْنُ وَلَآ أَنتَ مَكَانًا سُوًى ۝ قَالَ مَوْعِدُكُمْ يَوْمُ ٱلزِّينَةِ وَأَن يُحْشَرَ ٱلنَّاسُ ضُحًى ۝ فَتَوَلَّىٰ فِرْعَوْنُ فَجَمَعَ كَيْدَهُۥ ثُمَّ أَتَىٰ ۝ قَالَ لَهُم مُّوسَىٰ وَيْلَكُمْ لَا تَفْتَرُوا۟ عَلَى ٱللَّهِ كَذِبًا فَيُسْحِتَكُم بِعَذَابٍ وَقَدْ خَابَ مَنِ ٱفْتَرَىٰ ۝ فَتَنَازَعُوٓا۟ أَمْرَهُم بَيْنَهُمْ وَأَسَرُّوا۟ ٱلنَّجْوَىٰ ۝ قَالُوٓا۟ إِنْ هَٰذَٰنِ لَسَٰحِرَٰنِ يُرِيدَانِ أَن يُخْرِجَاكُم مِّنْ أَرْضِكُم بِسِحْرِهِمَا وَيَذْهَبَا بِطَرِيقَتِكُمُ ٱلْمُثْلَىٰ ۝ فَأَجْمِعُوا۟ كَيْدَكُمْ ثُمَّ ٱئْتُوا۟ صَفًّا وَقَدْ أَفْلَحَ ٱلْيَوْمَ مَنِ ٱسْتَعْلَىٰ ۝ قَالُوا۟ يَٰمُوسَىٰٓ إِمَّآ أَن تُلْقِىَ وَإِمَّآ أَن نَّكُونَ أَوَّلَ مَنْ أَلْقَىٰ ۝ قَالَ بَلْ أَلْقُوا۟ فَإِذَا حِبَالُهُمْ وَعِصِيُّهُمْ يُخَيَّلُ إِلَيْهِ مِن سِحْرِهِمْ أَنَّهَا تَسْعَىٰ ۝ فَأَوْجَسَ فِى نَفْسِهِۦ خِيفَةً مُّوسَىٰ ۝ قُلْنَا لَا تَخَفْ إِنَّكَ أَنتَ ٱلْأَعْلَىٰ ۝ وَأَلْقِ مَا فِى يَمِينِكَ تَلْقَفْ مَا صَنَعُوٓا۟ إِنَّمَا صَنَعُوا۟ كَيْدُ سَٰحِرٍ وَلَا يُفْلِحُ ٱلسَّاحِرُ حَيْثُ أَتَىٰ ۝ فَأُلْقِىَ ٱلسَّحَرَةُ سُجَّدًا قَالُوٓا۟ ءَامَنَّا بِرَبِّ هَٰرُونَ وَمُوسَىٰ ۝ قَالَ ءَامَنتُمْ لَهُۥ قَبْلَ أَنْ ءَاذَنَ لَكُمْ إِنَّهُۥ لَكَبِيرُكُمُ ٱلَّذِى عَلَّمَكُمُ ٱلسِّحْرَ فَلَأُقَطِّعَنَّ أَيْدِيَكُمْ وَأَرْجُلَكُم مِّنْ خِلَٰفٍ وَلَأُصَلِّبَنَّكُمْ فِى جُذُوعِ ٱلنَّخْلِ وَلَتَعْلَمُنَّ أَيُّنَآ أَشَدُّ عَذَابًا وَأَبْقَىٰ ۝ قَالُوا۟ لَن نُّؤْثِرَكَ عَلَىٰ مَا جَآءَنَا مِنَ ٱلْبَيِّنَٰتِ وَٱلَّذِى فَطَرَنَا فَٱقْضِ مَآ أَنتَ قَاضٍ إِنَّمَا تَقْضِى هَٰذِهِ ٱلْحَيَوٰةَ ٱلدُّنْيَآ ۝ إِنَّآ ءَامَنَّا بِرَبِّنَا لِيَغْفِرَ لَنَا خَطَٰيَٰنَا وَمَآ أَكْرَهْتَنَا عَلَيْهِ مِنَ ٱلسِّحْرِ وَٱللَّهُ خَيْرٌ وَأَبْقَىٰٓ ۝ إِنَّهُۥ مَن يَأْتِ رَبَّهُۥ مُجْرِمًا فَإِنَّ لَهُۥ جَهَنَّمَ لَا يَمُوتُ فِيهَا وَلَا يَحْيَىٰ ۝ وَمَن يَأْتِهِۦ مُؤْمِنًا قَدْ عَمِلَ ٱلصَّٰلِحَٰتِ فَأُو۟لَٰٓئِكَ لَهُمُ ٱلدَّرَجَٰتُ ٱلْعُلَىٰ ۝ جَنَّٰتُ عَدْنٍ تَجْرِى مِن تَحْتِهَا ٱلْأَنْهَٰرُ خَٰلِدِينَ فِيهَا وَذَٰلِكَ جَزَآءُ مَن تَزَكَّىٰ ۝ وَلَقَدْ أَوْحَيْنَآ إِلَىٰ مُوسَىٰٓ أَنْ أَسْرِ بِعِبَادِى فَٱضْرِبْ لَهُمْ طَرِيقًا فِى ٱلْبَحْرِ يَبَسًا لَّا تَخَٰفُ دَرَكًا وَلَا تَخْشَىٰ ۝ فَأَتْبَعَهُمْ فِرْعَوْنُ بِجُنُودِهِۦ فَغَشِيَهُم مِّنَ ٱلْيَمِّ

مَا غَشِيَهُمْ ۝ وَأَضَلَّ فِرْعَوْنُ قَوْمَهُ وَمَا هَدَىٰ ۝ يَـٰبَنِىٓ إِسْرَٰٓءِيلَ قَدْ أَنجَيْنَـٰكُم مِّنْ عَدُوِّكُمْ وَوَٰعَدْنَـٰكُمْ جَانِبَ ٱلطُّورِ ٱلْأَيْمَنَ وَنَزَّلْنَا عَلَيْكُمُ ٱلْمَنَّ وَٱلسَّلْوَىٰ ۝ كُلُوا۟ مِن طَيِّبَـٰتِ مَا رَزَقْنَـٰكُمْ وَلَا تَطْغَوْا۟ فِيهِ فَيَحِلَّ عَلَيْكُمْ غَضَبِى ۖ وَمَن يَحْلِلْ عَلَيْهِ غَضَبِى فَقَدْ هَوَىٰ ۝ وَإِنِّى لَغَفَّارٌ لِّمَن تَابَ وَءَامَنَ وَعَمِلَ صَـٰلِحًا ثُمَّ ٱهْتَدَىٰ ۝ ۞ وَمَآ أَعْجَلَكَ عَن قَوْمِكَ يَـٰمُوسَىٰ ۝ قَالَ هُمْ أُو۟لَآءِ عَلَىٰٓ أَثَرِى وَعَجِلْتُ إِلَيْكَ رَبِّ لِتَرْضَىٰ ۝ قَالَ فَإِنَّا قَدْ فَتَنَّا قَوْمَكَ مِنۢ بَعْدِكَ وَأَضَلَّهُمُ ٱلسَّامِرِىُّ ۝ فَرَجَعَ مُوسَىٰٓ إِلَىٰ قَوْمِهِۦ غَضْبَـٰنَ أَسِفًا ۚ قَالَ يَـٰقَوْمِ أَلَمْ يَعِدْكُمْ رَبُّكُمْ وَعْدًا حَسَنًا ۚ أَفَطَالَ عَلَيْكُمُ ٱلْعَهْدُ أَمْ أَرَدتُّمْ أَن يَحِلَّ عَلَيْكُمْ غَضَبٌ مِّن رَّبِّكُمْ فَأَخْلَفْتُم مَّوْعِدِى ۝ قَالُوا۟ مَآ أَخْلَفْنَا مَوْعِدَكَ بِمَلْكِنَا وَلَـٰكِنَّا حُمِّلْنَآ أَوْزَارًا مِّن زِينَةِ ٱلْقَوْمِ فَقَذَفْنَـٰهَا فَكَذَٰلِكَ أَلْقَى ٱلسَّامِرِىُّ ۝ فَأَخْرَجَ لَهُمْ عِجْلًا جَسَدًا لَّهُۥ خُوَارٌ فَقَالُوا۟ هَـٰذَآ إِلَـٰهُكُمْ وَإِلَـٰهُ مُوسَىٰ فَنَسِىَ ۝ أَفَلَا يَرَوْنَ أَلَّا يَرْجِعُ إِلَيْهِمْ قَوْلًا وَلَا يَمْلِكُ لَهُمْ ضَرًّا وَلَا نَفْعًا ۝ وَلَقَدْ قَالَ لَهُمْ هَـٰرُونُ مِن قَبْلُ يَـٰقَوْمِ إِنَّمَا فُتِنتُم بِهِۦ ۖ وَإِنَّ رَبَّكُمُ ٱلرَّحْمَـٰنُ فَٱتَّبِعُونِى وَأَطِيعُوٓا۟ أَمْرِى ۝ قَالُوا۟ لَن نَّبْرَحَ عَلَيْهِ عَـٰكِفِينَ حَتَّىٰ يَرْجِعَ إِلَيْنَا مُوسَىٰ ۝ قَالَ يَـٰهَـٰرُونُ مَا مَنَعَكَ إِذْ رَأَيْتَهُمْ ضَلُّوٓا۟ ۝ أَلَّا تَتَّبِعَنِ ۖ أَفَعَصَيْتَ أَمْرِى ۝ قَالَ يَبْنَؤُمَّ لَا تَأْخُذْ بِلِحْيَتِى وَلَا بِرَأْسِىٓ ۖ إِنِّى خَشِيتُ أَن تَقُولَ فَرَّقْتَ بَيْنَ بَنِىٓ إِسْرَٰٓءِيلَ وَلَمْ تَرْقُبْ قَوْلِى ۝ قَالَ فَمَا خَطْبُكَ يَـٰسَـٰمِرِىُّ ۝ قَالَ بَصُرْتُ بِمَا لَمْ يَبْصُرُوا۟ بِهِۦ فَقَبَضْتُ قَبْضَةً مِّنْ أَثَرِ ٱلرَّسُولِ فَنَبَذْتُهَا وَكَذَٰلِكَ سَوَّلَتْ لِى نَفْسِى ۝ قَالَ فَٱذْهَبْ فَإِنَّ لَكَ فِى ٱلْحَيَوٰةِ أَن تَقُولَ لَا مِسَاسَ ۖ وَإِنَّ لَكَ مَوْعِدًا لَّن تُخْلَفَهُۥ ۖ وَٱنظُرْ إِلَىٰٓ إِلَـٰهِكَ ٱلَّذِى ظَلْتَ عَلَيْهِ عَاكِفًا ۖ لَّنُحَرِّقَنَّهُۥ ثُمَّ لَنَنسِفَنَّهُۥ فِى ٱلْيَمِّ نَسْفًا ۝ إِنَّمَآ

إِلَٰهُكُمُ ٱللَّهُ ٱلَّذِي لَآ إِلَٰهَ إِلَّا هُوَ ۚ وَسِعَ كُلَّ شَيْءٍ عِلْمًا ۝ كَذَٰلِكَ نَقُصُّ عَلَيْكَ مِنْ أَنۢبَآءِ مَا قَدْ سَبَقَ ۚ وَقَدْ ءَاتَيْنَٰكَ مِن لَّدُنَّا ذِكْرًا ۝ مَّنْ أَعْرَضَ عَنْهُ فَإِنَّهُۥ يَحْمِلُ يَوْمَ ٱلْقِيَٰمَةِ وِزْرًا ۝ خَٰلِدِينَ فِيهِ ۖ وَسَآءَ لَهُمْ يَوْمَ ٱلْقِيَٰمَةِ حِمْلًا ۝ يَوْمَ يُنفَخُ فِى ٱلصُّورِ ۚ وَنَحْشُرُ ٱلْمُجْرِمِينَ يَوْمَئِذٍ زُرْقًا ۝ يَتَخَٰفَتُونَ بَيْنَهُمْ إِن لَّبِثْتُمْ إِلَّا عَشْرًا ۝ نَّحْنُ أَعْلَمُ بِمَا يَقُولُونَ إِذْ يَقُولُ أَمْثَلُهُمْ طَرِيقَةً إِن لَّبِثْتُمْ إِلَّا يَوْمًا ۝ وَيَسْـَٔلُونَكَ عَنِ ٱلْجِبَالِ فَقُلْ يَنسِفُهَا رَبِّى نَسْفًا ۝ فَيَذَرُهَا قَاعًا صَفْصَفًا ۝ لَّا تَرَىٰ فِيهَا عِوَجًا وَلَآ أَمْتًا ۝ يَوْمَئِذٍ يَتَّبِعُونَ ٱلدَّاعِىَ لَا عِوَجَ لَهُۥ ۖ وَخَشَعَتِ ٱلْأَصْوَاتُ لِلرَّحْمَٰنِ فَلَا تَسْمَعُ إِلَّا هَمْسًا ۝ يَوْمَئِذٍ لَّا تَنفَعُ ٱلشَّفَٰعَةُ إِلَّا مَنْ أَذِنَ لَهُ ٱلرَّحْمَٰنُ وَرَضِىَ لَهُۥ قَوْلًا ۝ يَعْلَمُ مَا بَيْنَ أَيْدِيهِمْ وَمَا خَلْفَهُمْ وَلَا يُحِيطُونَ بِهِۦ عِلْمًا ۝ ۞ وَعَنَتِ ٱلْوُجُوهُ لِلْحَىِّ ٱلْقَيُّومِ ۖ وَقَدْ خَابَ مَنْ حَمَلَ ظُلْمًا ۝ وَمَن يَعْمَلْ مِنَ ٱلصَّٰلِحَٰتِ وَهُوَ مُؤْمِنٌ فَلَا يَخَافُ ظُلْمًا وَلَا هَضْمًا ۝ وَكَذَٰلِكَ أَنزَلْنَٰهُ قُرْءَانًا عَرَبِيًّا وَصَرَّفْنَا فِيهِ مِنَ ٱلْوَعِيدِ لَعَلَّهُمْ يَتَّقُونَ أَوْ يُحْدِثُ لَهُمْ ذِكْرًا ۝ فَتَعَٰلَى ٱللَّهُ ٱلْمَلِكُ ٱلْحَقُّ ۗ وَلَا تَعْجَلْ بِٱلْقُرْءَانِ مِن قَبْلِ أَن يُقْضَىٰٓ إِلَيْكَ وَحْيُهُۥ ۖ وَقُل رَّبِّ زِدْنِى عِلْمًا ۝ وَلَقَدْ عَهِدْنَآ إِلَىٰٓ ءَادَمَ مِن قَبْلُ فَنَسِىَ وَلَمْ نَجِدْ لَهُۥ عَزْمًا ۝ وَإِذْ قُلْنَا لِلْمَلَٰٓئِكَةِ ٱسْجُدُوا۟ لِـَٔادَمَ فَسَجَدُوٓا۟ إِلَّآ إِبْلِيسَ أَبَىٰ ۝ فَقُلْنَا يَٰٓـَٔادَمُ إِنَّ هَٰذَا عَدُوٌّ لَّكَ وَلِزَوْجِكَ فَلَا يُخْرِجَنَّكُمَا مِنَ ٱلْجَنَّةِ فَتَشْقَىٰٓ ۝ إِنَّ لَكَ أَلَّا تَجُوعَ فِيهَا وَلَا تَعْرَىٰ ۝ وَأَنَّكَ لَا تَظْمَؤُا۟ فِيهَا وَلَا تَضْحَىٰ ۝ فَوَسْوَسَ إِلَيْهِ ٱلشَّيْطَٰنُ قَالَ يَٰٓـَٔادَمُ هَلْ أَدُلُّكَ عَلَىٰ شَجَرَةِ ٱلْخُلْدِ وَمُلْكٍ لَّا يَبْلَىٰ ۝ فَأَكَلَا مِنْهَا فَبَدَتْ لَهُمَا سَوْءَٰتُهُمَا وَطَفِقَا يَخْصِفَانِ عَلَيْهِمَا مِن وَرَقِ ٱلْجَنَّةِ ۚ وَعَصَىٰٓ ءَادَمُ رَبَّهُۥ فَغَوَىٰ ۝ ثُمَّ ٱجْتَبَٰهُ رَبُّهُۥ فَتَابَ

عَلَيْهِ وَهَدَىٰ ۝ قَالَ اهْبِطَا مِنْهَا جَمِيعًا ۖ بَعْضُكُمْ لِبَعْضٍ عَدُوٌّ ۖ فَإِمَّا يَأْتِيَنَّكُم مِّنِّي هُدًى فَمَنِ اتَّبَعَ هُدَايَ فَلَا يَضِلُّ وَلَا يَشْقَىٰ ۝ وَمَنْ أَعْرَضَ عَن ذِكْرِي فَإِنَّ لَهُ مَعِيشَةً ضَنكًا وَنَحْشُرُهُ يَوْمَ الْقِيَامَةِ أَعْمَىٰ ۝ قَالَ رَبِّ لِمَ حَشَرْتَنِي أَعْمَىٰ وَقَدْ كُنتُ بَصِيرًا ۝ قَالَ كَذَٰلِكَ أَتَتْكَ آيَاتُنَا فَنَسِيتَهَا ۖ وَكَذَٰلِكَ الْيَوْمَ تُنسَىٰ ۝ وَكَذَٰلِكَ نَجْزِي مَنْ أَسْرَفَ وَلَمْ يُؤْمِن بِآيَاتِ رَبِّهِ ۚ وَلَعَذَابُ الْآخِرَةِ أَشَدُّ وَأَبْقَىٰ ۝ أَفَلَمْ يَهْدِ لَهُمْ كَمْ أَهْلَكْنَا قَبْلَهُم مِّنَ الْقُرُونِ يَمْشُونَ فِي مَسَاكِنِهِمْ ۗ إِنَّ فِي ذَٰلِكَ لَآيَاتٍ لِّأُولِي النُّهَىٰ ۝ وَلَوْلَا كَلِمَةٌ سَبَقَتْ مِن رَّبِّكَ لَكَانَ لِزَامًا وَأَجَلٌ مُّسَمًّى ۝ فَاصْبِرْ عَلَىٰ مَا يَقُولُونَ وَسَبِّحْ بِحَمْدِ رَبِّكَ قَبْلَ طُلُوعِ الشَّمْسِ وَقَبْلَ غُرُوبِهَا ۖ وَمِنْ آنَاءِ اللَّيْلِ فَسَبِّحْ وَأَطْرَافَ النَّهَارِ لَعَلَّكَ تَرْضَىٰ ۝ وَلَا تَمُدَّنَّ عَيْنَيْكَ إِلَىٰ مَا مَتَّعْنَا بِهِ أَزْوَاجًا مِّنْهُمْ زَهْرَةَ الْحَيَاةِ الدُّنْيَا لِنَفْتِنَهُمْ فِيهِ ۚ وَرِزْقُ رَبِّكَ خَيْرٌ وَأَبْقَىٰ ۝ وَأْمُرْ أَهْلَكَ بِالصَّلَاةِ وَاصْطَبِرْ عَلَيْهَا ۖ لَا نَسْأَلُكَ رِزْقًا ۖ نَحْنُ نَرْزُقُكَ ۗ وَالْعَاقِبَةُ لِلتَّقْوَىٰ ۝ وَقَالُوا لَوْلَا يَأْتِينَا بِآيَةٍ مِّن رَّبِّهِ ۚ أَوَلَمْ تَأْتِهِم بَيِّنَةُ مَا فِي الصُّحُفِ الْأُولَىٰ ۝ وَلَوْ أَنَّا أَهْلَكْنَاهُم بِعَذَابٍ مِّن قَبْلِهِ لَقَالُوا رَبَّنَا لَوْلَا أَرْسَلْتَ إِلَيْنَا رَسُولًا فَنَتَّبِعَ آيَاتِكَ مِن قَبْلِ أَن نَّذِلَّ وَنَخْزَىٰ ۝ قُلْ كُلٌّ مُّتَرَبِّصٌ فَتَرَبَّصُوا ۖ فَسَتَعْلَمُونَ مَنْ أَصْحَابُ الصِّرَاطِ السَّوِيِّ وَمَنِ اهْتَدَىٰ ۝

(Ta-Ha 001-135)

INTRODUCTION TO CHAPTER (SURAH) 18: AL-KAHF (THE CAVE)

Ibn kathir's Introduction

What has been mentioned about the Virtues of this Surah and the first and last ten Ayat, which provide protection from the Dajjal

Imam Ahmad recorded that Al-Bara' said: "A man recited Al-Kahf and there was an animal in the house which began acting in a nervous manner. He looked, and saw a fog or cloud overhead. He mentioned this to the Prophet, who said:

Chapter 18: Al-Kahf (The Cave), Verses 075-110

«اقْرَأْ فُلَانُ، فَإِنَّهَا السَّكِينَةُ تَنْزِلُ عِنْدَ الْقُرْآنِ أَوْ تَنَزَّلَتْ لِلْقُرْآنِ»

(Keep on reciting so and so, for this is the tranquillity which descends when one reads Qur'an or because of reading Qur'an;) This was also recorded in the Two Sahihs. This man who recited it was Usayd bin Al-Hudayr, as we have previously mentioned in our Tafsir of Surat Al-Baqarah. Imam Ahmad recorded from Abu Ad-Darda' that the Prophet said:

«مَنْ حَفِظَ عَشْرَ آيَاتٍ مِنْ أَوَّلِ سُورَةِ الْكَهْفِ عُصِمَ مِنَ الدَّجَّالِ»

(Whoever memorizes ten Ayat from the beginning of Surat Al-Kahf will be protected from the Dajjal.) This was also recorded by Muslim, Abu Dawud, An-Nasa'i and At-Tirmidhi. According to the version recorded by At-Tirmidhi,

«مَنْ حَفِظَ ثَلَاثَ آيَاتٍ مِنْ أَوَّلِ الْكَهْفِ»

(Whoever memorizes three Ayat from the beginning of Al-Kahf.) He said, it is "Hasan Sahih." In his Mustadrak, Al-Hakim recorded from Abu Sa`id that the Prophet said:

«مَنْ قَرَأَ سُورَةَ الْكَهْفِ فِي يَوْمِ الْجُمُعَةِ أَضَاءَ لَهُ مِنَ النُّورِ مَا بَيْنَهُ وَبَيْنَ الْجُمُعَتَيْنِ»

(Whoever recites Surat Al-Kahf on Friday, it will illuminate him with light from one Friday to the next.) Then he said: "This Hadith has a Sahih chain, but they (Al-Bukhari and Muslim) did not record it." Al-Hafiz Abu Bakr Al-Bayhaqi also recorded it in his Sunan from Al-Hakim, then he narrated with his own chain that the Prophet said:

«مَنْ قَرَأَ سُورَةَ الْكَهْفِ كَمَا نَزَلَتْ، كَانَتْ لَهُ نُورًا يَوْمَ الْقِيَامَةِ»

(Whoever recites Surat Al-Kahf as it was revealed, it will be a light for him on the Day of Resurrection.)

CHAPTER (SURAH) 18: AL-KAHF (THE CAVE), VERSES 075 – 110

Surah: 18 Ayah: 74 (end of Part 15, included here for completing the tafsir that follows), Ayah: 75 (beginning of Part 16) & Ayah: 76

فَانطَلَقَا حَتَّىٰٓ إِذَا لَقِيَا غُلَٰمًا فَقَتَلَهُۥ قَالَ أَقَتَلْتَ نَفْسًا زَكِيَّةً بِغَيْرِ نَفْسٍ لَّقَدْ جِئْتَ شَيْئًا نُّكْرًا ۝

74. Then they both proceeded, till they met a boy, he (Khidr) killed him. Mûsa (Moses) said: "Have you killed an innocent person who had killed none? Verily, you have committed a thing "Nukr" (a great Munkar - prohibited, evil, dreadful thing)!"

۞ قَالَ أَلَمْ أَقُل لَّكَ إِنَّكَ لَن تَسْتَطِيعَ مَعِىَ صَبْرًا ۝

75. (Khidr) said: "Did I not tell you that you can have no patience with me?"

قَالَ إِن سَأَلْتُكَ عَن شَىْءٍ بَعْدَهَا فَلَا تُصَٰحِبْنِى قَدْ بَلَغْتَ مِن لَّدُنِّى عُذْرًا ۝

76. (Mûsa (Moses)) said: "If I ask you anything after this, keep me not in your company, you have received an excuse from me."

Transliteration

74. Faintalaqa hatta itha laqiya ghulaman faqatalahu qala aqatalta nafsan zakiyyatan bighayri nafsin laqad ji/ta shay-an nukran   75. Qala alam aqul laka innaka lan tastateeAAa maAAiya sabran   76. Qala in saaltuka AAan shay-in baAAdaha fala tusahibnee qad balaghta min ladunnee AAuthran

Tafsir Ibn Kathir

The Story of killing the Boy

(Then they both proceeded,) means, after the first incident,

(till they met a boy, and he (Khidr) killed him.) It has been stated previously that this boy was playing with other boys in one of the towns, and that Al-Khidr deliberately singled him out. He was the finest and most handsome of them all, and Al-Khidr killed him. When Musa, peace be upon him, saw that he denounced him even more fervently than in the first case, and said hastily:

(Have you killed an innocent person) meaning, a young person who had not yet committed any sin or done anything wrong, yet you killed him

(without Nafs) with no reason for killing him.

(Verily, you have committed a thing Nukr!) meaning, something that is clearly evil.

Chapter 18: Al-Kahf (The Cave), Verses 075-110

(He said: "Did I not tell you that you can have no patience with me") Once again, Al-Khidr reiterates the condition set in the first place, so Musa says to him:

(If I ask you anything after this,) meaning, `if I object to anything else you do after this,'

(keep me not in your company, you have received an excuse from me.) `you have accepted my apology twice.' Ibn Jarir narrated from Ibn `Abbas that Ubayy bin Ka`b said: "Whenever the Prophet mentioned anyone, he would pray for himself first. One day he said:

«رَحْمَةُ اللهِ عَلَيْنَا وَعَلَى مُوسَى لَوْ لَبِثَ مَعَ صَاحِبِهِ لَأَبْصَرَ الْعَجَبَ، وَلَكِنَّهُ قَالَ:

(إِن سَأَلْتُكَ عَن شَيْءٍ بَعْدَهَا فَلاَ تُصَاحِبْنِي قَدْ بَلَغْتَ مِن لَّدُنِّي عُذْراً)»

(May the mercy of Allah be upon us and upon Musa. If he had stayed with his companion he would have seen wonders, but he said, (`If I ask you anything after this, keep me not in your company, you have received an excuse from me.'))"

Surah: 18 Ayah: 77 & Ayah: 78

فَانطَلَقَا حَتَّىٰ إِذَآ أَتَيَآ أَهْلَ قَرْيَةٍ ٱسْتَطْعَمَآ أَهْلَهَا فَأَبَوْاْ أَن يُضَيِّفُوهُمَا فَوَجَدَا فِيهَا جِدَاراً يُرِيدُ أَن يَنقَضَّ فَأَقَامَهُ ۖ قَالَ لَوْ شِئْتَ لَتَّخَذْتَ عَلَيْهِ أَجْراً ۝

77. Then they both proceeded, till, when they came to the people of a town, they asked them for food, but they refused to entertain them. Then they found therein a wall about to collapse and he (Khidr) set it up straight. (Mûsa (Moses)) said: If you had wished, surely, you could have taken wages for it!"

قَالَ هَـٰذَا فِرَاقُ بَيْنِى وَبَيْنِكَ ۚ سَأُنَبِّئُكَ بِتَأْوِيلِ مَا لَمْ تَسْتَطِع عَّلَيْهِ صَبْراً ۝

78. (Khidr) said: "This is the parting between me and you, I will tell you the interpretation of (those) things over which you were unable to hold patience.

Transliteration

77. Faintalaqa hatta itha ataya ahla qaryatin istatAAama ahlaha faabaw an yudayyifoohuma fawajada feeha jidaran yureedu an yanqadda faaqamahu qala law shi/ta laittakhathta AAalayhi ajran 78. Qala hatha firaqu baynee wabaynika saonabbi-oka bita/weeli ma lam tastatiAA AAalayhi sabran

Tafsir Ibn Kathir

The Story of repairing the Wall Allah tells us that

(they both proceeded) after the first two instances,

(till when they came to the people of a town,) Ibn Jarir narrated from Ibn Sirin that this was Al-Aylah. According to the Hadith;

《حَتَّى إِذَا أَتَيَا أَهْلَ قَرْيَةٍ لِئَامًا》

(When they came there, the people of the town were mean.) i.e., miserly

(they asked them for food, but they refused to entertain them. Then they found therein a wall about to collapse and he (Khidr) set it up straight.) means, he fixed it so it was standing upright properly. We have already seen in the Hadith quoted above that he set it up with his own hands, supporting it until it was standing straight again, which is something extraordinary. At this point Musa said to him:

(If you had wished, surely you could have taken wages for it!) meaning, because they did not entertain us as guests, you should not have worked for them for free.

(He said: "This is the parting between you and I) meaning, because you said after the boy was killed that if you asked me anything after that, you would not accompany me any further. So this is the parting of the ways between me and you.

(I will tell you the interpretation) meaning explanation,

(of (those) things over which you were not able to be patient.)

Surah: 18 Ayah: 79

أَمَّا ٱلسَّفِينَةُ فَكَانَتْ لِمَسَٰكِينَ يَعْمَلُونَ فِى ٱلْبَحْرِ فَأَرَدتُّ أَنْ أَعِيبَهَا وَكَانَ وَرَآءَهُم مَّلِكٌ يَأْخُذُ كُلَّ سَفِينَةٍ غَصْبًا ۝

79. "As for the ship, it belonged to Masâkîn (poor people) working in the sea. So I wished to make a defective damage in it, as there was a king behind them who seized every ship by force.

Transliteration

79. Amma alssafeenatu fakanat limasakeena yaAAmaloona fee albahri faaradtu an aAAeebaha wakana waraahum malikun ya/khuthu kulla safeenatin ghasban

Chapter 18: Al-Kahf (The Cave), Verses 075-110

Tafsir Ibn Kathir

Interpretations of why the Ship was damaged

This is an explanation of what Musa found so hard to understand, and the appearence of which he condemed. Allah showed Al-Khidr the hidden reasons, so he said, "I damaged the ship to make it faulty, because they used to pass by a king who was one of the oppressors, who

(seized every boat), i.e., every good, sound boat

(by force.) `So I wanted to prevent him from taking this boat by making it appear faulty, so that its poor owners who had nothing else could benefit from it.' It was also said that they were orphans.

Surah: 18 Ayah: 80 & Ayah: 81

وَأَمَّا ٱلْغُلَٰمُ فَكَانَ أَبَوَاهُ مُؤْمِنَيْنِ فَخَشِينَآ أَن يُرْهِقَهُمَا طُغْيَٰنًا وَكُفْرًا ۝

80. "And as for the boy, his parents were believers, and we feared lest he should oppress them by rebellion and disbelief.

فَأَرَدْنَآ أَن يُبْدِلَهُمَا رَبُّهُمَا خَيْرًا مِّنْهُ زَكَوٰةً وَأَقْرَبَ رُحْمًا ۝

81. "So we intended that their Lord should change him for them for one better in righteousness and nearer to mercy.

Transliteration

80. Waamma alghulamu fakana abawahu mu/minayni fakhasheena an yurhiqahuma tughyanan wakufran 81. Faaradna an yubdilahuma rabbuhuma khayran minhu zakatan waaqraba ruhman

Tafsir Ibn Kathir

Interpretation of why the Boy was killed

Ibn `Abbas narrated from Ubayy bin Ka`b that the Prophet said:

«الْغُلَامُ الَّذِي قَتَلَهُ الْخَضِرُ طُبِعَ يَوْمَ طُبِعَ كَافِرًا»

(The boy Al-Khidr killed was destined to be a disbeliever from the day he was created.) It was recorded by Ibn Jarir from Ibn `Abbas. He said:

(his parents were believers, and we feared he would oppress them by rebellion and disbelief) Their love for him might make them follow him in disbelief. Qatadah said, "His parents rejoiced when he was born and grieved for him when he was killed. If he had stayed alive, he would have been the cause of their doom. So let a man be content with the decree of Allah, for the decree of Allah for the believer, if he dislikes it, is better for him than if He were to decree something that he likes for him." An authentic Hadith says;

«لَا يَقْضِي اللَّهُ لِلْمُؤْمِنِ مِنْ قَضَاءٍ إِلَّا كَانَ خَيْرًا لَهُ»

(Allah does not decree anything for the believer except it is good for him.) And Allah says:

(and it may be that you dislike a thing which is good for you.) (2:216).

(So we intended that their Lord should exchange him for them for one better in righteousness and nearer to mercy.) A child who was better than this one, a child for whom they would feel more compassion. This was the view of Ibn Jurayj.

Surah: 18 Ayah: 82

وَأَمَّا ٱلۡجِدَارُ فَكَانَ لِغُلَٰمَيۡنِ يَتِيمَيۡنِ فِي ٱلۡمَدِينَةِ وَكَانَ تَحۡتَهُۥ كَنزٌ لَّهُمَا وَكَانَ أَبُوهُمَا صَٰلِحٗا فَأَرَادَ رَبُّكَ أَن يَبۡلُغَآ أَشُدَّهُمَا وَيَسۡتَخۡرِجَا كَنزَهُمَا رَحۡمَةٗ مِّن رَّبِّكَۚ وَمَا فَعَلۡتُهُۥ عَنۡ أَمۡرِيۚ ذَٰلِكَ تَأۡوِيلُ مَا لَمۡ تَسۡطِع عَّلَيۡهِ صَبۡرٗا ۝

82. "And as for the wall, it belonged to two orphan boys in the town; and there was under it a treasure belonging to them; and their father was a righteous man, and your Lord intended that they should attain their age of full strength and take out their treasure as a mercy from your Lord. And I did them not of my own accord. That is the interpretation of those (things) over which you could not hold patience."

Transliteration

82. Waamma aljidaru fakana lighulamayni yateemayni fee almadeenati wakana tahtahu kanzun lahuma wakana aboohuma salihan faarada rabbuka an yablugha ashuddahuma wayastakhrija kanzahuma rahmatan min rabbika wama faAAaltuhu AAan amree thalika ta/weelu ma lam tastiAA AAalayhi sabran

Tafsir Ibn Kathir

Interpretation of why the Wall was repaired for no Charge

In this Ayah there is a proof that the word Qaryah (village) may be used to refer to a city (Madinah), because Allah first says,

(till when they came to the people of a town (Qaryah)) (18:77), but here He says:

(it belonged to two orphan boys in the town (Al-Madinah);) This is like the Ayat:

(And many a town (Qaryah), stronger than your town which has driven you out We have destroyed) (47:13) and;

(And they say: "Why is not this Qur'an sent down to some great man of the two towns (Al-Qaryatayn)")(43:31) meaning Makkah and At-Ta'if. The meaning of the Ayah (18:82) is: "I repaired this wall because it belonged to two orphan boys in the city, and underneath it was some treasure belonging to them." `Ikrimah, Qatadah and others said, "Underneath it there was some wealth that was buried for them." This meaning is apparent from the context of the Ayah, and is the view chosen by Ibn Jarir (may Allah have mercy on him).

(their father was a righteous man,) indicates that a righteous person's offspring will be taken care of, and that the blessing of his worship will extend to them in this world and in the Hereafter. This will occur through his intercession for them, as well as their status being raised to the highest levels of Paradise, so that he may find joy in them. This was stated in the Qur'an and reported in the Sunnah. Sa`id bin Jubayr narrated from Ibn `Abbas: "They were taken care of because their father was a righteous man, although it is not stated that they themselves were righteous."

(your Lord intended that they should attain their age of full strength and take out their treasure) Here will is attributed to Allah, the Exalted, because no one else is able to bring them to the age of full strength and puberty except Allah. In contrast, He said about the boy:

(So we intended that their Lord should exchange him for them for one better in righteousness) and concerning the ship:

(So I wished to make a defective damage in it,) And Allah knows best.

Was Al-Khidr a Prophet

(as a mercy from your Lord. And I did them not of my own accord.) Meaning, `These three things that I did, come from the mercy of Allah for those we have mentioned, the crew of the ship, the parents of the boy and the two sons of the righteous man; I was only commanded to do these things that were enjoined upon me.' This is proof and evidence in support of those who say that Al-Khidr, peace be upon him, was a Prophet, along with the Ayah which we have already quoted:

(Then they found one of Our servants, on whom We had bestowed mercy from Us, and whom We had taught knowledge from Us.) (18:65)

Why he was called Al-Khidr

Imam Ahmad recorded that Abu Hurayrah, may Allah be pleased with him, said that the Prophet said concerning Al-Khidr:

«إِنَّمَا سُمِّيَ خَضِرًا لِأَنَّهُ جَلَسَ عَلَى فَرْوَةٍ بَيْضَاءَ، فَإِذَا هِيَ تَهْتَزُّ مِنْ تَحْتِهِ خَضْرَاءُ»

(He was called Al-Khidr because he sat on a barren Farwah that turned white, then it turned green (Khadra') beneath him.) Imam Ahmad also recorded this from `Abdur-Razzaq. It was also recorded in Sahih Al-Bukhari from Hammam from Abu Hurayrah that the Messenger of Allah said,

«إِنَّمَا سُمِّي الْخَضِرَ لِأَنَّهُ جَلَسَ عَلَى فَرْوَةٍ، فَإِذَا هِيَ تَهْتَزُّ مِنْ تَحْتِهِ خَضْرَاءٌ»

(He was called Al-Khidr because he sat on a barren Farwah and it turned green (Khadra') beneath him.) The meaning of Farwah here is a patch of withered vegetation. This was the view of `Abdur-Razzaq. It was also said that it means the face of the earth.

(That is the interpretation of those (things) over which you could not be patient.) meaning, 'this is the explanation of the things which you could not put up with or be patient with until I took the initiative of explaining them to you.' When he explained them and made them clear and solved the confusion, he used a milder form of the verb,

(you could) When the matter was still confusing and very difficult, a more intensive form was used,

(I will tell you the interpretation of (those) things over which you were unable to be patient with) (18:78). The intensity of the verbal form used reflects the intensity of the confusion felt. This is like the Ayah:

(So they (Ya`juj and Ma`juj) were not able to scale it) (18:97) which means ascending to its highest point,

(nor are they able to dig through it) (18:97) which is more difficult than the former. The intensity of the verbal form used reflects the difficulty of the action, which has to do with the subtleties of meaning. And Allah knows best. If one were to ask, what happened to the boy-servant of Musa who appears at the beginning of the story but then is not mentioned The answer is that the objective of the story is what happened between Musa and Al-Khidr. Musa's boy-servant was with him, following him. It is clearly mentioned in the Sahih Hadiths referred to above that he was Yusha` bin Nun, who was the one who became the leader of the Children of Israel after Musa, peace be upon him.

Surah: 18 Ayah: 83 & Ayah: 84

وَيَسْـَٔلُونَكَ عَن ذِى ٱلْقَرْنَيْنِ ۖ قُلْ سَأَتْلُواْ عَلَيْكُم مِّنْهُ ذِكْرًا ۝

83. And they ask you about Dhul-Qarnain. Say: "I shall recite to you something of his story."

إِنَّا مَكَّنَّا لَهُۥ فِى ٱلْأَرْضِ وَءَاتَيْنَٰهُ مِن كُلِّ شَىْءٍ سَبَبًا ۝

Chapter 18: Al-Kahf (The Cave), Verses 075-110

84. Verily, We established him in the earth, and We gave him the means of everything.

Transliteration

83. Wayas-aloonaka AAan thee alqarnayni qul saatloo AAalaykum minhu thikran 84. Inna makkanna lahu fee al-ardi waataynahu min kulli shay-in sababan

Tafsir Ibn Kathir

The Story of Dhul-Qarnayn Allah says to His Prophet ,

(And they ask you) O Muhammad ,

(about Dhul-Qarnayn.) i.e., about his story. We have already mentioned how the disbelievers of Makkah sent word to the People of the Book and asked them for some information with which they could test the Prophet . They (the People of the Book) said, `Ask him about a man who traveled extensively throughout the earth, and about some young men who nobody knows what they did, and about the Ruh (the soul),' then Surat Al-Kahf was revealed. Dhul-Qarnayn had great Power

(Verily, We established him in the earth,) means, `We have given him great power, so that he had all that kings could have of might, armies, war equipment and siege machinery.' So he had dominion over the east and the west, all countries and their kings submitted to him, and all the nations, Arab and non-Arab, served him. Some of them said he was called Dhul-Qarnayn (the one with two horns) because he reached the two "Horns" of the sun, east and west, where it rises and where it sets.

(and We gave him the means of everything.) Ibn `Abbas, Mujahid, Sa`id bin Jubayr, `Ikrimah, As-Suddi, Qatadah, Ad-Dahhak and others said, "This means knowledge." Qatadah also said,

(and We gave him the means of everything.) "The different parts and features of the earth." Concerning Bilqis, Allah said,

(she has been given all things) (27:23), meaning all things that monarchs like her are given. Thus too was Dhul-Qarnayn: Allah gave him the means of all things, meaning the means and power to conquer all areas, regions and countries, to defeat enemies, suppress the kings of the earth and humiliate the people of Shirk. He was given all that a man like him would need. And Allah knows best.

Surah: 18 Ayah: 85, Ayah: 86, Ayah: 87 & Ayah: 88

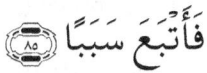

85. So he followed a way.

حَتَّىٰ إِذَا بَلَغَ مَغْرِبَ ٱلشَّمْسِ وَجَدَهَا تَغْرُبُ فِى عَيْنٍ حَمِئَةٍ وَوَجَدَ عِندَهَا قَوْمًا ۗ قُلْنَا يَـٰذَا ٱلْقَرْنَيْنِ إِمَّآ أَن تُعَذِّبَ وَإِمَّآ أَن تَتَّخِذَ فِيهِمْ حُسْنًا ۞

86. Until, when he reached the setting place of the sun, he found it setting in a spring of black muddy (or hot) water. And he found near it a people. We (Allâh) said (by inspiration): "O Dhul-Qarnain! Either you punish them, or treat them with kindness."

قَالَ أَمَّا مَن ظَلَمَ فَسَوْفَ نُعَذِّبُهُۥ ثُمَّ يُرَدُّ إِلَىٰ رَبِّهِۦ فَيُعَذِّبُهُۥ عَذَابًا نُّكْرًا ۞

87. He said: "As for him (a disbeliever in the Oneness of Allâh) who does wrong, we shall punish him, and then he will be brought back unto his Lord, Who will punish him with a terrible torment (Hell)."

وَأَمَّا مَنْ ءَامَنَ وَعَمِلَ صَـٰلِحًا فَلَهُۥ جَزَآءً ٱلْحُسْنَىٰ ۖ وَسَنَقُولُ لَهُۥ مِنْ أَمْرِنَا يُسْرًا ۞

88. "But as for him who believes (in Allâh's Oneness) and works righteousness, he shall have the best reward, (Paradise), and we (Dhul-Qarnain) shall speak unto him mild words (as instructions)."

Transliteration

85. FaatbaAAa sababan   86. Hatta itha balagha maghriba alshshamsi wajadaha taghrubu fee AAaynin hami-atin wawajada AAindaha qawman qulna ya tha alqarnayni imma an tuAAaththiba wa-imma an tattakhitha feehim husnan   87. Qala amma man thalama fasawfa nuAAaththibuhu thumma yuraddu ila rabbihi fayuAAaththibuhu AAathaban nukran   88. Waamma man amana waAAamila salihan falahu jazaan alhusna wasanaqoolu lahu min amrina yusran

Tafsir Ibn Kathir

His traveling and reaching the Place where the Sun sets (the West)

(So he followed a way.) Ibn `Abbas said that he followed different routes to achieve what he wanted.

(So he followed a way.) Mujahid said that he followed different routes, east and west. According to one report narrated from Mujahid, he said:

(a way) means, "A route through the land." Qatadah said, "It means he followed the routes and landmarks of the earth."

(Until, when he reached the setting place of the sun,) means, he followed a route until he reached the furthest point that could be reached in the direction of the sun's setting, which is the west of the earth. As for the idea of his reaching the place in the sky where the sun sets, this is something impossible, and the tales told by storytellers that he traveled so far to the west that the sun set behind him are not true at all.

Chapter 18: Al-Kahf (The Cave), Verses 075-110

Most of these stories come from the myths of the People of the Book and the fabrications and lies of their heretics.

(he found it setting in a spring of Hami'ah) meaning, he saw the sun as if it were setting in the ocean. This is something which everyone who goes to the coast can see: it looks as if the sun is setting into the sea but in fact it never leaves its path in which it is fixed. Hami'ah is, according to one of the two views, derived from the word Hama'ah, which means mud. This is like the Ayah:

("I am going to create a man (Adam) from dried clay of altered Hama'h (mud)) (15:28), which means smooth mud, as we have discussed above.

(And he found near it a people.) meaning a nation. They mentioned that they were a great nation from among the sons of Adam.

(We (Allah) said (by inspiration): "O Dhul-Qarnayn! Either you punish them or treat them with kindness") means, Allah gave him power over them and gave him the choice: if he wanted to, he could kill the men and take the women and children captive, or if he wanted to, he could set them free, with or without a ransom. His justice and faith became apparent in the ruling he pronounced:

(As for him who does wrong,) meaning who persists in his Kufr and in associating others in worship with his Lord,

(we shall punish him,) Qatadah said, i.e., by killing him.

(and then he will be brought back unto his Lord, Who will punish him with a terrible torment.) meaning a severe, far-reaching and painful punishment. This implies a confirmation of the Hereafter and the reward and punishment.

(But as for him who believes), meaning `who follows us in our call to worship Allah Alone with no partner or associate,'

(he shall have the best reward,) meaning in the Hereafter, with Allah.

(and we (Dhul-Qarnayn) shall speak unto him mild words.) Mujahid said, `(words of) kindness.'

Surah: 18 Ayah: 89, Ayah: 90 & Ayah: 91

$$ ثُمَّ أَتْبَعَ سَبَبًا ۝ $$

89. Then he followed another way,

$$ حَتَّىٰ إِذَا بَلَغَ مَطْلِعَ ٱلشَّمْسِ وَجَدَهَا تَطْلُعُ عَلَىٰ قَوْمٍ لَّمْ نَجْعَل لَّهُم مِّن دُونِهَا سِتْرًا ۝ $$

90. Until, when he came to the rising place of the sun, he found it rising on a people for whom We (Allâh) had provided no shelter against the sun.

$$ كَذَٰلِكَ وَقَدْ أَحَطْنَا بِمَا لَدَيْهِ خُبْرًا ﴿٩١﴾ $$

91. So (it was)! And We knew all about him (Dhul-Qarnain).

Transliteration

89. Thumma atbaAAa sababan 90. Hatta itha balagha matliAAa alshshamsi wajadaha tatluAAu AAala qawmin lam najAAal lahum min dooniha sitran 91. Kathalika waqad ahatna bima ladayhi khubran

Tafsir Ibn Kathir

His Journey East

Allah tells us that Dhul-Qarnayn then traveled from the west of the earth towards the east. Every time he passed a nation, he subjugated the people and called them to Allah. If they obeyed him, all well and good, otherwise he would humiliate them and take their wealth and possessions. From every nation he took what his armies needed to fight the next nation. When he reached the place where the sun rises, as Allah says,

(he found it rising on a people) meaning a nation,

(for whom We (Allah) had provided no shelter against the sun.) meaning, they had no buildings or trees to cover them and shade them from the heat of the sun. Qatadah said, "It was mentioned to us that they were in a land where nothing grew, so when the sun rose they would go into tunnels until it had passed its zenith, then they would come out to go about their daily lives and earn themselves a living."

(So (it was)! And We knew all about him.) Mujahid and As-Suddi said, "This means that Allah knew everything about him and his army, and nothing was hidden from Him, even though they came from so many different nations and lands. For,

(Truly, nothing is hidden from Allah, in the earth or in the heaven.)(3:5)"

Surah: 18 Ayah: 92, Ayah: 93, Ayah: 94, Ayah: 95 & Ayah: 96

$$ ثُمَّ أَتْبَعَ سَبَبًا ﴿٩٢﴾ $$

92. Then he followed (another) way,

$$ حَتَّىٰ إِذَا بَلَغَ بَيْنَ السَّدَّيْنِ وَجَدَ مِن دُونِهِمَا قَوْمًا لَّا يَكَادُونَ يَفْقَهُونَ قَوْلًا ﴿٩٣﴾ $$

93. Until, when he reached between two mountains, he found, before (near) them (those two mountains), a people who scarcely understood a word.

Chapter 18: Al-Kahf (The Cave), Verses 075-110

$$\text{قَالُوا۟ يَـٰذَا ٱلْقَرْنَيْنِ إِنَّ يَأْجُوجَ وَمَأْجُوجَ مُفْسِدُونَ فِى ٱلْأَرْضِ فَهَلْ نَجْعَلُ لَكَ خَرْجًا عَلَىٰٓ أَن تَجْعَلَ بَيْنَنَا وَبَيْنَهُمْ سَدًّا ۝}$$

94. They said: "O Dhul-Qarnain! Verily! Ya'jûj and Ma'jûj (Gog and Magog) are doing great mischief in the land. Shall we then pay you a tribute in order that you might erect a barrier between us and them?"

$$\text{قَالَ مَا مَكَّنِّى فِيهِ رَبِّى خَيْرٌ فَأَعِينُونِى بِقُوَّةٍ أَجْعَلْ بَيْنَكُمْ وَبَيْنَهُمْ رَدْمًا ۝}$$

95. He said: "That (wealth, authority and power) in which my Lord had established me is better (than your tribute). So help me with strength (of men), I will erect between you and them a barrier.

$$\text{ءَاتُونِى زُبَرَ ٱلْحَدِيدِ ۖ حَتَّىٰٓ إِذَا سَاوَىٰ بَيْنَ ٱلصَّدَفَيْنِ قَالَ ٱنفُخُوا۟ ۖ حَتَّىٰٓ إِذَا جَعَلَهُۥ نَارًا قَالَ ءَاتُونِىٓ أُفْرِغْ عَلَيْهِ قِطْرًا ۝}$$

96. "Give me pieces (blocks) of iron;" then, when he had filled up the gap between the two mountain-cliffs, he said: "Blow," then when he had made them (red as) fire, he said: "Bring me molten copper to pour over it."

Transliteration

92. Thumma atbaAAa sababan 93. Hatta itha balagha bayna alssaddayni wajada min doonihima qawman la yakadoona yafqahoona qawlan 94. Qaloo ya tha alqarnayni inna ya/jooja wama/jooja mufsidoona fee al-ardi fahal najAAalu laka kharjan AAala an tajAAala baynana wabaynahum saddan 95. Qala ma makkannee feehi rabbee khayrun faaAAeenoonee biquwwatin ajAAal baynakum wabaynahum radman 96. Atoonee zubara alhadeedi hatta itha sawa bayna alsadafayni qala onfukhoo hatta itha jaAAalahu naran qala atoonee ofrigh AAalayhi qitran

Tafsir Ibn Kathir

His Journey to the Land of Ya'juj and Ma'juj, and building the Barrier

Allah says of Dhul-Qarnayn:

(Then he followed (another) way) meaning, he traveled from the east of the earth until he reached a place between the two mountains which were next to one another with a valley in between, from which Ya'juj and Ma'juj (Gog and Magog) will emerge into the land of the Turks and spread mischief there, destroying crops and people. Ya'juj and Ma'juj are among the progeny of Adam, peace be upon him, as was recorded in the Two Sahihs;

$$\text{«إِنَّ اللهَ تَعَالَى يَقُولُ: يَا آدَمُ فَيَقُولُ: لَبَّيْكَ وَسَعْدَيْكَ فَيَقُولُ: ابْعَثْ بَعْثَ}$$

النَّارِ، فَيَقُولُ: وَمَا بَعْثُ النَّارِ؟ فَيَقُولُ: مِنْ كُلِّ أَلْفٍ تِسْعُمِائَةٍ وَتِسْعَةٌ وَتِسْعُونَ إِلَى النَّارِ وَوَاحِدٌ إِلَى الْجَنَّةِ، فَحِينَئِذٍ يَشِيبُ الصَّغِيرُ وَتَضَعُ كُلُّ ذَاتِ حَمْلٍ حَمْلَهَا. فَقَالَ: إِنَّ فِيكُمْ أُمَّتَيْنِ مَا كَانَتَا فِي شَيْءٍ إِلَّا كَثَّرَتَاهُ يَأْجُوجَ وَمَأْجُوجَ»

"Allah said: "O Adam." Adam said, "Here I am at Your service." Allah said, "Send forth the group of Hellfire." Adam said, "What is the group of Hellfire" Allah said: "Out of every thousand, nine hundred and ninety-nine will go to Hell and one will go to Paradise." At that time young men will turn grey and every pregnant female will drop her load. Among you are two nations who never come to anything but they overwhelm it with their huge numbers. (They are) Ya'juj and Ma'juj."

(he found before them a people who scarcely understood a word.) he could not understand their speech, because they were so isolated from other people.

(They said: "O Dhul-Qarnayn! Verily, Ya'juj and Ma'juj are doing great mischief in the land. Shall we then pay you a tribute") Ibn Jurayj reported from `Ata' from Ibn `Abbas that this meant a great reward, i.e., they wanted to collect money among themselves to give to him so that he would create a barrier between them and Ya'juj and Ma'juj. Dhul-Qarnayn said with kindness, righteousness and good intentions,

(That in which my Lord had established me is better (than your tribute).) meaning, the power and authority that Allah has given me is better for me than what you have collected. This is like when Sulayman (Solomon), peace be upon him, said:

(Will you help me in wealth. What Allah has given me is better than that which He has given you!) (27:36) Similarly, Dhul-Qarnayn said: `What I have is better than what you want to give me, but help me with strength,' i.e., with your labor and construction equipment,

(I will erect between you and them a barrier. Give me Zubar of iron,) Zubar is the plural of Zubrah, which means pieces or chunks of something. This was the view of Ibn `Abbas, Mujahid and Qatadah. These pieces were like bricks or blocks, and it was said that each block weighed one Damascene Qintar or more.

(then, when he had filled up the gap between the two mountain-cliffs,) means, he put the blocks on top of one another, starting at the bottom, until he reached the tops of the mountains, filling the width and height of the gap. The scholars differed about the precise width and height.

(he said: "Blow;") means, he lit a fire until the whole thing was burning hot.

Chapter 18: Al-Kahf (The Cave), Verses 075-110   27

(he said: "Bring me Qitran to pour over them.") Ibn `Abbas, Mujahid, `Ikrimah, Ad-Dahhak, Qatadah and As-Suddi said it was copper. Some of them added that it was molten. This is similar to the Ayah:

(And We caused a fount of Qitran to flow for him) (34:12). So it resembled a striped cloak. Then Allah said:

Surah: 18 Ayah: 97, Ayah: 98 & Ayah: 99

فَمَا اسْطَاعُوٓا۟ أَن يَظْهَرُوهُ وَمَا اسْتَطَاعُوا۟ لَهُۥ نَقْبًا ۝

97. So they (Ya'jûj and Ma'jûj (Gog and Magog)) were made powerless to scale it or dig through it.

قَالَ هَٰذَا رَحْمَةٌ مِّن رَّبِّى ۖ فَإِذَا جَآءَ وَعْدُ رَبِّى جَعَلَهُۥ دَكَّآءَ ۖ وَكَانَ وَعْدُ رَبِّى حَقًّا ۝

98. (Dhul-Qarnain) said: "This is a mercy from my Lord, but when the Promise of my Lord comes, He shall level it down to the ground. And the Promise of my Lord is ever true."

۞ وَتَرَكْنَا بَعْضَهُمْ يَوْمَئِذٍ يَمُوجُ فِى بَعْضٍ ۖ وَنُفِخَ فِى ٱلصُّورِ فَجَمَعْنَٰهُمْ جَمْعًا ۝

99. And on that Day (i.e. the Day Ya'jûj and Ma'jûj (Gog and Magog) will come out), We shall leave them to surge like waves on one another, and the Trumpet will be blown, and We shall collect them (the creatures) all together.

Transliteration

97. Fama istaAAoo an yathharoohu wama istataAAoo lahu naqban 98. Qala hatha rahmatun min rabbee fa-itha jaa waAAdu rabbee jaAAalahu dakkaa wakana waAAdu rabbee haqqan 99. Watarakna baAAdahum yawma-ithin yamooju fee baAAdin wanufikha fee alssoori fajamaAAnahum jamAAan

Tafsir Ibn Kathir

The Barrier restrains Them, but It will be breached when the Hour draws nigh

Allah tells us that Ya'juj and Ma'juj could not climb over the barrier or penetrate its lower portion. Varying forms of the verb are used here in the Arabic text to reflect the difficulty of the action referred to.

(So they (Ya'juj and Ma'juj) could not scale it or dig through it.) This indicates that they could not penetrate it or dig through it. Imam Ahmad recorded that Zaynab bint Jahsh, the wife of the Prophet said, "The Prophet woke from sleep, and he was red in the face. He said,

«لَا إِلَهَ إِلَّا اللَّهُ وَيْلٌ لِلْعَرَبِ مِنْ شَرٍّ قَدِ اقْتَرَبَ فُتِحَ الْيَوْمَ مِنْ رَدْمِ يَأْجُوجَ وَمَأْجُوجَ مِثْلُ هَذَا»

(La ilaha illallah! Woe to the Arabs from the evil that has approached (them). Today a hole has been opened in the barrier of Ya'juj and Ma'juj like this.) and he made a circle with his index finger and thumb. I (Zaynab) said, `O Messenger of Allah, will we be destroyed even though there will be righteous people among us' He said:

«نَعَمْ إِذَا كَثُرَ الْخَبَثُ»

(Yes, if evil increases.)" This is a Sahih Hadith, both Al-Bukhari and Muslim recorded it.

((Dhul-Qarnayn) said: "This is a mercy from my Lord...") meaning, after it was built by Dhul-Qarnayn.

(He said: This is a mercy from my Lord) for the people, when he placed a barrier between them and Ya'juj and Ma'juj, to stop them from spreading evil and corruption on earth.

(but when the promise of my Lord comes) means, when the true promise comes

(He shall Dakka' it down to the ground.) means, will make it flat. The Arabs use Dakka' to describe a female camel whose back is flat and has no hump. And Allah says:

(So when his Lord appeared to the mountain, He made it Dakkan) (7:143) meaning, level to the ground.

(And the promise of my Lord is ever true.) means, it will come to pass without a doubt.

(We shall leave some of them) meaning mankind, on that day, the day when the barrier will be breached and these people (Ya'juj and Ma'juj) will come out surging over mankind to destroy their wealth and property.

(We shall leave some of them to surge like waves on one another;) As-Suddi said: "That is when they emerge upon the people." All of this will happen before the Day of Resurrection and after the Dajjal, as we will explain when discussing the Ayat:

(Until, when Ya'juj and Ma'juj are let loose, and they swoop down from every Hadab. And the true promise shall draw near...) (21:96-97)

(and As-Sur will be blown.) As-Sur, as explained in the Hadith, is a horn that is blown into. The one who will blow into it is (the angel) Israfil, peace be upon him, as has been explained in the Hadith quoted at length above, and there are many Hadiths on this topic. According to a Hadith narrated from `Atiyah from Ibn `Abbas and Abu Sa`id, and attributed to the Prophet,

«كَيْفَ أَنْعَمُ وَصَاحِبُ الْقَرْنِ قَدِ الْتَقَمَ الْقَرْنَ وَحَنَى جَبْهَتَهُ وَاسْتَمَعَ مَتَى يُؤْمَرُ؟»

(How can I relax when the one with the Horn has put the Horn in his mouth and has knelt down, listening out for the command to be given to him) They said, "What should we say" He said:

«قُولُوا: حَسْبُنَا اللهُ وَنِعْمَ الْوَكِيلُ عَلَى اللهِ تَوَكَّلْنَا»

(Say: "Allah is Sufficient for us and the best Disposer of affairs, in Allah have we put our trust.")

(and We shall collect them (the creatures) all together.) means, `We shall bring them all together for Reckoning.'

(Say: "(Yes) verily, those of old, and those of later times. All will surely be gathered together for appointed meeting of a known Day.) (56:49-50)

(and we shall gather them all together so as to leave not one of them behind.) (18:47)

Surah: 18 Ayah: 100, Ayah: 101 & Ayah: 102

وَعَرَضْنَا جَهَنَّمَ يَوْمَئِذٍ لِّلْكَٰفِرِينَ عَرْضًا ۝

100. And on that Day We shall present Hell to the disbelievers, plain to view -

ٱلَّذِينَ كَانَتْ أَعْيُنُهُمْ فِى غِطَآءٍ عَن ذِكْرِى وَكَانُوا۟ لَا يَسْتَطِيعُونَ سَمْعًا ۝

101. (To) Those whose eyes had been under a covering from My Reminder (this Qur'ân), and who could not bear to hear (it).

أَفَحَسِبَ ٱلَّذِينَ كَفَرُوٓا۟ أَن يَتَّخِذُوا۟ عِبَادِى مِن دُونِىٓ أَوْلِيَآءَ ۚ إِنَّآ أَعْتَدْنَا جَهَنَّمَ لِلْكَٰفِرِينَ نُزُلًا ۝

102. Do then those who disbelieve think that they can take My slaves (i.e., the angels, Allâh's Messengers, 'Iesa (Jesus), son of Maryam (Mary)) as Auliyâ' (lords, gods, protectors) besides Me? Verily, We have prepared Hell as an entertainment for the disbelievers (in the Oneness of Allâh - Islâmic Monotheism).

Transliteration

100. WaAAaradna jahannama yawma-ithin lilkafireena AAardan 101. Allatheena kanat aAAyunuhum fee ghita-in AAan thikree wakanoo la yastateeAAoona samAAan 102. Afahasiba allatheena kafaroo an yattakhithoo AAibadee min doonee awliyaa inna aAAtadna jahannama lilkafireena nuzulan

Tafsir Ibn Kathir

Hell will be displayed before the Disbelievers on the Day of Resurrection

Allah tells us what He will do to the disbelievers on the Day of Resurrection. He will show Hell to them, meaning He will bring it forth for them to see its punishment and torment before they enter it. This will intensify their distress and grief. In Sahih Muslim it is recorded that Ibn Mas`ud said, "The Messenger of Allah said,

«يُؤْتَى بِجَهَنَّمَ تُقَادُ يَوْمَ الْقِيَامَةِ بِسَبْعِينَ أَلْفَ زِمَامٍ، مَعَ كُلِّ زِمَامٍ سَبْعُونَ أَلْفَ مَلَكٍ»

(Hell will be brought forth on the Day of Resurrection, pulled by means of seventy thousand reins, each of which will be held by seventy thousand angels.) Then Allah says of them:

((To) those whose eyes had been under a covering from My Reminder,) meaning, they neglected it, turning a blind eye and a deaf ear to it, refusing to accept guidance and follow the truth. As Allah says:

(And whosoever turns away blindly from the remembrance of the Most Gracious, We appoint for him a Shaytan to be a companion for him.) (43:36) And here Allah says:

(and they could not bear to hear (it).) meaning, they did not understand the commands and prohibitions of Allah. Then He says:

(Do then those who disbelieved think that they can take My servants as Awliya' (protectors) besides Me) meaning, do they think that this is right for them and that it is going to benefit them

(Nay, but they will deny their worship of them, and become opponents to them) (19:82). Allah says that He has prepared Hell as their abode on the Day of Resurrection

Surah: 18 Ayah: 103, Ayah: 104, Ayah: 105 & Ayah: 106

قُلْ هَلْ نُنَبِّئُكُم بِٱلْأَخْسَرِينَ أَعْمَٰلًا

103. Say (O Muhammad (peace be upon him)) "Shall We tell you the greatest losers in respect of (their) deeds?

$$\text{ٱلَّذِينَ ضَلَّ سَعْيُهُمْ فِى ٱلْحَيَوٰةِ ٱلدُّنْيَا وَهُمْ يَحْسَبُونَ أَنَّهُمْ يُحْسِنُونَ صُنْعًا ﴿١٠٤﴾}$$

104. "Those whose efforts have been wasted in this life while they thought that they were acquiring good by their deeds!

$$\text{أُوْلَـٰٓئِكَ ٱلَّذِينَ كَفَرُواْ بِـَٔايَـٰتِ رَبِّهِمْ وَلِقَآئِهِۦ فَحَبِطَتْ أَعْمَـٰلُهُمْ فَلَا نُقِيمُ لَهُمْ يَوْمَ ٱلْقِيَـٰمَةِ وَزْنًا ﴿١٠٥﴾}$$

105. "They are those who deny the Ayât (proofs, evidences, verses, lessons, signs, revelations, etc.) of their Lord and the Meeting with Him (in the Hereafter). So their works are in vain, and on the Day of Resurrection, We shall not give them any weight.

$$\text{ذَٰلِكَ جَزَآؤُهُمْ جَهَنَّمُ بِمَا كَفَرُواْ وَٱتَّخَذُوٓاْ ءَايَـٰتِى وَرُسُلِى هُزُوًا ﴿١٠٦﴾}$$

106. "That shall be their recompense, Hell; because they disbelieved and took My Ayât (proofs, evidences, verses, lessons, signs, revelations, etc.) and My Messengers by way of jest and mockery.

Transliteration

103. Qul hal nunabbi-okum bial-akhsareena aAAmalan   104. Allatheena dalla saAAyuhum fee alhayati alddunya wahum yahsaboona annahum yuhsinoona sunAAan   105. Ola-ika allatheena kafaroo bi-ayati rabbihim waliqa-ihi fahabitat aAAmaluhum fala nuqeemu lahum yawma alqiyamati waznan   106. Thalika jazaohum jahannamu bima kafaroo waittakhathoo ayatee warusulee huzuwan

Tafsir Ibn Kathir

The Greatest Losers in respect of (Their) Deeds

Al-Bukhari recorded from `Amr that Mus`ab who said: "I asked my father -- meaning Sa`d bin Abi Waqqas -- about Allah's saying,

(Say: "Shall We tell you the greatest losers in respect of (their) deeds") `Are they the Haruriyyah' He said, `No, they are the Jews and Christians. As for the Jews, they disbelieved in Muhammad , and as for the Christians, they disbelieved in Paradise and said that there is no food or drink there, and the Haruriyyah are those who break Allah's covenant after ratifying it.' Sa`d used to call them Al-Fasiqin (the corrupt). `Ali bin Abi Talib, Ad-Dahhak and others said: "They are the Haruriyyah," so this means, that according to `Ali, may Allah be pleased with him, this Ayah includes the Haruriyyah just as it includes the Jews, the Christians and others. This does not mean that the Ayah was revealed concerning any of these groups in particular; it is more general than that, because the Ayah was revealed in Makkah, before the Qur'an addressed the Jews and Christians, and before the Khawarij existed at all. So the Ayah is general and refers to everyone who worships Allah in a way that is not acceptable, thinking that he is right in doing that and that his deeds will be accepted, but he is mistaken and his deeds will be rejected, as Allah says:

(Some faces, that Day will be humiliated. Laboring, weary. They will enter in the hot blazing Fire.) (88:2-4)

(And We shall turn to whatever deeds they did, and We shall make such deeds as scattered floating particles of dust.) (25:23)

(As for those who disbelieved, their deeds are like a mirage in a desert. The thirsty one thinks it to be water, until he comes up to it, he finds it to be nothing) (24:39) And in this Ayah Allah says:

(Say: "Shall We tell you...") meaning, `Shall We inform you;'

(the greatest losers in respect of (their) deeds) Then Allah explains who they are, and says:

(Those whose efforts have been wasted in this life) meaning, they did deeds that do not count, deeds that are not in accordance with the prescribed way that is acceptable to Allah.

(while they thought that they were acquiring good by their deeds.) means, they thought that there was some basis for their deeds and that they were accepted and loved.

(They are those who deny the Ayat of their Lord and the meeting with Him.) they denied the signs of Allah in this world, the proofs that He has established of His Oneness and of the truth of His Messengers, and they denied the Hereafter.

(and on the Day of Resurrection, We shall assign no weight for them.) means, `We will not make their Balance heavy because it is empty of any goodness.' Al-Bukhari recorded that Abu Hurayrah said that the Messenger of Allah said:

«إِنَّهُ لَيَأْتِي الرَّجُلُ الْعَظِيمُ السَّمِينُ يَوْمَ الْقِيَامَةِ لَا يَزِنُ عِنْدَ اللهِ جَنَاحَ بَعُوضَةٍ وَقَالَ: اقْرَءُوا إِنْ شِئْتُمْ:

(فَلاَ نُقِيمُ لَهُمْ يَوْمَ الْقِيَـمَةِ وَزْناً)»

(A huge fat man will come forward on the Day of Resurrection and he will weigh no more than the wing of a gnat to Allah. Recite, if you wish:) (and on the Day of Resurrection, We shall assign no weight for them) It was also recorded by Muslim.

(That shall be their recompense, Hell; because they disbelieved) means, `We will punish them with that because of their disbelief and because they took the signs and Messengers of Allah as a joke, mocking them and disbelieving them in the worst way.'

Chapter 18: Al-Kahf (The Cave), Verses 075-110

Surah: 18 Ayah: 107 & Ayah: 108

إِنَّ ٱلَّذِينَ ءَامَنُوا۟ وَعَمِلُوا۟ ٱلصَّٰلِحَٰتِ كَانَتْ لَهُمْ جَنَّٰتُ ٱلْفِرْدَوْسِ نُزُلًا ۝

107. "Verily those who believe (in the Oneness of Allâh - Islâmic Monotheism) and do righteous deeds, shall have the Gardens of Al-Firdaus (the Paradise) for their entertainment.

خَٰلِدِينَ فِيهَا لَا يَبْغُونَ عَنْهَا حِوَلًا ۝

108. "Wherein they shall dwell (forever). No desire will they have for removal therefrom."

Transliteration

107. Inna allatheena amanoo waAAamiloo alssalihati kanat lahum jannatu alfirdawsi nuzulan 108. Khalideena feeha la yabghoona AAanha hiwalan

Tafsir Ibn Kathir

The Reward of the Righteous Believers

Allah tells us about His blessed servants, those who believed in Allah and His Messengers and accepted as truth what the Messengers brought. He tells us that they will have the Gardens of Al-Firdaws (Paradise). Abu Umamah said, "Al-Firdaws is the center of Paradise." Qatadah said, "Al-Firdaws is a hill in Paradise, at its center, the best of it." This was also narrated from Samurah and attributed to the Prophet ,

«الْفِرْدَوْسُ رَبْوَةُ الْجَنَّةِ أَوْسَطُهَا وَأَحْسَنُهَا»

(Al-Firdaws is a hill in Paradise, at its center, the best of it.) A similar report was narrated from Qatadah from Anas bin Malik, and attributed to the Prophet . All of the preceding reports were narrated by Ibn Jarir, may Allah have mercy on him. The following is in the Sahih,

«إِذَا سَأَلْتُمُ اللهَ الْجَنَّةَ، فَاسْأَلُوهُ الْفِرْدَوْسَ فَإِنَّهُ أَعْلَى الْجَنَّةِ وَأَوْسَطُ الْجَنَّةِ، وَمِنْهُ تَفَجَّرُ أَنْهَارُ الْجَنَّةِ»

(If you ask Allah for Paradise, then ask Him for Al-Firdaws, for it is the highest part of Paradise, in the middle of Paradise, and from it spring the rivers of Paradise.)

(entertainment) means offered to them as hospitality.

(Wherein they shall dwell (forever).) means, they will stay there and never leave.

(No desire will they have for removal therefrom.) means, they will never choose or want anything else. This Ayah tells us how much they love and desire it, even though one might imagine that a person who is to stay in one place forever would get tired and bored of it. But Allah tells us that despite this eternal stay, they will never choose to change or move from where they are.

Surah: 18 Ayah: 109

قُل لَّوْ كَانَ ٱلْبَحْرُ مِدَادًا لِّكَلِمَٰتِ رَبِّى لَنَفِدَ ٱلْبَحْرُ قَبْلَ أَن تَنفَدَ كَلِمَٰتُ رَبِّى وَلَوْ جِئْنَا بِمِثْلِهِۦ مَدَدًا ۝

109. Say (O Muhammad (peace be upon him) to mankind). "If the sea were ink for (writing) the Words of my Lord, surely, the sea would be exhausted before the Words of my Lord would be finished, even if We brought (another sea) like it for its aid."

Transliteration

109. Qul law kana albahru midadan likalimati rabbee lanafida albahru qabla an tanfada kalimatu rabbee walaw ji/na bimithlihi madadan

Tafsir Ibn Kathir

The Words of the Lord can never be finished

Allah says: `Say, O Muhammad, if the water of the sea were ink for a pen to write down the words, wisdom and signs of Allah, the sea would run dry before it all could be written down.

(even if We brought like it) means, another sea, then another, and so on, additional seas to be used for writing. The Words of Allah would still never run out. As Allah says:

(And if all the trees on the earth were pens and the sea (were ink), with seven seas behind it to increase it, yet the Words of Allah would not be exhausted. Verily, Allah is All-Mighty, All-Wise.) (31:27) Ar-Rabi` bin Anas said, "The parable of the knowledge of all of mankind, in comparison to the knowledge of Allah, is that of a drop of water in comparison to all of the oceans." Allah revealed that:

(Say: "If the sea were ink for the Words of my Lord, surely, the sea would be exhausted before the Words of my Lord would be finished,) Allah says that even if those oceans were ink for the Words of Allah, and all the trees were pens, the pens would be broken and the water of the sea would run dry, and the Words of Allah would remain, for nothing can outlast them. For no one can comprehend the greatness of Allah or praise Him as He deserves to be praised, except the One Who praises Himself. Our Lord is as He says He is and He is beyond what we can say. The blessings of this world, the beginning and end of it, in comparison to the blessings of the Hereafter, are like a mustard seed compared to the entire world.

Chapter 18: Al-Kahf (The Cave), Verses 075-110

Surah: 18 Ayah: 110

قُلْ إِنَّمَا أَنَا۠ بَشَرٌ مِّثْلُكُمْ يُوحَىٰٓ إِلَيَّ أَنَّمَا إِلَٰهُكُمْ إِلَٰهٌ وَاحِدٌ ۖ فَمَن كَانَ يَرْجُوا۟ لِقَآءَ رَبِّهِۦ فَلْيَعْمَلْ عَمَلًا صَٰلِحًا وَلَا يُشْرِكْ بِعِبَادَةِ رَبِّهِۦٓ أَحَدًۢا ۝

110. Say (O Muhammad (peace be upon him)) "I am only a man like you. It has been revealed to me that your Ilâh (God) is One Ilâh (God - i.e. Allâh). So whoever hopes for the Meeting with his Lord, let him work righteousness and associate none as a partner in the worship of his Lord."

Transliteration

110. Qul innama ana basharun mithlukum yooha ilayya annama ilahukum ilahun wahidun faman kana yarjoo liqaa rabbihi falyaAAmal AAamalan salihan wala yushrik biAAibadati rabbihi ahadan

Tafsir Ibn Kathir

Muhammad is a Human Being and a Messenger, and the God is One

Allah says to His Messenger Muhammad ,

(Say) to these idolators who reject your message to them,

(`I am only a man like you.) Whoever claims that I am lying, let him bring something like this that I have brought. For I did not know the Unseen, the matters of the past which you asked me about and I told you about, the story of the people of the Cave and of Dhul-Qarnayn, stories which are true -- I did not know any of this except for what Allah made known to me. And I tell you,

(that your God), Who calls you to worship Him,

(is One God), with no partner or associate.'

(So whoever hopes for the meeting with his Lord,) i.e., hopes for a good reward and recompense,

(let him work righteousness) meaning, in accordance with the prescribed laws of Allah,

(and associate none as a partner in the worship of his Lord.) This is what is meant by seeking the pleasure of Allah alone with no associate or partner. These are the two basic features of acceptable deeds: their intent is for the sake of Allah alone, and are done in accordance with the way of the Messenger of Allah . Imam Ahmad recorded that Mahmud bin Labid said that the Messenger of Allah said:

«إِنَّ أَخْوَفَ مَا أَخَافُ عَلَيْكُمُ الشِّرْكُ الْأَصْغَرُ»

(What I fear the most for you is the small Shirk.) "They said: What is the small Shirk, O Messenger of Allah" He said,

«إِذَا جَمَعَ اللَّهُ الْأَوَّلِينَ وَالْآخِرِينَ لِيَوْمِ الْقِيَامَةِ لِيَوْمٍ لَا رَيْبَ فِيهِ نَادَى مُنَادٍ: مَنْ كَانَ أَشْرَكَ فِي عَمَلٍ عَمِلَهُ لِلَّهِ أَحَدًا فَلْيَطْلُبْ ثَوَابَهُ مِنْ عِنْدِ غَيْرِ اللَّهِ، فَإِنَّ اللَّهَ أَغْنَى الشُّرَكَاءِ عَنِ الشِّرْكِ»

(Showing off (Ar-Riya'). Allah will say on the Day of Resurrection, when the people are rewarded or punished for their deeds, "Go to the one for whom you were showing off in the world and see if you will find any reward with him.") Imam Ahmad recorded that Abu Sa`id bin Abi Fadalah Al-Ansari, who was one of the Companions, said: "I heard the Messenger of Allah say,

(Allah will gather the first and the last on the Day of Resurrection, the Day concerning which there is no doubt. A voice will call out, "Whoever used to associate anyone with Allah in the deeds which he did, let him seek his reward from someone other than Allah, for Allah is the least in need of any partner or associate.) It was also recorded by At-Tirmidhi and Ibn Majah. This is the end of the Tafsir of Surat Al-Kahf. Praise be to Allah, the Lord of all that exists.

INTRODUCTION TO CHAPTER (SURAH) 19: MARYAM (MARY)

Ibn kathir's introduction

(Chapter - 19) Which was revealed in Makkah

Muhammad bin Ishaq recorded a Hadith of Umm Salamah in his Sirah, and Ahmad bin Hanbal recorded from Ibn Mas`ud, the story of the Hijrah (migration) to Ethiopia from Makkah. The narration mentions that Ja`far bin Abi Talib recited the first part of this Surah to An-Najashi and his companions.

CHAPTER (SURAH) 19: MARYAM (MARY), VERSES 001 – 098

(بِسْمِ اللَّهِ الرَّحْمَـنِ الرَّحِيمِ)

In the Name of Allah, the Most Gracious, the Most Merciful.

Surah: 19 Ayah: 1, Ayah: 2, Ayah: 3, Ayah: 4, Ayah: 5 & Ayah: 6

1. Kâf- Hâ-Yâ-'Aîn-Sâd. [These letters are one of the miracles of the Qur'ân, and none but Allâh (Alone) knows their meanings].

Chapter 19: Maryam (Mary), Verses 001-098

$$ذِكْرُ رَحْمَتِ رَبِّكَ عَبْدَهُ زَكَرِيَّا$$

2. (This is) a mention of the mercy of your Lord to His slave Zakariyyâ (Zachariah).

$$إِذْ نَادَىٰ رَبَّهُ نِدَآءً خَفِيًّا$$

3. When he called out his Lord (Allâh) a call in secret.

$$قَالَ رَبِّ إِنِّى وَهَنَ الْعَظْمُ مِنِّى وَاشْتَعَلَ الرَّأْسُ شَيْبًا وَلَمْ أَكُن بِدُعَآئِكَ رَبِّ شَقِيًّا$$

4. Saying: "My Lord! Indeed my bones have grown feeble, and gray hair has spread on my head, And I have never been unblest in my invocation to You, O my Lord!

$$وَإِنِّى خِفْتُ الْمَوَالِىَ مِن وَرَآءِى وَكَانَتِ امْرَأَتِى عَاقِرًا فَهَبْ لِى مِن لَّدُنكَ وَلِيًّا$$

5. "And verily I fear my relatives after me, and my wife is barren. So give me from Yourself an heir.

$$يَرِثُنِى وَيَرِثُ مِنْ ءَالِ يَعْقُوبَ وَاجْعَلْهُ رَبِّ رَضِيًّا$$

6. "Who shall inherit me, and inherit (also) the posterity of Ya'qûb (Jacob) (inheritance of the religious knowledge and Prophethood, not the wealth.). And make him, my Lord, one with whom You are Well-pleased!"

Transliteration

1. Kaf-ha-ya-AAayn-sad 2. Thikru rahmati rabbika AAabdahu zakariyya 3. Ith nada rabbahu nidaan khafiyyan 4. Qala rabbi innee wahana alAAathmu minnee waishtaAAala alrra/su shayban walam akun biduAAaika rabbi shaqiyyan 5. Wa-innee khiftu almawaliya min wara-ee wakanati imraatee AAaqiran fahab lee min ladunka waliyyan 6. Yarithunee wayarithu min ali yaAAqooba waijAAalhu rabbi radiyyan

Tafsir Ibn Kathir

The Story of Zakariyya and His Supplication for a Son The discussion about the separate letters has already preceded at the beginning of Surat Al-Baqarah.

Concerning Allah's statement,

(A reminder of the mercy of your Lord) This means that this is a reminder of Allah's mercy upon His servant Zakariyya. Yahya bin Ya`mar recited it, "He has reminded of your Lord's mercy to His servant Zakariyya." The word Zakariyya in the Ayah has been recited with elongation and also shortened. Both recitations are well-known. He was a great Prophet from the Prophets of the Children of Israel. In Sahih Al-Bukhari, it is recorded (that the Prophet said about Zakariyya) that He was a carpenter who used to eat from what he earned with his own hand through carpentry. Concerning Allah's statement,

(When he called his Lord (with) a call in secret.) He only made his supplication secretly because it is more beloved to Allah. This is similar to what Qatadah said concerning this Ayah,

(When he called out his Lord (with) a call in secret.) "Verily, Allah knows the pious heart and he hears the hidden voice."

(He said: "My Lord! Indeed my bones have grown feeble...") meaning, "I have become weak and feeble in strength."

(and gray hair has Ashta`al on my head,) means the gray hair has burned into the black hair. The intent is to inform of weakness and old age, and its external and internal traces. Concerning Allah's statement,

(and I have never been unblessed in my invocation to You, O my Lord!) This means, "I have not experienced from You except that You would respond to my supplication and that You would never refuse me in whatever I ask of You." Concerning His statement,

(And verily, I fear Mawali after me,) Mujahid, Qatadah and As-Suddi, all said, "In saying the word Mawali, he (Zakariyya) meant his succeeding relatives." The reason for his fear was that he was afraid that the generation that would succeed him would be a wicked generation. Thus, he asked Allah for a son who would be a Prophet after him, who would guide them with his prophethood and that which was revealed to him. In response to this I would like to point out that he was not afraid of them inheriting his wealth. For a Prophet is too great in status, and too lofty in esteem to become remorseful over his wealth in this fashion. A Prophet would not disdain to leave his wealth to his successive relatives, and thus ask to have a son who would receive his inheritance instead of them. This is one angle of argument. The second argument is that Allah did not mention that he (Zakariyya) was wealthy. On the contrary, he was a carpenter who ate from the earnings of his own hand. This type of person usually does not have a mass of wealth. Amassing wealth is not something normal for Prophets, for verily, they are the most abstentious in matters of this worldly life. The third argument is that it is confirmed in the Two Sahihs, in more than one narration, that the Messenger of Allah said,

«لَا نُورَثُ، مَا تَرَكْنَا فَهُوَ صَدَقَةٌ»

(We (the Prophets) do not leave behind inheritance (of wealth). Whatever we leave behind, then it is charity.) In a narration recorded by At-Tirmidhi with an authentic chain of narrations, he said,

Chapter 19: Maryam (Mary), Verses 001-098

$$\langle\langle \text{نَحْنُ مَعْشَرَ الْأَنْبِيَاءِ لَا نُورَثُ} \rangle\rangle$$

(We Prophets do not leave behind inheritance (of wealth).) Therefore, the meaning in these Hadiths restricts the meaning of Zakariyya's statement,

(So give me from yourself an heir. Who shall inherit me,) inheritance of prophethood. For this reason Allah said,

(and inherit (also) the posterity of Ya`qub.) This is similar to Allah's statement,

(And Sulayman inherited from Dawud.)(27:16) This means that he inherited prophethood from him. If this had meant wealth, he would not have been singled with it among his other brothers. There also would have been no important benefit in mentioning it if it was referring to wealth. It is already well-known and established in all of the previous laws and divinely revealed creeds, that the son inherits the wealth of his father. Therefore, if this was not referring to a specific type of inheritance, then Allah would not have mentioned it. All of this is supported and affirmed by what is in the authentic Hadith:

$$\langle\langle \text{نَحْنُ مَعَاشِرَ الْأَنْبِيَاءِ لَا نُورَثُ، مَا تَرَكْنَا فَهُوَ صَدَقَةٌ} \rangle\rangle$$

(We Prophets do not leave behind any inheritance (of wealth). Whatever we leave behind, then it is charity.) Mujahid said concerning his statement,

(Who shall inherit me, and inherit (also) the posterity of Ya'qub.) (19:6) "His inheritance was knowledge, and Zakariyya was one of the descendants of Ya`qub." Hushaym said, "Isma'il bin Abi Khalid informed us that Abu Salih commented about the Ayah:

(who shall inherit me, and inherit (also) the posterity of Ya`qub.) "He would be a Prophet like his forefathers were Prophets." Allah's statement,

(and make him, my Lord, one with whom You are well-pleased!) means "Make him pleasing to You (Allah) and your creation. Love him and make him beloved to your creatures, in both his religion and his character."

Surah: 19 Ayah: 7

$$\text{يَـٰزَكَرِيَّآ إِنَّا نُبَشِّرُكَ بِغُلَـٰمٍ ٱسْمُهُۥ يَحْيَىٰ لَمْ نَجْعَل لَّهُۥ مِن قَبْلُ سَمِيًّا ۝}$$

7. (Allâh said) "O Zakariyyâ (Zachariah)! Verily, We give you the glad tidings of a son, whose name will be Yahyâ (John). We have given that name to none before (him)."

Transliteration

7. Ya zakariyya inna nubashshiruka bighulamin ismuhu yahya lam najAAal lahu min qablu samiyyan

Tafsir Ibn Kathir

The acceptance of His Supplication

This statement implies what is not mentioned, that his supplication was answered. It was said to him,

((Allah said:) "O Zakariyya! Verily, We give you the glad tidings of a son, whose name will be Yahya...") Similarly Allah, the Exalted, said;

(At that time Zakariyya invoked his Lord, saying: "O my Lord! Grant me from You, a good offspring. You are indeed the All-Hearer of invocation." Then the angels called him, while he was standing in prayer in the Mihrab, (saying): "Allah gives you glad tidings of Yahya, confirming (believing in) the word from Allah, noble, keeping away from sexual relations with women, a Prophet, from among the righteous.")(3:38-39) Allah said,

(We have given that name to none before (him).) Qatadah, Ibn Jurayj and Ibn Zayd said, "This means that no one had this name before him." Ibn Jarir preferred this interpretation, may Allah have mercy upon him.

Surah: 19 Ayah: 8 & Ayah: 9

قَالَ رَبِّ أَنَّىٰ يَكُونُ لِى غُلَـٰمٌ وَكَانَتِ ٱمْرَأَتِى عَاقِرًا وَقَدْ بَلَغْتُ مِنَ ٱلْكِبَرِ عِتِيًّا ۝

8. He said: "My Lord! How can I have a son, when my wife is barren, and I have reached the extreme old age."

قَالَ كَذَٰلِكَ قَالَ رَبُّكَ هُوَ عَلَىَّ هَيِّنٌ وَقَدْ خَلَقْتُكَ مِن قَبْلُ وَلَمْ تَكُ شَيْـًٔا ۝

9. He said: "So (it will be). Your Lord says: It is easy for Me. Certainly I have created you before, when you had been nothing!"

Transliteration

8. Qala rabbi anna yakoonu lee ghulamun wakanati imraatee AAaqiran waqad balaghtu mina alkibari AAitiyyan 9. Qala kathalika qala rabbuka huwa AAalayya hayyinun waqad khalaqtuka min qablu walam taku shay-an

Chapter 19: Maryam (Mary), Verses 001-098

Tafsir Ibn Kathir

His amazement after the acceptance of His Supplication

Zakariyya was amazed when his supplication was answered and he was given the good news of a son. He became extremely overjoyed and asked how this child would be born to him, and in what manner he would come. This was particularly amazing because his wife was an old woman who was barren and had not given birth to any children in her entire life. Even Zakariyya himself had become old and advanced in years, his bones had become feeble and thin, and he had no potent semen or vigor for sexual intercourse. The Answer of the Angel

(He said:) That is, the angel, in his response to Zakariyya and his was amazement.

("Thus says your Lord: `It is easy for Me...'") Meaning the birth of the son will be from you and from this wife of yours and not from any other (woman).

(easy) Meaning, it is simple and easy for Allah to do. Then he (the angel) mentioned to him that which is more amazing than what he was asking about. The angel said that the Lord said,

(Certainly I have created you before, when you had been nothing!) This is similar to Allah's statement,

(Has there not been over man a period of time, when he was not a thing worth mentioning) (76:1)

Surah: 19 Ayah: 10 & Ayah: 11

قَالَ رَبِّ اجْعَل لِّى ءَايَةً قَالَ ءَايَتُكَ أَلَّا تُكَلِّمَ ٱلنَّاسَ ثَلَٰثَ لَيَالٍ سَوِيًّا ۝

10. (Zakariyyâ (Zachariah)) said: "My Lord! Appoint for me a sign." He said: "Your sign is that you shall not speak unto mankind for three nights, though having no bodily defect."

فَخَرَجَ عَلَىٰ قَوْمِهِۦ مِنَ ٱلْمِحْرَابِ فَأَوْحَىٰ إِلَيْهِمْ أَن سَبِّحُوا۟ بُكْرَةً وَعَشِيًّا ۝

11. Then he came out to his people from Al-Mihrâb (a praying place or a private room), he told them by signs to glorify Allâh's Praises in the morning and in the afternoon.

Transliteration

10. Qala rabbi ijAAal lee ayatan qala ayatuka alla tukallima alnnasa thalatha layalin sawiyyan   11. Fakharaja AAala qawmihi mina almihrabi faawha ilayhim an sabbihoo bukratan waAAashiyyan

Tafsir Ibn Kathir

The Sign of the Pregnancy

Allah, the Exalted, informed about Zakariyya that he said,

(He (Zakariyya) said: "My Lord! Appoint for me a sign.") "Give me a sign and a proof of the existence of that which You have promised me, so that my soul will be at rest and my heart will be at ease with Your promise." Similarly Ibrahim said,

(My Lord! Show me how You give life to the dead. He (Allah) said: "Do you not believe" He said: "Yes (I believe), but to put my heart at ease.")(2:260) Then Allah says,

(He said: "Your sign is...") meaning, "Your sign will be..."

(that you shall not speak unto mankind for three nights, though having no bodily defect.) Meaning, `your tongue will be prevented from speaking for three nights while you are healthy and fit, without any sickness or illness.' Ibn `Abbas, Mujahid, `Ikrimah, Wahb, As-Suddi, Qatadah and others said, "His tongue was arrested without any sickness or illness." `Abdur-Rahman bin Zayd bin Aslam said, "He used to recite and glorify Allah, but he was not able to speak to his people except by gestures. " Al-`Awfi reported that Ibn `Abbas said,

(three nights, though having no bodily defect.) "The nights were consecutive." However, the first statement that is reported from him and the majority is more correct. This Ayah is similar to what Allah, the Exalted, said in Surah Al `Imran,

(He said: "O my Lord! Make a sign for me." (Allah) said "Your sign is that you shall not speak to mankind for three days except with signals. And remember your Lord much, and glorify (Him) in the afternoon and in the morning.)(3:41) This is a proof that he did not speak to his people for these three nights and their days as well.

(except with signals.) Meaning, with bodily gestures, this is why Allah says in this noble Ayah,

(Then he came out to his people from the Mihrab) referring to the place where he was given the good news of the child.

(he indicated to them by signs) Meaning he made a gesture to them that was subtle and swift.

(to glorify (Allah) in the morning and in the afternoon.) That they should be agreeable to what he was commanded to do during these three days, to increase in his deeds and gratitude to Allah for what He had given him. Mujahid said,

(he indicated to them by signs) "He made a gesture." Wahb and Qatadah said the same.

Chapter 19: Maryam (Mary), Verses 001-098

Surah: 19 Ayah: 12, Ayah: 13, Ayah: 14 & Ayah: 15

يَٰيَحْيَىٰ خُذِ ٱلْكِتَٰبَ بِقُوَّةٍ وَءَاتَيْنَٰهُ ٱلْحُكْمَ صَبِيًّا ﴿١٢﴾

12. (It was said to his son): "O Yahyâ (John)! Hold fast the Scripture (the Taurât (Torah))" And We gave him wisdom while yet a child.

وَحَنَانًا مِّن لَّدُنَّا وَزَكَوٰةً وَكَانَ تَقِيًّا ﴿١٣﴾

13. And (made him) sympathetic to men as a mercy (or a grant) from Us, and pure from sins (i.e. Yahyâ (John)) and he was righteous,

وَبَرًّۢا بِوَٰلِدَيْهِ وَلَمْ يَكُن جَبَّارًا عَصِيًّا ﴿١٤﴾

14. And dutiful towards his parents, and he was neither arrogant nor disobedient (to Allâh or to his parents).

وَسَلَٰمٌ عَلَيْهِ يَوْمَ وُلِدَ وَيَوْمَ يَمُوتُ وَيَوْمَ يُبْعَثُ حَيًّا ﴿١٥﴾

15. And Salâm (peace) be on him the day he was born, the day he dies, and the day he will be raised up to life (again)!

Transliteration

12. Ya yahya khuthi alkitaba biquwwatin waataynahu alhukma sabiyyan   13. Wahananan min ladunna wazakatan wakana taqiyyan   14. Wabarran biwalidayhi walam yakun jabbaran AAasiyyan   15. Wasalamun AAalayhi yawma wulida wayawma yamootu wayawma yubAAathu hayyan

Tafsir Ibn Kathir

The Birth of the Boy and His Characteristics

This also implies what is not mentioned, that this promised boy was born and he was Yahya. There is also the implication that Allah taught him the Book, the Tawrah which they used to study among themselves. The Prophets who were sent to the Jews used to rule according to the Tawrah, as did the scholars and rabbis among them. He was still young in age when Allah gave him this knowledge. This is the reason that Allah mentioned it. Because of how Allah favored him and his parents, He says,

(O Yahya! Hold fast to the Scripture (the Tawrah).) Means, "Learn the Book with strength." In other words, learn it well, with zeal and studious effort.

(And We gave him wisdom while yet a child.) This means he was given understanding, knowledge, fortitude, diligence and zeal for good and the pursuit of good. He was blessed with these characteristics even though he was young. Allah said,

(And (made him) Hananan from Us,) (19:13) Ali bin Abi Talhah reported that Ibn `Abbas said,

(And Hananan from Us,) "This means mercy from Us." `Ikrimah, Qatadah and Ad-Dahhak all said the same. Ad-Dahhak added, "Mercy that no one would be able to give except Us." Qatadah added, "With it, Allah had mercy upon Zakariyya." Mujahid said,

(And Hananan from Us,) "This was gentleness from His Lord upon him." The apparent meaning is that Allah's statement Hananan (affection, compassion) is directly related to His statement,

(and We gave him wisdom while yet a child.) meaning, "We gave him wisdom, compassion and purity." This means that he was a compassionate man, who was righteous. Hanan means the love for affection and tenderness (towards others). Concerning Allah's statement,

(and Zakatan,) This is related to His statement,

(And Hananan) The word Zakah means purity from filth, wickedness and sins. Qatadah said, "The word Zakah means the righteous deed." Ad-Dahhak and Ibn Jurayj both said, "The righteous deed is the pure (Zakah) deed." Al-`Awfi reported that Ibn `Abbas said,

(and Zakatan,) "This means that he was a blessing."

(and he was pious.)(19:13) meaning that he was pure and had no inclination to do sins. Allah said;

(And dutiful to his parents, and he was not arrogant or disobedient.) After Allah mentioned Yahya's obedience to his Lord and that Allah created him full of mercy, purity and piety, He attached to it his obedience to his parents and his good treatment of them. Allah mentioned that he refrained from disobeying them in speech, actions, commands and prohibitions. Due to this Allah says,

(and he was not arrogant or disobedient.) Then, after mentioning these beautiful characteristics, Allah mentions his reward for this,

(And Salam (peace) be on him the day he was born, and the day he dies, and the day he will be raised up to life (again)!) This means that he had security and safety in these three circumstances. Sufyan bin `Uyaynah said, "The loneliest that a man will ever feel is in three situations. The first situation is on the day that he is born, when he sees himself coming out of what he was in. The second situation is on the day that he dies, when he sees people that he will not see anymore. The third situation is on the day when he is resurrected, when he sees himself in the great gathering. Allah has exclusively honored Yahya, the son of Zakariyya, by granting him peace in these situations. Allah says,

(And Salam (peace) be on him the day he was born, and the day he dies, and the day he will be raised up to life (again)!) This narration was reported by Ibn Jarir, from Ahmad bin Mansur Al-Marwazi, from Sadaqah bin Al-Fadl, from Sufyan bin `Uyaynah.

Surah: 19 Ayah: 16, Ayah: 17, Ayah: 18, Ayah: 19, Ayah: 20 & Ayah: 21

وَٱذْكُرْ فِى ٱلْكِتَٰبِ مَرْيَمَ إِذِ ٱنتَبَذَتْ مِنْ أَهْلِهَا مَكَانًا شَرْقِيًّا ﴿١٦﴾

16. And mention in the Book (the Qur'ân, O Muhammad (peace be upon him) the story of) Maryam (Mary), when she withdrew in seclusion from her family to a place facing east.

فَٱتَّخَذَتْ مِن دُونِهِمْ حِجَابًا فَأَرْسَلْنَا إِلَيْهَا رُوحَنَا فَتَمَثَّلَ لَهَا بَشَرًا سَوِيًّا ﴿١٧﴾

17. She placed a screen (to screen herself) from them; then We sent to her Our Ruh (angel Jibrîl (Gabriel)) and he appeared before her in the form of a man in all respects.

قَالَتْ إِنِّى أَعُوذُ بِٱلرَّحْمَٰنِ مِنكَ إِن كُنتَ تَقِيًّا ﴿١٨﴾

18. She said: "Verily! I seek refuge with the Most Gracious (Allâh) from you, if you do fear Allâh."

قَالَ إِنَّمَا أَنَا۠ رَسُولُ رَبِّكِ لِأَهَبَ لَكِ غُلَامًا زَكِيًّا ﴿١٩﴾

19. (The angel) said: "I am only a Messenger from your Lord, (to announce) to you the gift of a righteous son."

قَالَتْ أَنَّىٰ يَكُونُ لِى غُلَامٌ وَلَمْ يَمْسَسْنِى بَشَرٌ وَلَمْ أَكُ بَغِيًّا ﴿٢٠﴾

20. She said: "How can I have a son, when no man has touched me, nor am I unchaste?"

قَالَ كَذَٰلِكِ قَالَ رَبُّكِ هُوَ عَلَىَّ هَيِّنٌ وَلِنَجْعَلَهُۥ ءَايَةً لِلنَّاسِ وَرَحْمَةً مِّنَّا وَكَانَ أَمْرًا مَّقْضِيًّا ﴿٢١﴾

21. He said: "So (it will be), your Lord said: 'That is easy for Me (Allâh): And (We wish) to appoint him as a sign to mankind and a mercy from Us (Allâh), and it is a matter (already) decreed, (by Allâh).'"

Transliteration

16. Waothkur fee alkitabi maryama ithi intabathat min ahliha makanan sharqiyyan 17. Faittakhathat min doonihim hijaban faarsalna ilayha roohana fatamaththala laha basharan sawiyyan 18. Qalat innee aAAoothu bialrrahmani minka in kunta taqiyyan Translation 19. Qala innama ana rasoolu rabbiki li-ahaba laki ghulaman zakiyyan Translation 20. Qalat anna yakoonu lee ghulamun walam yamsasnee basharun walam aku baghiyyan 21. Qala kathaliki qala rabbuki huwa AAalayya hayyinun walinajAAalahu ayatan lilnnasi warahmatan minna wakana amran maqdiyyan

Tafsir Ibn Kathir

The Story of Maryam and Al-Masih (`Isa)

After Allah, the Exalted, mentioned the story of Zakariyya, and that He blessed him with a righteous, purified and blessed child even in his old age while his wife was barren, He then mentions the story of Maryam. Allah informs of His granting her a child named `Isa without a father being involved (in her pregnancy). Between these two stories there is an appropriate and similar relationship. Due to their closeness in meaning, Allah mentioned them here together, as well as in Surahs Al `Imran and Al-Anbiya'. Allah has mentioned these stories to show His servants His ability, the might of His authority and that He has power over all things. Allah says,

(And mention in the Book, Maryam,) She was Maryam bint `Imran from the family lineage of Dawud. She was from a good and wholesome family of the Children of Israel. Allah mentioned the story of her mother's pregnancy with her in Surah Al `Imran, and that she (Maryam's mother) dedicated her freely for the service of Allah. This meant that she dedicated the child (Maryam) to the service of the Masjid of the Sacred House (in Jerusalem). Thus, they (Zakariyya, Maryam's mother and Maryam) were similar in that aspect.

(So her Lord (Allah) accepted her with goodly acceptance. He made her grow in a good manner.)(3:37) Thus, Maryam was raised among the Children of Israel in an honorable way. She was one of the female worshippers, well-known for her remarkable acts of worship, devotion and perseverance. She lived under the care of her brother-in-law, Zakariyya, who was a Prophet of the Children of Israel at that time. He was a great man among them, whom they would refer to in their religious matters. Zakariyya saw astonishing miracles occur from her that amazed him.

(Every time Zakaiyya entered the Mihrab to (visit) her, he found her supplied with sustenance. He said: "O Maryam! From where have you got this" She said, "This is from Allah." Verily, Allah provides to whom He wills, without limit.) (3:37) It has been mentioned that he would find her with winter fruit during the summer and summer fruit during the winter. This has already been explained in Surah Al `Imran. Then, when Allah wanted to grant her His servant and Messenger, `Isa, one of the five Great Messengers.

(she withdrew in seclusion from her family to place facing east.) (19:16) This means that she withdrew from them and secluded herself from them. She went to the eastern side of the Sacred Masjid (in Jerusalem). It is reported from Ibn `Abbas that he said, "Verily, I am the most knowledgeable of Allah's creation of why the Christians took the east as the direction of devotional worship. They did because of Allah's statement,

(When she withdrew in seclusion from her family to a place facing east.) Therefore, they took the birthplace of `Isa as their direction of worship." Concerning Allah's statement,

(She placed a screen before them;) This means that she hid herself from them and concealed herself. Then, Allah sent Jibril to her.

Chapter 19: Maryam (Mary), Verses 001-098

(and he appeared before her in the form of a man in all respects.) (19:17) This means that he came to her in the form of a perfect and complete man. Mujahid, Ad-Dahhak, Qatadah, Ibn Jurayj, Wahb bin Munabbih and As-Suddi all commented on Allah's statement,

(then We sent to her Our Ruh,) "It means Jibril."

(She said: "Verily, I seek refuge with the Most Gracious from you, if you do fear Allah.") This means that when the angel (Jibril) appeared to her in the form of a man, while she was in a place secluded by herself with a partition between her and her people, she was afraid of him and thought that he wanted to rape her. Therefore, she said,

(Verily, I seek refuge with the Most Gracious from you, if you do fear Allah.) She meant, "If you fear Allah," as a means of reminding him of Allah. This is what is legislated in defense against (evil), so that it may be repulsed with ease. Therefore, the first thing she did was try to make him fear Allah, the Mighty and Sublime. Ibn Jarir reported from `Asim that Abu Wa'il said when mentioning the story of Maryam, "She knew that the pious person would refrain (from committing evil) when she said,

("Verily, I seek refuge with the Most Gracious from you, if you do fear Allah." He said: "I am only a messenger from your Lord...") This means that the angel said to her in response, and in order to remove the fear that she felt within herself, "I am not what you think, but I am the messenger of your Lord." By this he meant, "Allah has sent me to you." It is said that when she mentioned the (Name of the) Most Beneficent (Ar-Rahman), Jibril fell apart and returned to his true form (as an angel). He responded, (زَكِيًّا غُلَامًا لَكِ لِيَهَبَ رَبِّكِ رَسُولُ أَنَا إِنَّمَا) `I am only a messenger from your Lord, to provide to you the gift of a righteous son.'

(She said: "How can I have a son...") This means that Maryam was amazed at this. She said, "How can I have a son" She said this to mean, "In what way would a son be born to me when I do not have a husband and I do not commit any wicked acts (i.e. fornication)" For this reason she said,

(when no man has touched me, nor am I Baghiyya) The Baghiyy is a female fornicator. For this reason, a Hadith has been reported prohibiting the money earned from Baghiyy.

(He said: "Thus said your Lord: `That is easy for Me (Allah)...'") This means that the angel said to her in response to her question, "Verily, Allah has said that a boy will be born from you even though you do not have a husband and you have not committed any lewdness. Verily, He is Most Able to do whatever He wills." Due to this, he (Jibril) conveyed Allah's Words,

(And (We wish) to appoint him as a sign to mankind) This means a proof and a sign for mankind of the power of their Maker and Creator, Who diversified them in their creation. He created their father, Adam, without a male (father) or female (mother). Then, He created Hawwa' (Adam's spouse) from a male (father) without a female (mother). Then, He created the rest of their progeny from male and female, except

`Isa. He caused `Isa to be born from a female without a male. Thus, Allah completed the four types of creation (of the human being), which proves the perfection of His power and the magnificence of His authority. There is no god worthy of worship except Him and there is no true Lord other than Him. Concerning Allah's statement,

(and a mercy from Us,) This means, "We will make this boy a mercy from Allah and a Prophet from among the Prophets. He will call to the worship of Allah and monotheistic belief in Him. This is as Allah, the Exalted, said in another Ayah,

((Remember) when the angels said: "O Maryam! Verily, Allah gives you the good news of a Word from Him, his name will be Al-Masih, `Isa, the son of Maryam, held in honor in this world and in the Hereafter, and will be one of those who are near to Allah. And he will speak to the people, in the cradle and in manhood, and he will be one of the righteous.) (3:45-46) This means that he will call to the worship of his Lord in his cradle and while and adult. Concerning His statement,

(and it is a matter (already) decreed (by Allah).) This is the completion of Jibril's dialogue with Maryam. He informed her that this matter was preordained by Allah's power and will. Muhammad bin Ishaq said,

(and it is a matter (already) decreed (by Allah).) "This means that Allah determined to do this, so there is no avoiding it."

Surah: 19 Ayah: 22 & Ayah: 23

فَحَمَلَتْهُ فَٱنتَبَذَتْ بِهِۦ مَكَانًا قَصِيًّا ۝

22. So she conceived him, and she withdrew with him to a far place (i.e. Bethlehem valley about 4-6 miles from Jerusalem).

فَأَجَاءَهَا ٱلْمَخَاضُ إِلَىٰ جِذْعِ ٱلنَّخْلَةِ قَالَتْ يَٰلَيْتَنِى مِتُّ قَبْلَ هَٰذَا وَكُنتُ نَسْيًا مَّنسِيًّا ۝

23. And the pains of childbirth drove her to the trunk of a date-palm. She said: "Would that I had died before this, and had been forgotten and out of sight!"

Transliteration

22. Fahamalat-hu faintabathat bihi makanan qasiyyan 23. Faajaaha almakhadu ila jithAAi alnnakhlati qalat ya laytanee mittu qabla hatha wakuntu nasyan mansiyyan

Tafsir Ibn Kathir

The Conception and the Birth

Allah, the Exalted, informs about Maryam that when Jibril had spoken to her about what Allah said, she accepted the decree of Allah. Many scholars of the predecessors (Salaf) have mentioned that at this point the angel (who was Jibril) blew into the opening of the garment that she was wearing. Then the breath descended until it entered into her vagina and she conceived the child by the leave of Allah. Muhammad bin Ishaq said, "When she conceived him and filled her water jug (at a well), she returned (to her people). After this, her menstrual bleeding ceased and she experienced what the pregnant woman experiences of sickness, hunger, change of color and there was even a change in the manner of her speech. After this, no people came to visit any house like they did the house of Zakariyya. The word spread among the Children of Israel and the people were saying, `Verily, her partner (in fornication) was Yusuf, because there was no one else in the temple with her except him.' So she hid herself from the people and placed a veil between herself and them. No one saw her and she did not see anyone else." Allah said;

(And the pains of childbirth drove her to the trunk of a date palm.) This means that her pains of labor compelled her to go to the trunk of a date-palm tree that was at the place where she had secluded herself. The scholars differed over its location. As-Suddi said, "Her place of seclusion was to the east and that was where she would pray at the Sacred House of Jerusalem." Wahb bin Munabbih said, "She ran away and when she reached an area between Ash-Sham and Egypt, she was overcome by labor pains." In another narration from Wahb, he said, "This took place eight miles from the Sacred House of Jerusalem in a village that was known as Bayt Al-Lahm (Bethlehem)." I say, there are Hadiths about the Isra' (Night Journey of the Prophet) that are reported by An-Nasa'i on the authority of Anas, and Al-Bayhaqi on the authority of Shadad bin Aws, that say that this took place at Bait Al-Lahm. Allah knows best. This is what is well known that the people all relate from each other. The Christians have no doubt held that the place of this occurrence was Bethlehem and this is what all the people relate. It has been related in a Hadith also, if the Hadith is authentic. Allah says, informing about her,

(She said: "Would that I had died before this, and had been forgotten and out of sight!") In this is an evidence of the permissibility to wish for death when a calamity strikes. She knew that she was going to be tested with the birth, the people would not assist her, and they would not believe her story. After she was known as a devout worshipper among them, they now thought that she had become a fornicating whore. She said,

(Would that I had died before this,) She said this to mean before this situation.

(and I had been forgotten and out of sight!) This means, "I wish I had not been created and I was nothing." This was mentioned by Ibn `Abbas. Qatadah said,

(and I had been forgotten and out of sight!) "This means something unknown, forgotten and no one knew who I was."

Surah: 19 Ayah: 24, Ayah: 25 & Ayah: 26

$$\text{فَنَادَىٰهَا مِن تَحْتِهَآ أَلَّا تَحْزَنِى قَدْ جَعَلَ رَبُّكِ تَحْتَكِ سَرِيًّا}$$

24. Then (the babe 'Iesa (Jesus) or Jibrîl (Gabriel)) cried unto her from below her, saying: "Grieve not: your Lord has provided a water stream under you.

وَهُزِّي إِلَيْكِ بِجِذْعِ ٱلنَّخْلَةِ تُسَٰقِطْ عَلَيْكِ رُطَبًا جَنِيًّا ۝

25. "And shake the trunk of date-palm towards you, it will let fall fresh ripe-dates upon you."

فَكُلِي وَٱشْرَبِي وَقَرِّي عَيْنًا ۖ فَإِمَّا تَرَيِنَّ مِنَ ٱلْبَشَرِ أَحَدًا فَقُولِي إِنِّي نَذَرْتُ لِلرَّحْمَٰنِ صَوْمًا فَلَنْ أُكَلِّمَ ٱلْيَوْمَ إِنسِيًّا ۝

26. "So eat and drink and be glad. And if you see any human being, say: 'Verily! I have vowed a fast unto the Most Gracious (Allâh) so I shall not speak to any human being this day.'"

Transliteration

24. Fanadaha min tahtiha alla tahzanee qad jaAAala rabbuki tahtaki sariyyan 25. Wahuzzee ilayki bijithAAi alnnakhlati tusaqit AAalayki rutaban janiyyan 26. Fakulee waishrabee waqarree AAaynan fa-imma tarayinna mina albashari ahadan faqoolee innee nathartu lilrrahmani sawman falan okallima alyawma insiyyan

Tafsir Ibn Kathir

What was said to Her after the Birth Some reciters read the Ayah as, (Who was below her)

(Who was below her) Meaning the one who was below her called to her. Others recited it as,

(from below her) With the meaning of a preposition (from) instead of a pronoun (who). The scholars of Tafsir have differed over the interpretation of who was calling out. Al-`Awfi and others reported from Ibn `Abbas that he said,

(Then cried unto her from below her,) "This is referring to Jibril because `Isa did not speak until she brought him to her people." Similarly, Sa`id bin Jubayr, Ad-Dahhak, `Amr bin Maymun, As-Suddi and Qatadah all said, "Verily, this is referring to the angel Jibril." This means that he (Jibril) called out to her from the bottom of the valley. Mujahid said,

(Then cried unto her from below her,) "This is referring to `Isa bin Maryam." Likewise, `Abdur-Razzaq reported from Ma`mar that Qatadah said that Al-Hasan said, "This is referring to her son (`Isa)." This is also one of the two opinions reported from Sa`id bin Jubayr -- that it was her son, `Isa, speaking. Sa`id said, "Have you not heard Allah saying,

(Then she pointed to him.) Ibn Zayd and Ibn Jarir preferred this opinion in his Tafsir. Allah said,

(Grieve not:) He called to her saying, "Do not grieve."

Chapter 19: Maryam (Mary), Verses 001-098 51

(your Lord has provided a Sariy under you.) Sufyan Ath-Thawri and Shu`bah reported from Abu Ishaq that Al-Bara' bin `Azib said,

(your Lord has provided a Sariy under you.) "This means a small stream." Likewise, `Ali bin Abi Talhah reported that Ibn `Abbas said, "Sariy means a river." `Amr bin Maymun held the same view, as he said, "It means a river for her to drink from." Mujahid said, "It means river in the Syrian language." Sa`id bin Jubayr said, "Sariy is a small flowing river." Others said that Sariy refers to `Isa. This was said by Al-Hasan, Ar-Rabi` bin Anas, Muhammad bin `Abbad bin Ja`far, and it is one of the two opinions reported from Qatadah. It is also the view of `Abdur-Rahman bin Zayd bin Aslam. However, the first view seems to be the most obvious meaning. For this reason, Allah said after it,

(And shake the trunk of date palm towards you,) meaning, "Grab the trunk of the date-palm tree and shake it towards yourself." Therefore, Allah blessed her by giving her food and drink. Then He said,

(It will let fall fresh ripe dates upon you. So eat and drink and rejoice.) Meaning to be happy. This is why `Amr bin Maymun said, "Nothing is better for the woman confined in childbed than dried dates and fresh dates." Then he recited this noble Ayah. Concerning Allah's statement,

(And if you see any human being,) This means any person that you see,

(Say: `Verily, I have vowed a fast unto the Most Gracious (Allah) so I shall not speak to any human being today.') Meaning, by signaling with gestures, not a statement by speech. This is so that she does not negate her oath itself,

(so I shall not speak to any human being today.) Anas bin Malik commented on,

(I have vowed a fast unto the Most Gracious) He said; "A vow of silence." Likewise said Ibn `Abbas and Ad-Dahhak. The meaning here is that in their Law, when fasting, it was forbidden for them to eat and speak. As-Suddi, Qatadah and `Abdur-Rahman bin Zayd have all stated this view. `Abdur-Rahman bin Zayd said, "When `Isa said to Maryam,

(Grieve not) She said, `How can I not grieve when you are with me and I have no husband nor am I an owned slave woman. What excuse do I have with the people. Woe unto me, if I had only died before this, and had been a thing forgotten and unknown.' Then, `Isa said to her, `I will suffice you with a statement,

(And if you see any human being, say: `Verily, I have vowed a fast unto the Most Gracious so I shall not speak to any human being this day.')' All of this is from the speech of `Isa to his mother." Wahb said the same as well.

Surah: 19 Ayah: 27, Ayah: 28, Ayah: 29, Ayah: 30, Ayah: 31, Ayah: 32 & Ayah: 33

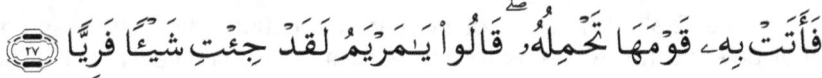

27. Then she brought him (the baby) to her people, carrying him. They said: "O Mary! Indeed you have brought a thing Fariyy (a mighty thing). (Tafsir Al-Tabari)

$$ يَٰٓأُخْتَ هَٰرُونَ مَا كَانَ أَبُوكِ ٱمْرَأَ سَوْءٍ وَمَا كَانَتْ أُمُّكِ بَغِيًّا ﴿٢٨﴾ $$

28. "O sister (i.e. the like) of Hârûn (Aaron)! Your father was not a man who used to commit adultery, nor your mother was an unchaste woman."

$$ فَأَشَارَتْ إِلَيْهِ ۖ قَالُوا۟ كَيْفَ نُكَلِّمُ مَن كَانَ فِى ٱلْمَهْدِ صَبِيًّا ﴿٢٩﴾ $$

29. Then she pointed to him. They said: "How can we talk to one who is a child in the cradle?"

$$ قَالَ إِنِّى عَبْدُ ٱللَّهِ ءَاتَىٰنِىَ ٱلْكِتَٰبَ وَجَعَلَنِى نَبِيًّا ﴿٣٠﴾ $$

30. "He ('Iesa (Jesus)) said: Verily I am a slave of Allâh, He has given me the Scripture and made me a Prophet;"

$$ وَجَعَلَنِى مُبَارَكًا أَيْنَ مَا كُنتُ وَأَوْصَٰنِى بِٱلصَّلَوٰةِ وَٱلزَّكَوٰةِ مَا دُمْتُ حَيًّا ﴿٣١﴾ $$

31. "And He has made me blessed wheresoever I be, and has enjoined on me Salât (prayer), and Zakât, as long as I live."

$$ وَبَرًّۢا بِوَٰلِدَتِى وَلَمْ يَجْعَلْنِى جَبَّارًا شَقِيًّا ﴿٣٢﴾ $$

32. "And dutiful to my mother, and made me not arrogant, unblest."

$$ وَٱلسَّلَٰمُ عَلَىَّ يَوْمَ وُلِدتُّ وَيَوْمَ أَمُوتُ وَيَوْمَ أُبْعَثُ حَيًّا ﴿٣٣﴾ $$

33. "And Salâm (peace) be upon me the day I was born, and the day I die, and the day I shall be raised alive!"

Transliteration

27. Faatat bihi qawmaha tahmiluhu qaloo ya maryamu laqad ji/ti shay-an fariyyan 28. Ya okhta haroona ma kana abooki imraa saw-in wama kanat ommuki baghiyyan 29. Faasharat ilayhi qaloo kayfa nukallimu man kana fee almahdi sabiyyan 30. Qala innee AAabdu Allahi ataniya alkitaba wajaAAalanee nabiyyan 31. WajaAAalanee mubarakan aynama kuntu waawsanee bialssalati waalzzakati ma dumtu hayyan 32. Wabarran biwalidatee walam yajAAalnee jabbaran shaqiyyan 33. Waalssalamu AAalayya yawma wulidtu wayawma amootu wayawma obAAathu hayyan

Tafsir Ibn Kathir

Maryam with Al-Masih before the People, Their Rejection of Her and His Reply to Them

Allah, the Exalted, informs of Maryam's situation when she was commanded to fast that day and not to speak to any human being. For verily, her affair would be taken

Chapter 19: Maryam (Mary), Verses 001-098

care of and her proof would be established. Thus, she accepted the command of Allah and she readily received His decree. She took her child and brought him to her people, carrying him. When they saw her like this they made a big deal about her situation and they sternly protested against of it, and

(They said: "O Mary! Indeed you have brought a thing Fariy.") Fariy means a mighty thing. This was said by Mujahid, Qatadah, As-Suddi and others. Ibn Abi Hatim reported from Nawf Al-Bikali that he said, "Her people went out searching for her, she was from a family that was blessed with prophethood and nobility. However, they could not find any trace of her. They came across a cow herder and they asked him, `Have you seen a girl whose description is such and such' He replied, `No, but tonight I saw my cows doing something that I've never seen them do before.' They asked, `What did you see' He said, `Tonight I saw them prostrating in the direction of that valley.'" `Abdullah bin Ziyad said (adding to the narration), "I memorized from Sayyar that he (the cattle herder) said, `I saw a radiant light.' " So they went towards the direction that he told him, and Maryam was coming towards them from that direction. When she saw them she sat down and she was holding her child in her lap. They came towards her until they were standing over her.

(They said: "O Mary! Indeed you have brought a mighty thing (Fariy).") This means it was a mighty thing that she had brought.

(O sister of Harun!) This means, "O one resembling Harun (Aaron) in worship."

(Your father was not a man who used to commit adultery, nor your mother was an unchaste woman.) They meant, "You are from a good, pure family, well-known for its righteousness, worship and abstinence from worldy indulgence. How could you do such a thing" `Ali bin Abi Talhah and As-Suddi both said, "It was said to her,

(O sister of Harun!) referring to the brother of Musa, because she was of his descendants. This is similar to the saying, `O brother of Tamim,' to one who is from the Tamimi tribe, and `O brother of Mudar,' to one who is from the Mudari tribe. It has also been said that she was related to a righteous man among them whose name was Harun and she was comparable to him in her abstinence and worship. Concerning Allah's statement,

(Then she pointed to him. They said: "How can we talk to one who is a child in the cradle") This is what took place while they were in doubt about her situation, condeming her circumstances, saying what they wanted to say. At that time they were slandering her and falsely accusing her of a horrendous act. On that day she was fasting and keeping silent. Therefore, she referred all speech to him (the child) and she directed them to his address and speech to them. They scoffed at her because they thought that she was mocking at them and playing with them. They said,

(How can we talk to one who is a child in the cradle) Maymun bin Mahran said,

(Then she pointed to him.) "She indicated, `Speak to him.' They then said, `After she has come to us with this calamity, she now commands us to speak to one who is a child in the cradle!'" As-Suddi said, "When she pointed to him they became angry and said, `Her mocking us, to the extent of commanding us to speak to this child, is worse to us than her fornication.' "

(They said: "How can we talk to one who is a child in the cradle") This means, "How can someone speak who is in his cradle, in the state of infancy and a child" `Isa said,

(Verily, I am a servant of Allah,) The first thing that he said was a declaration of the lofty honor of his Lord and His being free of having a child. Also, he affirmed that he himself was a worshipper of his Lord. Allah said,

(He has given me the Scripture and made me a Prophet.) This was a declaration of innocence for his mother from the immorality that was attributed to her. Nawf Al-Bikali said, "When they said what they said to his mother, he (`Isa) was nursing from her breast. At their statement he released the breast from his mouth and reclined on his left saying,

(Verily, I am a servant of Allah, He has given me the Scripture and made me a Prophet.) And he continued speaking until he said,

(as long as I live.)" Concerning his statement,

(And He has made me blessed wherever I be,) Mujahid, `Amr bin Qays and Ath-Thawri all said that this means, "And He made me a teacher of goodness." In another narration from Mujahid, he said, "A person of great benefit." Ibn Jarir reported from Wuhayb bin Al-Ward, a freed slave of the Bani Makhzum tribe, that he said, "A scholar met another scholar who had more knowledge than himself. So he said to him, `May Allah have mercy upon you, what acts of mine should I perform openly' The other replied, `Commanding good and forbidding evil, for verily, it is the religion of Allah, which He sent His Prophets with to His servants.' The scholars have indeed agreed upon the statement of Allah,

(And He has made me blessed wherever I be,) Then it was said, `What was his blessing' He (Wuhayb) replied, `Commanding good and forbidding evil wherever he was.' " His saying,

(and He has enjoined on me (Awsani) Salah and Zakah, as long as I live.) This is similar to the statement of Allah to Muhammad ,

(And worship your Lord until there comes unto you the certainty (i.e. death).) (15:99) `Abdur-Rahman bin Al-Qasim reported from Malik bin Anas that he commented on Allah's statement,

(and He has enjoined on me (Awsani) Salah and Zakah, as long as I live.) He said, "Allah informed him of what would be of his affair until his death. This is the firmest evidence against the people who deny Allah's preordained decree." Concerning Allah's statement,

(And to be dutiful to my mother.) This means, "He (Allah) has commanded me to treat my mother well." He mentioned this after mentioning obedience to his Lord,

Allah. This is because Allah often combines the command to worship Him with obedience to the parents. This is similar to Allah's statement,

(And your Lord has decreed that you worship none but Him and that you be dutiful to your parents.) (17:23) And He, the Exalted, said,

(Give thanks to Me and to your parents. Unto Me is the final destination.) (31:14) Concerning his statement,

(and He made me not arrogant, unblessed.) This means, "He (Allah) has not made me too proud or arrogant to worship Him, obey Him and be dutiful to my mother, and thus be unblessed." Concerning Allah's statement,

(And Salam (peace) be upon me the day I was born, and the day I die, and the day I shall be raised alive!) This is his affirmation that `he is a worshipper of Allah, the Mighty and Sublime, and that he is a creature created by Allah. He (`Isa) will live, die and be resurrected, just like the other creatures that Allah has created. However, he will have peace in these situations, which are the most difficult situations for Allah's creatures.' May Allah's peace and blessings be upon him.

Surah: 19 Ayah: 34, Ayah: 35, Ayah: 36 & Ayah: 37

ذَٰلِكَ عِيسَى ٱبْنُ مَرْيَمَ قَوْلَ ٱلْحَقِّ ٱلَّذِى فِيهِ يَمْتَرُونَ ﴿٣٤﴾

34. Such is 'Iesa (Jesus), son of Maryam (Mary). (It is) a statement of truth, about which they doubt (or dispute).

مَا كَانَ لِلَّهِ أَن يَتَّخِذَ مِن وَلَدٍ سُبْحَٰنَهُۥٓ إِذَا قَضَىٰٓ أَمْرًا فَإِنَّمَا يَقُولُ لَهُۥ كُن فَيَكُونُ

35. It befits not (the Majesty of) Allâh that He should beget a son (this refers to the slander of Christians against Allâh, by saying that 'Iesa (Jesus) is the son of Allâh). Glorified (and Exalted be He above all that they associate with Him). When He decrees a thing, He only says to it, "Be!" - and it is.

وَإِنَّ ٱللَّهَ رَبِّى وَرَبُّكُمْ فَٱعْبُدُوهُ هَٰذَا صِرَٰطٌ مُّسْتَقِيمٌ ﴿٣٦﴾

36. ('Iesa (Jesus) said): "And verily Allâh is my Lord and your Lord. So worship Him (Alone). That is the Straight Path. (Allâh's religion of Islâmic Monotheism which He did ordain for all of His Prophets)." (Tafsir At-Tabarî)

فَٱخْتَلَفَ ٱلْأَحْزَابُ مِنۢ بَيْنِهِمْ فَوَيْلٌ لِّلَّذِينَ كَفَرُوا۟ مِن مَّشْهَدِ يَوْمٍ عَظِيمٍ ﴿٣٧﴾

37. Then the sects differed (i.e. the Christians about 'Iesa (Jesus) (peace be upon him)) so woe unto the disbelievers (those who gave false witness by saying that 'Iesa (Jesus) is the son of Allâh) from the Meeting of a great Day (i.e. the Day of Resurrection, when they will be thrown in the blazing Fire).

Transliteration

34. Thalika AAeesa ibnu maryama qawla alhaqqi allathee feehi yamtaroona 35. Ma kana lillahi an yattakhitha min waladin subhanahu itha qada amran fa-innama yaqoolu lahu kun fayakoonu 36. Wa-inna Allaha rabbee warabbukum faoAAbudoohu hatha siratun mustaqeemun 37. Faikhtalafa al-ahzabu min baynihim fawaylun lillatheena kafaroo min mashhadi yawmin AAatheemin

Tafsir Ibn Kathir

`Isa is the Servant of Allah and not His Son

Allah, the Exalted, says to His Messenger Muhammad , `This is the story which We have related to you about `Isa,' upon him be peace.

((It is) a statement of truth about which they doubt.) lThis means that the people of falsehood and the people of truth are in disagreement, of those who believe in him and those who disbelieve believe in him. For this reason most of the reciters recited this Ayah with Qawlul-Haqq (statement of truth) as the subject, referring to `Isa himself. `Asim and `Abdullah bin `Amir both recited it Qawlal-Haqq (statement of truth) referring to the story in its entirety that the people differed about. It is reported from Ibn Mas`ud that he recited it as Qalal-Haqqa, which means that he (`Isa) said the truth. The recitation of the Ayah with the Qawlul-Haqq being the subject referring to `Isa, is the most apparent meaning grammatically. It has support for it in the statement of Allah (after the story of `Isa),

((This is) the truth from your Lord, so be not of those who doubt.) (3:60) When Allah mentioned that He created him as a servant and a Prophet, He extolled Himself, the Most Holy, by saying,

(It befits not (the majesty of) Allah that He should beget a son. Glorified be He.) Means glory be unto Him, He is far exalted above that which these ignorant, wrongdoing, transgressing people say about Him.

(When He decrees a thing, He only says to it: "Be!" -- and it is.) Whenever He wants something, He merely commands it and it happens as He wills. This is as Allah says,

(Verily, the likeness of `Isa before Allah is the likeness of Adam. He created him from dust, then said to him: "Be" -- and he was. (This is) the truth from your Lord, so be not of those who doubt.) (3:59-60)

`Isa commanded the Worship of Allah Alone, then the People differed after Him

Allah said;

(And verily, Allah is my Lord and your Lord. So worship Him. That is the straight path.) Among those things which `Isa said to his people while he was in his cradle is that Allah was his Lord and their Lord, and he commanded them to worship Him alone. He said,

Chapter 19: Maryam (Mary), Verses 001-098

(So worship Him. That is the straight path.) Meaning, "That which I have come to you with from Allah is the straight path." This means that the path is correct; whoever follows it will be rightly guided and whoever opposes it will deviate and go astray. Allah's statement,

(Then the sects differed,) means that the opinions of the People of the Book differed concerning `Isa even after the explanation of his affair and the clarification of his situation. They disagreed about his being the servant of Allah, His Messenger, and His Word that He cast upon Maryam and a spirit from Himself. So a group of them -- who were the majority of the Jews (may Allah's curses be upon them) -- determined that he was a child of fornication and that his speaking in his cradle was merely sorcery. Another group said that it was Allah Who was speaking (not `Isa). Others said that he (`Isa) was the son of Allah. Some said that he was the third part of a divine trinity with Allah. Yet, others said that he was the servant of Allah and His Messenger. This latter view is the statement of truth, which Allah guided the believers to. A report similar with this meaning has been reported from `Amr bin Maymun, Ibn Jurayj, Qatadah and others from the Salaf (predecessors) and the Khalaf (later generations). Allah said,

(so woe unto the disbelievers from the meeting of a great Day.) This is a threat and severe warning for those who lie about Allah, invent falsehood and claim that He (Allah) has a son. However, Allah has given them respite until the Day of Resurrection, and He has delayed their term out of gentleness and confident reliance upon His divine decree overcoming them. Verily, Allah does not hasten the affair of those who disobey Him. This has been related in a Hadith collected in the Two Sahihs,

«إِنَّ اللَّهَ لَيُمْلِي لِلظَّالِمِ حَتَّى إِذَا أَخَذَهُ لَمْ يُفْلِتْهُ»

(Verily, Allah gives respite to the wrongdoer until He seizes him and he will not be able to escape Him.) Then, the Messenger of Allah recited the Ayah,

(Such is the punishment of your Lord when He punishes the towns while they are doing wrong. Verily, His punishment is painful, (and) severe.) (11:102) In the Two Sahihs it is also reported that the Messenger of Allah said,

«لَا أَحَدَ أَصْبَرُ عَلَى أَذًى سَمِعَهُ مِنَ اللَّهِ، إِنَّهُمْ يَجْعَلُونَ لَهُ وَلَدًا وَهُوَ يَرْزُقُهُمْ وَيُعَافِيهِم»

(No one is more patient with something harmful that he hears than Allah. Verily, they attribute to Him a son, while He is the One Who provides them sustenance and good health.) Allah says,

(And many a township did I give respite while it was given to wrongdoing. Then I punished it. And to me is the (final) return (of all).) (22:48) Allah, the Exalted, also says,

(Consider not that Allah is unaware of that which the wrongdoers do, but He gives them respite up to a Day when the eyes will stare in horror.)(14:42) This is the reason that Allah says here,

(So woe unto the disbelievers from the meeting of a great Day.) referring to the Day of Resurrection. It has been related in an authentic Hadith that is agreed upon (in Al-Bukhari and Muslim), on the authority of `Ubadah bin As-Samit who said that the Messenger of Allah said,

«مَنْ شَهِدَ أَنْ لَا إِلَهَ إِلَّا اللهُ وَحْدَهُ لَا شَرِيكَ لَهُ، وَأَنَّ مُحَمَّدًا عَبْدُهُ وَرَسُولُهُ، وَأَنَّ عِيسَى عَبْدُاللهِ وَرَسُولُهُ وَكَلِمَتُهُ أَلْقَاهَا إِلَى مَرْيَمَ وَرُوحٌ مِنْهُ، وَأَنَّ الْجَنَّةَ حَقٌّ وَالنَّارَ حَقٌّ، أَدْخَلَهُ اللهُ الْجَنَّةَ عَلَى مَا كَانَ مِنَ الْعَمَلِ»

(Whoever testifies that there is no deity worthy of worship except Allah alone, Who has no partners, and that Muhammad is His servant and Messenger, and that `Isa was Allah's servant and Messenger, and His Word that He cast upon Maryam, and a spirit from Him, and that Paradise and Hell are both real, then Allah will admit him into Paradise regardless of whatever he did.)

Surah: 19 Ayah: 38, Ayah: 39 & Ayah: 40

أَسْمِعْ بِهِمْ وَأَبْصِرْ يَوْمَ يَأْتُونَنَا لَكِنِ الظَّالِمُونَ الْيَوْمَ فِي ضَلَالٍ مُبِينٍ ﴿٣٨﴾

38. How clearly will they (polytheists and disbelievers in the Oneness of Allâh) see and hear the Day when they will appear before Us! But the Zalimûn (polytheists and wrong-doers) today are in plain error.

وَأَنذِرْهُمْ يَوْمَ الْحَسْرَةِ إِذْ قُضِيَ الْأَمْرُ وَهُمْ فِي غَفْلَةٍ وَهُمْ لَا يُؤْمِنُونَ ﴿٣٩﴾

39. And warn them (O Muhammad (peace be upon him)) of the Day of grief and regrets, when the case has been decided, while (now) they are in a state of carelessness, and they believe not.

إِنَّا نَحْنُ نَرِثُ الْأَرْضَ وَمَنْ عَلَيْهَا وَإِلَيْنَا يُرْجَعُونَ ﴿٤٠﴾

40. Verily! We will inherit the earth and whatsoever is thereon. And to Us they all shall be returned,

Transliteration

38. AsmiAA bihim waabsir yawma ya/toonana lakini aththalimoona alyawma fee dalalin mubeenin 39. Waanthirhum yawma alhasrati ith qudiya al-amru wahum fee ghaflatin wahum la yu/minoona 40. Inna nahnu narithu al-arda waman AAalayha wa-ilayna yurjaAAoona

Tafsir Ibn Kathir

The Disbeliever's warning of the Day of Distress

Allah, the Exalted, says informing about the disbelievers on the Day of Resurrection that they will be made to have the clearest hearing and sight. This is as Allah says,

(And if you only could see when the criminals hang their heads before their Lord (saying): "Our Lord! We have now seen and heard.") (32:12) They will say that when it will not benefit them, nor will it be of any use to them. If they had used these senses properly before seeing the torment, then it would have brought them some benefit and saved them from the Allah's punishment. This is why Allah says,

(How clearly will they (disbelievers) see and hear,) This means that no one will hear and see better than they will.

(the day when they will appear before Us.) The Day of Resurrection.

(But the wrongdoers today are...) now, in the life of this world,

(...in plain error.) They do not hear, see or think. When they are requested to follow guidance, they are not guided and they succumb to those things that do not benefit them. Then, Allah says,

(And warn them of the Day of grief and regrets,) warn the creation of the Day of Distress,

(when the case has been decided,) when the people of Paradise and the people of Hell will be sorted out, and everyone will reach his final abode which he was destined to remain in forever.

(while (now) they are) today, in the present life of this world,

(in a state of carelessness.) with the warning of the Day of grief and regret, they are heedless.

(and they believe not.) meaning they do not believe that it is true. Imam Ahmad recorded that Abu Sa`id said that the Messenger of Allah said,

«إِذَا دَخَلَ أَهْلُ الْجَنَّةِ الْجَنَّةَ وَأَهْلُ النَّارِ النَّارَ، يُجَاءُ بِالْمَوْتِ كَأَنَّهُ كَبْشٌ أَمْلَحُ فَيُوقَفُ بَيْنَ الْجَنَّةِ وَالنَّارِ، فَيُقَالُ: يَا أَهْلَ الْجَنَّةِ هَلْ تَعْرِفُونَ هَذَا، قَالَ: فَيَشْرَئِبُّونَ وَيَنْظُرُونَ وَيَقُولُونَ: نَعَمْ هَذَا الْمَوْتُ قَالَ: فَيُقَالُ: يَاأَهْلَ النَّارِ، هَلْ تَعْرِفُونَ هَذَا؟ قَالَ: فَيَشْرَئِبُّونَ وَيَنْظُرُونَ وَيَقُولُونَ: نَعَمْ هَذَا الْمَوْتُ قَالَ: فَيُؤْمَرُ

بِهِ فَيُذْبَحُ، قَالَ: وَيُقَالُ: يَا أَهْلَ الْجَنَّةِ، خُلُودٌ وَلَا مَوْتَ، وَيَا أَهْلَ النَّارِ، خُلُودٌ وَلَا مَوْت»

(When the people of Paradise enter Paradise and the people of the Hellfire enter the Hellfire, death will be brought in the form of a handsome ram and it will be placed between Paradise and the Hellfire. Then, it will be said, "O people of Paradise, do you know what this is" Then, they will turn their gazes and look, and they will say, "Yes, this is death." Then, it will be said, "O people of the Hellfire, do you know what this is" Then, they will turn their gazes and look, and they will say, "Yes, this is death." Then, the order will be given for it to be slaughtered and it will be said, "O people of Paradise, eternity and no more death, O people of Hellfire, eternity and no more death.") Then the Messenger of Allah recited the Ayah,

(And warn them of the Day of grief and regret, when the case has been decided, while (now) they are in a state of carelessness, and they believe not.) Then, the Messenger of Allah made a gesture with his hand and said,

«أَهْلُ الدُّنْيَا فِي غَفْلَةِ الدُّنْيَا»

(The people of this life are in the state of heedlessness of this life.) Thus recorded Imam Ahmad and it was also recorded by Al-Bukhari and Muslim in their Sahihs with wording similar to this. It is reported from `Abdullah bin Mas`ud that he mentioned a story in which he said, "There is not a soul except that it will see a residence in Paradise and a residence in the Hellfire, and this will be the Day of distress. So the people of the Hellfire will see the residence that Allah prepared for them if they had believed. Then, it will be said to them, `If you had believed and worked righteous deeds, you would have had this, which you see in Paradise.' Then, they will be overcome with distress and grief. Likewise, the people of Paradise will see the residence that is in the Hellfire and it will be said to them, `If Allah had not bestowed His favor upon you (this would have been your place).' " Concerning Allah's statement,

(Verily, We will inherit the earth and whatsoever is thereon. And to Us they all shall be returned.) Allah is informing that He is the Creator, the Owner and the Controller of all matters. All of the creation will be destroyed and only He, the Most High and Most Holy, will remain. There is no one who can claim absolute ownership and control of affairs besides Him. He is the Inheritor of all His creation. He is the Eternal, Who will remain after they are gone and He is the Judge of their affairs. Therefore, no soul will be done any injustice, nor wronged even the weight of a mosquito or an atom. Ibn Abi Hatim recor- ded that Hazm bin Abi Hazm Al-Quta`i said, "`Umar bin `Abdul-Aziz wrote to `Abdul-Hamid bin `Abdur-Rahman, who was the governor of Kufah: `Thus, to proceed: Verily, Allah prescribed death for His creatures when He created them and He determined their final destination. He said in that which He revealed in His truthful Book, which He guarded with His knowledge and made His angels testify to its preservation, that He will inherit the earth and all who are on it, and they will all be returned to Him.'"

Surah: 19 Ayah: 41, Ayah: 42, Ayah: 43, Ayah: 44 & Ayah: 45

وَاذْكُرْ فِى ٱلْكِتَٰبِ إِبْرَٰهِيمَ ۚ إِنَّهُۥ كَانَ صِدِّيقًا نَّبِيًّا ۝

41. And mention in the Book (the Qur'ân) Ibrâhîm (Abraham). Verily he was a man of truth, a Prophet.

إِذْ قَالَ لِأَبِيهِ يَٰٓأَبَتِ لِمَ تَعْبُدُ مَا لَا يَسْمَعُ وَلَا يُبْصِرُ وَلَا يُغْنِى عَنكَ شَيْـًٔا ۝

42. When he said to his father: "O my father! Why do you worship that which hears not, sees not and cannot avail you in anything?

يَٰٓأَبَتِ إِنِّى قَدْ جَآءَنِى مِنَ ٱلْعِلْمِ مَا لَمْ يَأْتِكَ فَٱتَّبِعْنِىٓ أَهْدِكَ صِرَٰطًا سَوِيًّا ۝

43. "O my father! Verily there has come to me of the knowledge that which came not unto you. So follow me, I will guide you to the Straight Path.

يَٰٓأَبَتِ لَا تَعْبُدِ ٱلشَّيْطَٰنَ ۖ إِنَّ ٱلشَّيْطَٰنَ كَانَ لِلرَّحْمَٰنِ عَصِيًّا ۝

44. "O my father! Worship not Shaitân (Satan). Verily! Shaitân (Satan) has been a rebel against the Most Gracious (Allâh).

يَٰٓأَبَتِ إِنِّىٓ أَخَافُ أَن يَمَسَّكَ عَذَابٌ مِّنَ ٱلرَّحْمَٰنِ فَتَكُونَ لِلشَّيْطَٰنِ وَلِيًّا ۝

45. "O my father! Verily! I fear lest a torment from the Most Gracious (Allâh) should overtake you, so that you become a companion of Shaitân (Satan) (in the Hell-fire)." (Tafsir Al-Qurtubî)

Transliteration

41. Waothkur fee alkitabi ibraheema innahu kana siddeeqan nabiyyan   42. Ith qala li-abeehi ya abati lima taAAbudu ma la yasmaAAu wala yubsiru wala yughnee AAanka shay-an   43. Ya abati innee qad jaanee mina alAAilmi ma lam ya/tika faittabiAAnee ahdika siratan sawiyyan   44. Ya abati la taAAbudi alshshaytana inna alshshaytana kana lilrrahmani AAasiyyan   45. Ya abati innee akhafu an yamassaka AAathabun mina alrrahmani fatakoona lilshshyatani waliyyan

Tafsir Ibn Kathir

Ibrahim's Admonition of His Father

Allah, the Exalted, tells His Prophet, Muhammad ,

(And mention in the Book, Ibrahim.) "Recite this to your people who are worshipping idols and mention to them what happened with Ibrahim, the intimate Friend (Khalil) of the Most Beneficent. These idol worshippers (Arabs) are his descendants and they claim to follow his religion. Inform them that he was a truthful Prophet. Tell them about what took place with his father and how he forbade him from worshipping idols." Ibrahim said,

(O my father! Why do you worship that which hears not, sees not and cannot avail you in anything) Meaning that these idols will not benefit you, nor can they protect you from any harm.

(O my father! Verily, there has come to me the knowledge of that which came not unto you.) This means, "Even though I am from your loins and you see me as inferior to you because I am your son, know that I have received knowledge from Allah that you do not know and it has not reached you."

(So follow me, I will guide you to the straight path.) meaning, "a straight path that will carry you to the desired objective and save you from that which is dreaded (Hell)."

(O my father! Worship not Shaytan.) This is means, "Do not obey him by worshipping these idols. He invites to this (idolatry) and he is pleased with it." This is as Allah says,

(Did I not command you, O Children of Adam, that you should not worship Shaytan. Verily, he is a plain enemy to you.) (36:60) Allah also says,

(They invoke nothing but females (idols) besides Him (Allah), and they invoke nothing but Shaytan, a persistent rebel!) (4:117) Concerning Allah's statement,

(Verily, Shaytan has been a rebel against the Most Gracious.) This means obstinate and too arrogant to obey his Lord. Therefore, Allah expelled him and made him an outcast. Therefore, "do not follow him or you will become like him."

(O my father! Verily, I fear lest a torment from the Most Gracious should overtake you,) "because of your associating partners with Allah and your disobedience in what I am commanding you with."

(so that you become a companion of Shaytan.) This means, "there will be no one who will protect you, or help you, or assist you, except Iblis. However, neither he, nor anyone else, has any power over the outcome of matters. Following him will only cause you to be surrounded by the torment (of Allah)." This is as Allah says,

(By Allah, We indeed sent (Messengers) to the nations before you, but Shaytan made their deeds fair seeming to them. So he is their helper today (in this world), and theirs will be a painful torment.) (16:63)

Surah: 19 Ayah: 46, Ayah: 47 & Ayah: 48

قَالَ أَرَاغِبٌ أَنتَ عَنْ ءَالِهَتِى يَـٰإِبْرَٰهِيمُ لَئِن لَّمْ تَنتَهِ لَأَرْجُمَنَّكَ وَٱهْجُرْنِى مَلِيًّا ۝

46. He (the father) said: "Do you reject my gods, O Ibrâhîm (Abraham)? If you stop not (this), I will indeed stone you. So get away from me safely (before I punish you)."

Chapter 19: Maryam (Mary), Verses 001-098

$$\text{قَالَ سَلَـٰمٌ عَلَيْكَ ۖ سَأَسْتَغْفِرُ لَكَ رَبِّىٓ ۖ إِنَّهُۥ كَانَ بِى حَفِيًّا ﴿٤٧﴾}$$

47. Ibrâhîm (Abraham) said: "Peace be on you! I will ask Forgiveness of my Lord for you. Verily He is unto me Ever Most Gracious.

$$\text{وَأَعْتَزِلُكُمْ وَمَا تَدْعُونَ مِن دُونِ ٱللَّهِ وَأَدْعُوا۟ رَبِّى عَسَىٰٓ أَلَّآ أَكُونَ بِدُعَآءِ رَبِّى شَقِيًّا ﴿٤٨﴾}$$

48. "And I shall turn away from you and from those whom you invoke besides Allâh. And I shall call on my Lord and I hope that I shall not be unblest in my invocation to my Lord."

Transliteration

46. Qala araghibun anta AAan alihatee ya ibraheemu la-in lam tantahi laarjumannaka waohjurnee maliyyan 47. Qala salamun AAalayka saastaghfiru laka rabbee innahu kana bee hafiyyan 48. WaaAAtazilukum wama tadAAoona min dooni Allahi waadAAoo rabbee AAasa alla akoona biduAAa-i rabbee shaqiyyan

Tafsir Ibn Kathir

The Reply of Ibrahim's Father

Allah, the Exalted, informs of the reply of Ibrahim's father to his son, Ibrahim, in reference to what he was calling him to. He said,

(Do you revile my gods, O Ibrahim) This means, "If you do not want to worship them (the idols) and you are not pleased with them, then at least stop cursing, abusing, and reviling them. For verily, if you do not cease, I will punish you, curse you and revile you." This is the meaning of his statement;

(La'arjumannaka.) Ibn `Abbas, As-Suddi, Ibn Jurayj, Ad-Dahhak and others said this. Concerning His statement,

(So get away from me Maliyan.) Mujahid, `Ikrimah, Sa`id bin Jubayr and Mujahid bin Ishaq all said, "Maliyan means forever." Al-Hasan Al-Basri said, "For a long time." As-Suddi said,

(So get away from me safely Maliyan.) "This means forever." Ali bin Abi Talhah and Al-`Awfi both reported that Ibn `Abbas said,

(So get away from me safely Maliyan.) "This means to go away in peace and safety before you are afflicted with a punishment from me." Ad-Dahhak, Qatadah, `Atiyah Al-Jadali, Malik and others said the same. This is also the view preferred by Ibn Jarir.

The Reply of Allah's Friend (Khalil)

With this, Ibrahim said to his father,

(Peace be on you!) This is as Allah said concerning the description of the believers, (and when the foolish address them (with bad words) they say, "Salaman (peace).") (25:63) Allah also says,

(And when they hear Al-Laghw (false speech), they withdraw from it and say: "To us our deeds, and to you your deeds. Peace be to you. We seek not (the way of) the ignorant.") (28:55) The meaning of Ibrahim's statement to his father,

(Peace be on you!) "You will not receive any insult or harm from me." This is due to the respect and honor of fatherhood.

(I will ask forgiveness of my Lord for you.) meaning "But, I will ask Allah to guide you and forgive you for your sin."

(Verily, He is unto me Hafiyya.) Ibn `Abbas and others said that Hafiyyan means, "Kind." Meaning, "since He guided me to worship Him and direct my religious devotion to Him alone." As-Suddi said, "Al-Hafi is One Who is concerned with his (Ibrahim's) affair." Thus, Ibrahim sought forgiveness for his father for a very long time, even after he migrated to Ash-Sham. He continued to seek forgiveness for him even after building the Sacred Masjid (in Makkah) and after the birth of his two sons, Isma`il and Ishaq. This can be seen in his statement,

(Our Lord! Forgive me and my parents, and (all) the believers on the Day when the reckoning will be established.) (14:41) From this tradition, during the beginning stages of Islam, the Muslims used to seek forgiveness for their relatives and their family members who were polytheists. They did this following the way of Ibrahim, the Khalil (Friend) of Allah, until Allah revealed,

(Indeed there has been an excellent example for you in Ibrahim and those with him, when they said to their people: "Verily, we are free from you and whatever you worship besides Allah.") (60:4) Until Allah's statement,

(Except the saying of Ibrahim to his father: "Verily, I will ask forgiveness (from Allah) for you, but I have no power to do anything for you before Allah.") (60:4) meaning, except for this statement, so do not follow it. Then Allah explains that Ibrahim abandoned this statement and retracted it. Allah, the Exalted, says,

(It is not (proper) for the Prophet and those who believe to ask Allah's forgiveness for the idolators.) (9:113) Until Allah's statement,

(And Ibrahim's invoking for his father's forgiveness was only because of a promise he had made to him. But when it became clear to him that he is an enemy of Allah, he dissociated himself from him. Verily, Ibrahim was Awwah, forbearing.) (9:114) Concerning Allah's statement,

(And I shall turn away from you and from those whom you invoke besides Allah. And I shall call upon my Lord,) This means, "And I worship my Lord alone, associating no partners with Him."

(I certainly hope that I shall not be unblessed in my invocation to my Lord.) The word `Asa (I hope) here means that which will necessarily occur and not that which is hoped for from the impossible. For verily, he (Ibrahim) is the leader of the Prophets other than Muhammad .

Surah: 19 Ayah: 49 & Ayah: 50

فَلَمَّا ٱعْتَزَلَهُمْ وَمَا يَعْبُدُونَ مِن دُونِ ٱللَّهِ وَهَبْنَا لَهُۥ إِسْحَٰقَ وَيَعْقُوبَ ۖ وَكُلًّا جَعَلْنَا نَبِيًّا ۝

49. So when he had turned away from them and from those whom they worshipped besides Allâh, We gave him Ishâq (Isaac) and Ya'qûb (Jacob), and each one of them We made a Prophet.

وَوَهَبْنَا لَهُم مِّن رَّحْمَتِنَا وَجَعَلْنَا لَهُمْ لِسَانَ صِدْقٍ عَلِيًّا ۝

50. And We gave them of Our Mercy (a good provision in plenty), and We granted them honor on the tongues (of all the nations, i.e. everybody remembers them with a good praise).

Transliteration

49. Falamma iAAtazalahum wama yaAAbudoona min dooni Allahi wahabna lahu ishaqawayaAAqooba wakullan jaAAalna nabiyyan   50. Wawahabna lahum min rahmatina wajaAAalna lahum lisana sidqin AAaliyyan

Tafsir Ibn Kathir

Allah gave Ibrahim Ishaq and Ya`qub

Allah, the Exalted, says that when the Friend of Allah (Ibrahim) withdrew from his father and his people for the sake of Allah, Allah gave him in exchange those who were better than them. He gave him Ishaq (Isaac) and Ya`qub (Jacob), meaning his son, Ishaq, and Ishaq's son, Ya`qub. This is as Allah said in another Ayah,

(and Ya`qub, a grandson.) (21:72) Also, Allah says,

(and after Ishaq, of Ya`qub.) (11:71) There is no difference of opinion about Ishaq being the father of Ya`qub. This is what is recorded in the Qur'an in Surah Al-Baqarah.

(Or were you witnesses when death approached Ya`qub When he said unto his sons, "What will you worship after me" They said, "We shall worship your God the God of your fathers, Ibrahim, Isma`il and Ishaq.")(2:133) Allah only mentioned Ishaq and Ya`qub here to show that He made Prophets from among his descendants and successors in order to give him relief and happiness in his life. This is why Allah says,

(and each one of them We made a Prophet.) (19:49) If Ya`qub had not become a Prophet in the lifetime of Ibrahim, then Allah would not have limited the promise of prophethood to him, but He would have mentioned his son Yusuf as well. For verily,

Yusuf was also a Prophet, just as the Messenger of Allah said in a Hadith whose authenticity is agreed upon, when he was asked who was the best of people. He said,

«يُوسُفُ نَبِيُّ اللَّهِ ابْنُ يَعْقُوبَ نَبِيِّ اللَّهِ ابْنِ إِسْحَاقَ نَبِيِّ اللَّهِ ابْنِ إِبْرَاهِيمَ خَلِيلِ اللَّهِ»

(The Prophet of Allah, Yusuf, the son of the Prophet of Allah Ya`qub, the son of the Prophet of Allah Ishaq, the son of the Friend of Allah Ibrahim.) In another wording of this Hadith, he said,

«إِنَّ الْكَرِيمَ ابْنَ الْكَرِيمِ ابْنِ الْكَرِيمِ ابْنِ الْكَرِيمِ يُوسُفَ بْنَ يَعْقُوبَ بْنِ إِسْحَاقَ بْنِ إِبْرَاهِيمَ»

(Verily, the noble one is the son of the noble one, who is the son of the noble one, who is the son of the noble one. That is Yusuf, the son of Ya`qub, the son of Ishaq, the son of Ibrahim.) Concerning Allah's statement,

(And We gave them of Our mercy, and We granted Sidqin `Aliyyan on the tongues.) `Ali bin Abi Talhah reported that Ibn `Abbas said, "Sidqin `Aliyyan means the good praise." As-Suddi and Malik bin Anas said the same thing. Ibn Jarir said, "Allah only said `Aliyyan (loftiness, exalted) because all of the religions commend them and mention them with praises, may Allah's peace and blessing be upon them all."

Surah: 19 Ayah: 51, Ayah: 52 & Ayah: 53

وَاذْكُرْ فِي الْكِتَابِ مُوسَىٰ إِنَّهُ كَانَ مُخْلَصًا وَكَانَ رَسُولًا نَبِيًّا ۝

51. And mention in the Book (this Qur'ân) Mûsa (Moses). Verily he was chosen and he was a Messenger (and) a Prophet.

وَنَادَيْنَاهُ مِن جَانِبِ الطُّورِ الْأَيْمَنِ وَقَرَّبْنَاهُ نَجِيًّا ۝

52. And We called him from the right side of the Mount, and made him draw near to Us for a talk with him (Mûsa (Moses))

وَوَهَبْنَا لَهُ مِن رَّحْمَتِنَا أَخَاهُ هَارُونَ نَبِيًّا ۝

53. And We bestowed on him his brother Hârûn (Aaron), (also) a Prophet, out of Our Mercy.

Transliteration

51. Waothkur fee alkitabi moosa innahu kana mukhlasan wakana rasoolan nabiyyan
52. Wanadaynahu min janibi alttoori al-aymani waqarrabnahu najiyyan
53. Wawahabna lahu min rahmatina akhahu haroona nabiyyan

Tafsir Ibn Kathir

Mentioning Musa and Harun

After Allah had mentioned Ibrahim, the Friend of Allah, and commended him, he next mentioned Al-Kalim (the one spoken to by Allah directly). Allah said,

(And mention in the Book, Musa. Verily, he was Mukhlasan) Ath-Thawri reported from `Abdul-Aziz bin Rafi`, from Abu Lubabah that he said, "The Disciples (of `Isa) said, `O Spirit of Allah, inform us about the one who is Mukhlis (purely devoted) to Allah.' He said, `That is one who does a deed solely for Allah and he does not like for the people to praise him.'" Others recited the word as Mukhlas, which means that he was chosen. This is as Allah says,

(Verily, I have chosen you above men.) (7:144) Concerning Allah's statement,

(and he was a Messenger, (and) a Prophet.) Allah combined these two descriptions for him. For verily, he was one of the greatest Messengers and one of the five Messengers of Strong Will. They are Nuh, Ibrahim, Musa, `Isa and Muhammad. May the blessings of Allah be upon them and all of the Prophets. Allah said,

(And We called him from the side of the Tur.) means Mount

(right) It was on the right side of Musa when he went seeking a burning wood from that fire. He saw its glow in the distance, so he set out towards it and found it on the right side of the mountain from his direction, at the edge of the valley that he was in. This is when Allah, the Exalted, spoke to him and called out to him. Allah summoned him to come near and He conversed Ayah with him. Concerning His statement,

(And We granted him his brother Harun, (also) a Prophet, out of Our mercy.) This means, "We responded to his request and his plea on behalf of his brother and We made him a Prophet as well." This is as Allah says in another Ayah,

(And my brother Harun he is more eloquent in speech than me: so send him with me as a helper to confirm me. Verily, I fear that they will belie me.) (28:34) Also, Allah said,

((Allah said:) "You are granted your request, O Musa.") (20:36) He also said,

(So send for Harun. And they have a charge of crime against me, and I fear they will kill me.) (26:13-14) Because of this, some of the Salaf (predecessors) said, "No one in this life pleaded on behalf of someone else more than Musa pleaded for his brother to be a Prophet." Allah, the Exalted said,

(And We granted him his brother Harun, (also) a Prophet, out of Our mercy.)

Surah: 19 Ayah: 54 & Ayah: 55

$$\text{وَاذْكُرْ فِي الْكِتَابِ إِسْمَاعِيلَ ۚ إِنَّهُ كَانَ صَادِقَ الْوَعْدِ وَكَانَ رَسُولًا نَّبِيًّا}$$

54. And mention in the Book (the Qur'ân) Ismâ'il (Ishmael). Verily! He was true to what he promised, and he was a Messenger, (and) a Prophet.

$$\text{وَكَانَ يَأْمُرُ أَهْلَهُ بِالصَّلَاةِ وَالزَّكَاةِ وَكَانَ عِندَ رَبِّهِ مَرْضِيًّا}$$

55. And he used to enjoin on his family and his people As-Salât (the prayers) and the Zakât, and his Lord was pleased with him.

Transliteration

54. Waothkur fee alkitabi ismaAAeela innahu kana sadiqa alwaAAdi wakana rasoolan nabiyyan 55. Wakana ya/muru ahlahu bialssalati waalzzakati wakana AAinda rabbihi mardiyyan

Tafsir Ibn Kathir

Mentioning Isma`il

Here Allah has commended Isma`il, the son of Ibrahim, the Friend of Allah. He (Isma`il) is the father of all of the Arabs of the Hijaz because he was true to what he promised. Ibn Jurayj said, "He did not make any promise to his Lord, except that he fulfilled it." He never obligated himself to do any act of worship with a vow, except that he fulfilled it and carried it out, giving it its full due. Some said,

((he was) true to what he promised.) "This was said about him because he said to his father,

(If Allah wills you will find me of the patient.) (37:102) So he was truthful in that." Being true to one's promise is one of the praiseworthy characteristics, just as breaking one's promise is of the detested characteristics. Allah, the Exalted, says,

(O you who believe! Why do you say that which you do not do Most hateful it is with Allah that you say that which you do not do.) (61:2-3) The Messenger of Allah said,

$$\text{«آيَةُ الْمُنَافِقِ ثَلَاثٌ: إِذَا حَدَّثَ كَذَبَ، وَإِذَا وَعَدَ أَخْلَفَ، وَإِذَا اؤْتُمِنَ خَانَ»}$$

(The sign of the hypocrite is three things. When he speaks, he lies; when he promises, he breaks his promise; and when he is entrusted with something, he is disloyal to his trust.) Thus, if these are the characteristics of the hypocrites, then behaving contrary to these is a characteristic of the true believer. For this reason, Allah commended His servant and Messenger Isma`il, for he was true to his promise. Likewise, the Messenger of Allah was true to his promise. He did not promise anyone anything, except that he fulfilled his promise to that person. He also commended Abu Al-`As bin Ar-Rabi`, the husband of his daughter Zaynab, by saying,

Chapter 19: Maryam (Mary), Verses 001-098

《حَدَّثَنِي فَصَدَقَنِي، وَوَعَدَنِي فَوَفَى لِي》

(He spoke to me and he told me the truth, and he promised me and he fulfilled his promise to me.) When the Prophet died, the Khalifah (his successor), Abu Bakr As-Siddiq said, "Whoever received any promise from the Messenger of Allah or was owed any debt by him, then let him come to me and I will fulfill it on his behalf." So Jabir bin `Abdullah came and related that the Messenger of Allah said,

《لَوْ قَدْ جَاءَ مَالُ الْبَحْرَيْنِ أَعْطَيْتُكَ هَكَذَا وَهَكَذَا وَهَكَذَا》

(If the wealth of Bahrain comes (to me), then I would give you such and such and such.) This meant that he would fill his hands with wealth. Therefore, when the wealth of Bahrain came (to them), Abu Bakr commanded Jabir to come and fill his hands from that wealth. Then, he commanded him to do so again, until he collected five hundred Dirhams. Then, Abu Bakr gave him its double along with it.(i.e. one thousand extra Dirhams). Concerning Allah's statement,

(and he was a Messenger, (and) a Prophet.) In this is a proof of Isma`il's favored status over his brother, Ishaq. Ishaq was only described as being a Prophet, but Isma`il was described with both prophethood and messengership. It is confirmed in Sahih Muslim that the Messenger of Allah said,

《إِنَّ اللَّهَ اصْطَفَى مِنْ وَلَدِ إِبْرَاهِيمَ إِسْمَاعِيلَ》

(Verily, Allah chose Isma`il from the sons of Ibrahim...) Then, Imam Muslim mentions the rest of the Hadith in its entirety. However, this statement proves the correctness of what we have said. Allah said,

(And he would enjoin on his family and his people the Salah and the Zakah, and his Lord was pleased with him.) This is also a beautiful form of praise, a commendable quality, and and upright characteristic. He was commanded in this way because of his persistence in obedience of his Lord, and enjoining his family to do so. This is as Allah said to His Messenger ,

(And enjoin the Salah on your family, and be patient with them.) (20:132) Also, Allah, the Exalted, said,

(O you who believe! Protect yourselves and your families against a Fire (Hell) whose fuel is men and stones, over which are (appointed) angels stern (and) severe, who disobey not, (from executing) the commands they receive from Allah, but do that which they are commanded.) (66:6) This means to command them to do good, forbid them from evil and do not neglect them. If you do so, and they obey your command, the Fire (of Hell) will not devour them on the Day of Resurrection. It has been reported in a Hadith from Abu Hurayrah that the Messenger of Allah said,

«رَحِمَ اللهُ رَجُلًا قَامَ مِنَ اللَّيْلِ فَصَلَّى وَأَيْقَظَ امْرَأَتَهُ، فَإِنْ أَبَتْ نَضَحَ فِي وَجْهِهَا الْمَاءَ. رَحِمَ اللهُ امْرَأَةً قَامَتْ مِنَ اللَّيْلِ فَصَلَّتْ وَأَيْقَظَتْ زَوْجَهَا، فَإِنْ أَبَى نَضَحَتْ فِي وَجْهِهِ الْمَاءَ»

(May Allah have mercy upon a man who gets up at night to pray and he wakes his wife. If she refuses to get up, he sprinkles water in her face. May Allah have mercy upon a woman who gets up at night to pray and she wakes her husband. If he refuses to get up, she sprinkles water in his face.) This Hadith was recorded by Abu Dawud and Ibn Majah.

Surah: 19 Ayah: 56 & Ayah: 57

وَاذْكُرْ فِي الْكِتَٰبِ إِدْرِيسَ إِنَّهُۥ كَانَ صِدِّيقًا نَّبِيًّا ۝

56. And mention in the Book (the Qur'ân) Idrîs (Enoch). Verily he was a man of truth, (and) a Prophet.

وَرَفَعْنَٰهُ مَكَانًا عَلِيًّا ۝

57. And We raised him to a high station.

Transliteration

56. Waothkur fee alkitabi idreesa innahu kana siddeeqan nabiyyan   57. WarafaAAnahu makanan AAaliyyan

Tafsir Ibn Kathir

Mentioning Idris

Allah complimented Idris for being a truthful Prophet and He mentioned that he raised him to a high station. It has previously been mentioned that in the Sahih it is recorded that the Messenger of Allah passed by Idris on the night of the Isra (Night Journey) and he (Idris) was in the fourth heaven. Sufyan reported from Mansur that Mujahid said,

(And We raised him to a high station.) "This means the fourth heaven." Al-Hasan and others said concer- ning Allah's statement,

(And We raised him to a high station.) "This means Paradise."

Surah: 19 Ayah: 58

أُوْلَٰٓئِكَ ٱلَّذِينَ أَنْعَمَ ٱللَّهُ عَلَيْهِم مِّنَ ٱلنَّبِيِّـۧنَ مِن ذُرِّيَّةِ ءَادَمَ وَمِمَّنْ حَمَلْنَا مَعَ نُوحٍ وَمِن ذُرِّيَّةِ إِبْرَٰهِيمَ وَإِسْرَٰٓءِيلَ وَمِمَّنْ هَدَيْنَا وَٱجْتَبَيْنَآ إِذَا تُتْلَىٰ عَلَيْهِمْ ءَايَٰتُ ٱلرَّحْمَٰنِ خَرُّوا۟ سُجَّدًا وَبُكِيًّا ۩

58. Those were they unto whom Allâh bestowed His Grace from among the Prophets, of the offspring of Adam, and of those whom We carried (in the ship) with Nûh (Noah), and of the offspring of Ibrâhîm (Abraham) and Israel, and from among those whom We guided and chose. When the Verses of the Most Gracious (Allâh) were recited unto them, they fell down prostrate and weeping.

Transliteration

58. Ola-ika allatheena anAAama Allahu AAalayhim mina alnnabiyyeena min thurriyyati adama wamimman hamalna maAAa noohin wamin thurriyyati ibraheema wa-isra-eela wamimman hadayna waijtabayna itha tutla AAalayhim ayatu alrrahmani kharroo sujjadan wabukiyyan

Tafsir Ibn Kathir

These Prophets are the Chosen Ones

Allah, the Exalted, says that these Prophets (were favored), but this does not mean only these Prophets who were mentioned in this Surah. Rather, it is referring to all of those who were Prophets. Allah merely changes the implication of the discussion from specific individuals to the entire group of Prophets.

(they unto whom Allah bestowed His grace from among the Prophets, of the offspring of Adam.) As-Suddi and Ibn Jarir both said, "That which is meant by the offspring of Adam is Idris, and what is meant by the offspring of those `whom We carried with Nuh' is Ibrahim, and what is meant by the offspring of Ibrahim is Ishaq, Ya`qub and Isma`il, and what is meant by the offspring of Isra`il is Musa, Harun, Zakariyya, Yayha and `Isa bin Maryam." Ibn Jarir said, "And that is the distinction of their genealogies, even though Adam gathers all of them (as their original father). This is because among them is he who was not a descendant of those who were on the ship with Nuh, and he that is Idris. For verily, he was the grandfather of Nuh." I say that this is the most apparent meaning, which concludes that Idris is amongst the pillars of Nuh's ancestral lineage. The view that this Ayah refers to the ancestral lineage of the Prophets, is the fact that it is similar to Allah's statement in Surah Al-An`am,

(And that was our proof which We gave Ibrahim against his people. We raise whom We will in degrees. Certainly your Lord is All-Wise, All-Knowing. And We bestowed upon him Ishaq and Ya`qub, each of them We guided; and before him We guided Nuh, and among his progeny Dawud, Sulayman, Ayyub, Yusuf, Musa and Harun. Thus do We reward the doers of good. And Zakariyya, and Yahya, and `Isa and Ilyas, each one of them was of the righteous. And Isma`il and Al-Yasa` and Yunus and Lut and each one of them We preferred above the `Alamin. And also some of their fathers and their progeny and their brethren, We chose them, and We guided them to the straight path.)(6:83-87) Until Allah's statement,

(They are those whom Allah had guided. So follow their guidance.) (6: 90) Allah, the Exalted, says,

(Of some of them We have related to you their story. And of some We have not related to you their story.) (40:78) In Sahih Al-Bukhari it is reported from Mujahid that he asked Ibn `Abbas, "Is there a prostration in Surah Sad" Ibn `Abbas replied, "Yes." Then he recited,

(They are those whom Allah had guided. So follow their guidance.) (6:90) Ibn `Abbas then said, "So your Prophet is one of those who have been commanded to follow them. And he is of those who should be followed." -- referring to Dawud. Allah, the Exalted, said in this noble Ayah,

(When the Ayah of the Most Gracious were recited unto them, they fell down prostrate and weeping.) This means that when they heard the Words of Allah, mentioning His proofs and evidences, they prostrated to their Lord in humility, humbleness, praise and thanks for the great favors they were blessed with. The word Bukiyan at the end of the Ayah means those who are crying, and it is the plural of Baki. Due to this the scholars agree that it is legislated to prostrate upon reading this Ayah, in following them and adhering to their manner of worship.

Surah: 19 Ayah: 59 & Ayah: 60

❁ فَخَلَفَ مِنۢ بَعْدِهِمْ خَلْفٌ أَضَاعُوا۟ ٱلصَّلَوٰةَ وَٱتَّبَعُوا۟ ٱلشَّهَوَٰتِ ۖ فَسَوْفَ يَلْقَوْنَ غَيًّا ﴿٥٩﴾

59. Then, there has succeeded them a posterity who have given up As-Salât (the prayers) (i.e. made their Salât (prayers) to be lost, either by not offering them or by not offering them perfectly or by not offering them in their proper fixed times) and have followed lusts. So they will be thrown in Hell.

إِلَّا مَن تَابَ وَءَامَنَ وَعَمِلَ صَٰلِحًا فَأُو۟لَٰٓئِكَ يَدْخُلُونَ ٱلْجَنَّةَ وَلَا يُظْلَمُونَ شَيْـًٔا

60. Except those who repent and believe (in the Oneness of Allâh and His Messenger Muhammad (peace be upon him)) and work righteousness. Such will enter Paradise and they will not be wronged in aught.

Transliteration

59. Fakhalafa min baAAdihim khalfun adaAAoo alssalata waittabaAAoo alshshahawati fasawfa yalqawna ghayyan 60. Illa man taba waamana waAAamila salihan faola-ika yadkhuloona aljannata wala yuthlamoona shay-an

Chapter 19: Maryam (Mary), Verses 001-098   73

Tafsir Ibn Kathir

They were succeeded by Wicked People and Good People

After Allah mentioned the party of blessed ones -- the Prophets and those who followed them by maintainig the limits set by Allah and His commandments, fulfilling what Allah ordered and avoiding His prohibitions -- then He mentions,

(there has succeeded them a posterity.) This means later generations.

(who have lost Salah) Losing their prayers is when they do not consider the prayers obligatory. Therefore they lose, because the prayer is the pillar and foundation of the religion. It is the best of the servants' deeds. Thus, these people will occupy themselves with worldly desires and delights, and they will be pleased with the life of this world. They will be tranquil and at ease in the worldly appetites. Therefore, these people will meet with Ghaiy, which means loss on the Day of Resurrection. Al-Awza`i reported from Musa bin Sulayman, who reported from Al-Qasim bin Mukhaymirah that he said concerning Allah's statement,

(Then, there has succeeded them a posterity who have lost the Salah) "This means that they will not keep up with the proper times of the prayer, because if it meant complete abandonment of the prayer, this would be disbelief." It is also reported that it was said to Ibn Mas`ud, "Allah often mentions the prayer in the Qur'an. He says,

(Those who neglect their Salah.) (107:5) And He says,

(Those who remain constant in their Salah.) (70:23) And He says,

(Who guard their Salah.)" (23:9) Then, Ibn Mas`ud said, "This means at its designated times." The people said, "We thought that this was referring to the abandonment of the prayer." He replied, "That would be disbelief." Masruq said, "No one who guards the five daily prayers will be written among the heedless. In their neglect is destruction. Their neglect is delaying them past their fixed times." Al-Awza`i reported from Ibrahim bin Zayd that Umar bin `Abdul-`Aziz recited the Ayah,

(Then, there has succeeded them a posterity who have lost the Salah and have followed lusts. So they will meet Ghayy.) Then, he said, "Their loss was not their abandonment of the prayers, but it was by not offering them during their proper and prescribed times." Allah said,

(So they will meet Ghayy.) `Ali bin Abi Talhah reported from Ibn `Abbas that he said,

(So they will meet Ghayy.) "This means loss." Qatadah said, "This means evil." Sufyan Ath-Thawri, Shu`bah and Muhammad bin Ishaq all reported from Abu Ishaq As-Sabi`i, who reported from Abu `Ubaydah, who reported from `Abdullah bin Mas`ud that he said,

(So they will meet Ghayy.) "This is a valley in the Hellfire which is very deep and its food is filthy." Al-A`mash reported from Ziyad, who reported from Abu `Iyad, who commented Allah's statement,

(So they will meet Ghayy.) He said, "This is a valley in Hell made of puss and blood." Allah said,

(Except those who repent and believe and work righteousness.) This means, "Except those who recant from giving up the prayers and following the desires, for verily, Allah will accept their repentance, give them a good end and make them of those who inherit the Garden of Delight (Paradise). " For this reason Allah says,

(Such will enter Paradise and they will not be wronged in aught.) This is because repentance wipes away that which was before it. In another Hadith, the Prophet said,

(The one who repents from sin is like he who has no sin.) Because of this, those who repent will not lose anything from the (good) deeds that they did. They will not be held accountable for what they did before their repentance, thus causing a decrease in their reward for deeds that they do after their repentance. That is because whatever they did before repenting is lost, forgotten and not taken to account. This is an honor from the Most Generous and a kindness from the Most Gentle. This is an exception that is made for these people, similar to Allah's statement in Surah Al-Furqan,

(And those who invoke not any other god along with Allah, nor kill such person as Allah has forbidden, except for just cause...) until Allah's statement,

(and Allah is Oft-Forgiving, Most Merciful.) (25:68-70)

Surah: 19 Ayah: 61 & Ayah: 62 & Ayah: 63

جَنَّـٰتِ عَدْنٍ ٱلَّتِى وَعَدَ ٱلرَّحْمَـٰنُ عِبَادَهُۥ بِٱلْغَيْبِ إِنَّهُۥ كَانَ وَعْدُهُۥ مَأْتِيًّا ۝

61. (They will enter) 'Adn (Eden) Paradise (everlasting Gardens), which the Most Gracious (Allâh) has promised to His slaves in the Unseen: Verily His Promise must come to pass.

لَّا يَسْمَعُونَ فِيهَا لَغْوًا إِلَّا سَلَـٰمًا ۖ وَلَهُمْ رِزْقُهُمْ فِيهَا بُكْرَةً وَعَشِيًّا ۝

62. They shall not hear therein (in Paradise) any Laghw (dirty, false, evil vain talk), but only Salâm (salutations of peace). And they will have therein their sustenance, morning and afternoon. (See (V.40:55))

تِلْكَ ٱلْجَنَّةُ ٱلَّتِى نُورِثُ مِنْ عِبَادِنَا مَن كَانَ تَقِيًّا ۝

63. Such is the Paradise which We shall give as an inheritance to those of Our slaves who have been Al-Muttaqûn (the pious and righteous persons - See V.2:2).

Transliteration

61. Jannati AAadnin allatee waAAada alrrahmanu AAibadahu bialghaybi innahu kana waAAduhu ma/tiyyan 62. La yasmaAAoona feeha laghwan illa salaman walahum rizquhum feeha bukratan waAAashiyyan 63. Tilka aljannatu allatee noorithu min AAibadina man kana taqiyyan

Tafsir Ibn Kathir

The Description of the Gardens of the Truthful and Those Who repent

Allah, the Exalted, says that the Gardens (of Paradise), which the penitent will enter, will be Gardens of `Adn, meaning, eternity. These are Gardens that the Most Beneficent promises His servants in the unseen. This means that these Gardens are from the unseen things that they believe in, even though they have never witnessed them. They believe in the unseen out of their strong conviction and the strength of their faith. Concerning Allah's statement,

(Verily, His promise must come to pass.) This affirms the fact that this will occur, and that it is a settled matter. Allah does not break His promise, nor does He change it. This is similar to His statement,

(His promise is certainly to be accomplished.) (73:18) This means that His promise will be and there is no avoiding it. Allah's statement here,

(must come to pass.) This means that it will come to His servants who are striving towards it and they will reach it. There are those commentators who said,

(must come to pass.) "This means it is coming, because everything that comes to you, you also come to it. This is as the Arabs say, `Fifty years came to me, and I came to fifty years.' They both mean the same thing (I'm fifty years old)." Concerning Allah's statement,

(They shall not hear therein any Laghw.) This means that in these gardens of Paradise there is no ignorant, wasteful and useless speech, like there is in this life. He said,

(...but only Salam.) This is an indifferent exception, similar to Allah's statement,

(No Laghw will they hear therein, nor any sinful speech. But only the saying of: Salam! Salam!) (56:25-26) Concerning His statement,

(And they will have therein their sustenance, morning and afternoon.) This means, in what is similar to mornings and evenings. This does not mean that there is a night and a day (in Paradise), but they will be living in times that alternate. They will know its lighted times from its lights and illumination. This is as Imam Ahmad recorded from Abu Hurayrah, who said that the Messenger of Allah said,

«أَوَّلُ زُمْرَةٍ تَلِجُ الْجَنَّةَ صُوَرُهُمْ عَلَى صُورَةِ الْقَمَرِ لَيْلَةَ الْبَدْرِ لَا يَبْصُقُونَ فِيهَا، وَلَا يَتَمَخَّطُونَ فِيهَا. وَلَا يَتَغَوَّطُونَ، آنِيَتُهُمْ وَأَمْشَاطُهُمُ الذَّهَبُ وَالْفِضَّةُ وَبَخَامِرُهُمُ الْأَلُوَّةُ، وَرَشْحُهُمُ الْمِسْكُ وَلِكُلِّ وَاحِدٍ مِنْهُمْ زَوْجَتَانِ، يُرَى مُخُّ سَاقِهَا مِنْ

«وَرَاءِ اللَّحْمِ مِنَ الْحُسْنِ، لَا اخْتِلَافَ بَيْنَهُمْ وَلَا تَبَاغُضَ، قُلُوبُهُمْ عَلَى قَلْبِ رَجُلٍ وَاحِدٍ، يُسَبِّحُونَ اللهَ بُكْرَةً وَعَشِيًّا»

(The first group to enter into Paradise will have forms like the form of the moon on a night when it is full. They will not spit, nor will they blow their noses therein. They also will not defecate. Their containers and combs will be made of gold and silver and their censers will be of aloeswood. Their sweat will be the fragrance of musk and each of them will have two wives. The marrow of their shins will be visible from beneath the skin due to their beauty. They will not have any disputes between them, or any hatred. Their hearts will be united like the heart of one man. They will glorify Allah in the morning and evening.) Al-Bukhari and Muslim both recorded this narration in the Two Sahihs. Imam Ahmad also recorded that Ibn `Abbas said that the Messenger of Allah said,

«الشُّهَدَاءُ عَلَى بَارِقٍ نَهْرٍ بِبَابِ الْجَنَّةِ فِي قُبَّةٍ خَضْرَاءَ، يَخْرُجُ عَلَيْهِمْ رِزْقُهُمْ مِنَ الْجَنَّةِ بُكْرَةً وَعَشِيًّا»

(The martyrs will be upon the banks of a river by the gates of Paradise. Over them will be a green dome. Their sustenance will be brought out to them from Paradise, morning and evening.) Ahmad is the only one who collected this narration. Ad-Dahhak reported that Ibn `Abbas said,

(And they will have therein their sustenance, morning and afternoon.) "This means the amount of time equal to night and day." Allah said,

(Such is the Paradise which We shall give as an inheritance to those of Our servants who had Taqwa.) This means, `This Paradise that We have described with these magnificent attributes, it is that which We will cause are pious servants to inherit.' They are those who obey Allah in happiness and times of hardship. They are those who suppress their anger and they pardon people's offenses. This is as Allah says at the beginning of Surah Al-Mu'minun,

(Successful indeed are the believers. Those who are humble in their Salah.) (23:1-2) Until His saying,

(These are indeed the inheritors. Who shall inherit the Firdaws. In it they shall dwell forever.) (23:10-11)

Chapter 19: Maryam (Mary), Verses 001-098

Surah: 19 Ayah: 64 & Ayah: 65

وَمَا نَتَنَزَّلُ إِلَّا بِأَمْرِ رَبِّكَ ۖ لَهُ مَا بَيْنَ أَيْدِينَا وَمَا خَلْفَنَا وَمَا بَيْنَ ذَٰلِكَ ۚ وَمَا كَانَ رَبُّكَ نَسِيًّا ﴿٦٤﴾

64. And we (angels) descend not except by the Command of your Lord (O Muhammad (peace be upon him)) To Him belongs what is before us and what is behind us, and what is between those two; and your Lord is never forgetful -

رَبُّ السَّمَاوَاتِ وَالْأَرْضِ وَمَا بَيْنَهُمَا فَاعْبُدْهُ وَاصْطَبِرْ لِعِبَادَتِهِ ۚ هَلْ تَعْلَمُ لَهُ سَمِيًّا ﴿٦٥﴾

65. Lord of the heavens and the earth, and all that is between them, so worship Him (Alone) and be constant and patient in His worship. Do you know of any who is similar to Him? (of course none is similar or co-equal or comparable to Him, and He has none as partner with Him). (There is nothing like unto Him and He is the All-Hearer, the All-Seer).

Transliteration

64. Wama natanazzalu illa bi-amri rabbika lahu ma bayna aydeena wama khalfana wama bayna thalika wama kana rabbuka nasiyyan 65. Rabbu alssamawati waal-ardi wama baynahuma faoAAbudhu waistabir liAAibadatihi hal taAAlamu lahu samiyyan

Tafsir Ibn Kathir

The Angels do not descend, except by Allah's Command

Imam Ahmad recorded that Ibn `Abbas said that the Messenger of Allah said to Jibril,

«مَا يَمْنَعُكَ أَنْ تَزُورَنَا أَكْثَرَ مِمَّا تَزُورُنَا؟»

(What prevents you from visiting us more than you do) Then this Ayah was revealed,

(And we descend not except by the command of your Lord.) Al-Bukhari was alone in recording it and he related it with the Tafsir of this Ayah. Al-`Awfi reported from Ibn `Abbas that he said, "Jibril was kept from visiting the Messenger of Allah, so he was disturbed and grieved because of this. Then, Jibril came to him and said, `O Muhammad,

(And we descend not except by the command of your Lord.)'" Allah said,

(To Him belongs what is before us and what is behind us,) It has been said that the meaning of "what is before us" refers to that which is in this life and "what is behind us" refers to the Hereafter.

(and what is between those two;) This means what is between two blows of the Sur. This is the opinion of Abu Al-`Aliyah, `Ikrimah and Mujahid. This was also stated by Sa`id bin Jubayr and Qatadah in one narration from them. As-Suddi and Ar-Rabi` bin Anas held this opinion as well. It has also been said,

(what is before us) means the future matters of the Hereafter.

(what is behind us,) means what has taken place in this life,

(what is between those two;) means what happens between this life and the Hereafter. A statement like this explanation has been reported from Ibn `Abbas, Sa`id bin Jubayr, Ad-Dahhak, Qatadah, Ibn Jurayj and Ath-Thawri. Ibn Jarir also preferred this latter interpretation. And Allah knows best. Concerning Allah's statement,

(and your Lord is never forgetful.) Mujahid said, "This means that your Lord has not forgotten you." Allah said,

(Lord of the heavens and the earth, and all that is between them,) He created all of that, He is the Disposer of its affairs, He is the Legislator over it and He is in absolute control of it, having no one to oppose His decisions.

(so worship Him and abide patiently in his worship. Do you know of any who is similar to Him) `Ali bin Abi Talhah related that Ibn `Abbas said that this means, "Do you know any comparison or something similar to the Lord" Mujahid, Sa`id bin Jubayr, Qatadah, Ibn Jurayj and others all said the same. `Ikrimah related that Ibn `Abbas said, "There is no one named Ar-Rahman (the Most Beneficent) other than Him, Blessed and Exalted is He. Most Holy is His Name."

Surah: 19 Ayah: 66, Ayah: 67, Ayah: 68, Ayah: 69 & Ayah: 70

وَيَقُولُ ٱلْإِنسَٰنُ أَءِذَا مَا مِتُّ لَسَوْفَ أُخْرَجُ حَيًّا

66. And man (the disbeliever) says: "When I am dead, shall I then be raised up alive?"

أَوَلَا يَذْكُرُ ٱلْإِنسَٰنُ أَنَّا خَلَقْنَٰهُ مِن قَبْلُ وَلَمْ يَكُ شَيْـًٔا

67. Does not man remember that We created him before, while he was nothing?

فَوَرَبِّكَ لَنَحْشُرَنَّهُمْ وَٱلشَّيَٰطِينَ ثُمَّ لَنُحْضِرَنَّهُمْ حَوْلَ جَهَنَّمَ جِثِيًّا

68. So by your Lord, surely, We shall gather them together, and (also) the Shayâtîn (devils) (with them), then We shall bring them round Hell on their knees.

ثُمَّ لَنَنزِعَنَّ مِن كُلِّ شِيعَةٍ أَيُّهُمْ أَشَدُّ عَلَى ٱلرَّحْمَٰنِ عِتِيًّا

69. Then indeed We shall drag out from every sect all those who were worst in obstinate rebellion against the Most Gracious (Allâh).

ثُمَّ لَنَحْنُ أَعْلَمُ بِالَّذِينَ هُمْ أَوْلَىٰ بِهَا صِلِيًّا ﴿٧٠﴾

70. Then, verily, We know best those who are most worthy of being burnt therein.

Transliteration

66. Wayaqoolu al-insanu a-itha ma mittu lasawfa okhraju hayyan 67. Awa la yathkuru al-insanu anna khalaqnahu min qablu walam yaku shay-an 68. Fawarabbika lanahshurannahum waalshshayateena thumma lanuhdirannahum hawla jahannama jithiyyan 69. Thumma lananziAAanna min kulli sheeAAatin ayyuhum ashaddu AAala alrrahmani AAitiyyan 70. Thumma lanahnu aAAlamu biallatheena hum awla biha siliyyan Translation

Tafsir Ibn Kathir

Man's Amazement about Life after Death and the Refutation against this Amazement

Allah, the Exalted, informs that mankind is amazed that he could be returned to life after death and he thinks that this is something farfetched. As Allah says,

(And if you wonder, then wondrous is their saying: "When we are dust, shall we indeed then be (raised) in a new creation")(13:5) Allah also says,

(Does not man see that We have created him from Nutfah. Yet behold he (stands forth) as an open opponent. And he puts forth for Us a parable and forgets his own creation. He says: "Who will give life to these bones after they are rotten and have become dust" Say: "He will give life to them Who created them for the first time! And He is the All-Knower of every creation!")(36:77-79) And Allah says here in this Surah,

(And man says: "When I am dead, shall I then be raised up alive" Does not man remember that We created him before, while he was nothing) Allah uses the beginning of creation as a proof for its repetition. This means that He, the Exalted, created the human being while he was nothing. So can he not repeat this creation after the human had actually become something Similalry Allah says;

(And He it is Who originates the creation, then He will repeat it; and this is easier for Him.) (30:27) In the Sahih it is recorded that the Messenger of Allah said,

«يَقُولُ اللهُ تَعَالَى: كَذَّبَنِي ابْنُ آدَمَ وَلَمْ يَكُنْ لَهُ أَنْ يُكَذِّبَنِي، وَآذَانِي ابْنُ آدَمَ وَلَمْ يَكُنْ لَهُ أَنْ يُؤْذِيَنِي، أَمَّا تَكْذِيبُهُ إِيَّايَ فَقَوْلُهُ لَنْ يُعِيدَنِي كَمَا بَدَأَنِي، وَلَيْسَ أَوَّلُ الْخَلْقِ بِأَهْوَنَ عَلَيَّ مِنْ آخِرِهِ، وَأَمَّا أَذَاهُ إِيَّايَ فَقَوْلُهُ إِنَّ لِي وَلَدًا وَأَنَا الْأَحَدُ الصَّمَدُ الَّذِي لَمْ يَلِدْ وَلَمْ يُولَدْ وَلَمْ يَكُنْ لَهُ كُفُوًا أَحَد»

(Allah, the Exalted said, "The son of Adam denies Me and he has no right to deny Me. The son of Adam harms Me and he has no right to harm Me. His denial of Me is his statement that I will never repeat His creation like I created him the first time. Yet, the second creation is not more difficult upon Me than the first. His harming Me is his statement that I have a son. Yet, I am One Alone, the Self-Sufficient Whom all creatures need. He Who does not beget children, nor was He born and there is none coequal or comparable unto Him.") Concerning Allah's statement,

(So by your Lord, surely We shall gather them together, and the Shayatin,) The Lord, Blessed be He the Most High, swears by His Noble Self that He will definitely gather all of those who worshipped other than Allah and their devils as well.

(then We shall bring them round Hell, Jithiyya.) Al-`Awfi related that Ibn `Abbas said, "This means sitting and it is similar to His statement,

(And you will see each nation Jathiyah.)" (45:28) As-Suddi commented on the word Jithiyya, "It means standing." It has been reported from Murrah that Ibn Mas`ud said the same. Concerning Allah's statement,

(Then indeed We shall drag out from every sect) This means from every nation. This is what Mujahid said.

(all those who were worst in obstinate rebellion against the Most Gracious.) Ath-Thawri reported from `Ali bin Al-Aqmar, from Abu Al-Ahwas, from Ibn Mas`ud that he said, "The first of them will be bound to the last of them until their number is complete. Then, they will be brought all together. Then, Allah will begin with the greatest of them in crime and continue in succession. That is Allah's statement,

(Then indeed We shall drag out from every sect all those who were worst in obstinate rebellion against the Most Gracious.) This is similar to Allah's statement,

(Until they will be gathered all together in the Fire. The last of them will say to the first of them: "Our Lord! These misled us, so give them a double torment of the Fire.") Until His saying,

(For what you used to earn.) (7:38-39) The first of them will say to the last of them: "Your were not better than us, so taste the torment for what you used to earn." Concerning Allah's statement,

(Then, verily, We know best those who are most worthy of being burnt therein.) Then, at this point Allah attaches one piece of information to another. The meaning here is that Allah best knows which of His creatures deserve to be burned in the fire of Hell and remain there forever and who deserves to have his punishment doubled. This is as He says in the Ayah that was previously mentioned,

(He will say: "For each one there is double (torment), but you know not.") (7:38)

Surah: 19 Ayah: 71 & Ayah: 72

وَإِن مِّنكُمْ إِلَّا وَارِدُهَا ۚ كَانَ عَلَىٰ رَبِّكَ حَتْمًا مَّقْضِيًّا ﴿٧١﴾

71. There is not one of you but will pass over it (Hell): this is with your Lord; a Decree which must be accomplished.

ثُمَّ نُنَجِّي الَّذِينَ اتَّقَوا وَّنَذَرُ الظَّالِمِينَ فِيهَا جِثِيًّا ﴿٧٢﴾

72. Then We shall save those who used to fear Allâh and were dutiful to Him. And We shall leave the Zâlimûn (polytheists and wrongdoers) therein (humbled) to their knees (in Hell).

Transliteration

71. Wa-in minkum illa wariduha kana AAala rabbika hatman maqdiyyan 72. Thumma nunajjee allatheena ittaqaw wanatharu alththalimeena feeha jithiyyan

Tafsir Ibn Kathir

Everyone will be brought to Hell, then the Righteous will be saved

Ibn Jarir reported from `Abdullah that he said concerning Allah's statement,

(There is not one of you but will pass over it.) "The bridge over Hell is like the sharp edge of a sword. The first group to cross it will pass like a flash of lightning. The second group will pass like the wind. The third group will pass like the fastest horse. The fourth group will pass like the fastest cow. Then, the rest will pass while the angels will be saying, `O Allah save them, save them.'" This narration has supporting narrations similar to it from the Prophet in the Two Sahihs and other collections as well. These narrations have been related by Anas, Abu Sa`id, Abu Hurayrah, Jabir and other Companions, may Allah be pleased with them all. Ahmad also recorded that Umm Mubashshar, the wife of Zayd bin Harithah, said, "The Messenger of Allah was in the house of Hafsah when he said,

«لَا يَدْخُلُ النَّارَ أَحَدٌ شَهِدَ بَدْرًا وَالْحُدَيْبِيَّةَ»

(No one who was present at the battles of Badr and Hudaybiyyah (of the Muslims) will enter into the Hellfire.) Then, Hafsah said, "Doesn't Allah say,

(There is not one of you but will pass over it (Hell);) The Messenger of Allah replied by reciting,

(Then We shall save those who had Taqwa.) In the Two Sahihs there is a Hadith reported from Az-Zuhri, from Sa`id from Abu Hurayrah that the Messenger of Allah said,

«لَا يَمُوتُ لِأَحَدٍ مِنَ الْمُسْلِمِينَ ثَلَاثَةٌ مِنَ الْوَلَدِ تَمَسُّهُ النَّارُ إِلَّا تَحِلَّةَ الْقَسَمِ»

(No one of the Muslims who has had three children, who all died, will be touched by the Hellfire, except for an oath that must be fulfilled.) `Abdur-Rahman bin Zayd bin Aslam commented on Allah's statement,

(There is not one of you but will pass over it;) "The passing of the Muslims (over the Hellfire) means their passing over a bridge that is over it. But the passing of the idolators over the Hellfire refers to their admission to the Fire." As-Suddi reported from Murrah, from Ibn Mas`ud, that he said concerning Allah's statement,

(this is with your Lord; a Hatman decree.) "An oath that must be fulfilled." Mujahid said, "Hatman means preordainment." Ibn Jurayj said the same. Concerning Allah's statement,

(Then We shall save those who had Taqwa.) When all of the creatures passed over the Hellfire, and those disbelievers and the disobedient people who are destined to fall into it because of their disobedience, Allah will save the believers and the righteous people from it because of their deeds. Therefore, their passing over the bridge and their speed will be based upon their deeds that they did in this life. Then, the believers who performed major sins will be allowed intercession. The angels, the Prophets and the believers will all intercede. Thus, a large number of the sinners will be allowed to come out of Hell. The fire will have devoured much of their bodies, except the places of prostration on their faces. Their removal from the Hellfire will be due to the faith in their hearts. The first to come out will be he who has the weight of a Dinar of faith in his heart. Then, whoever has the next least amount after him. Then, whoever is next to that after him, and so forth. This will continue until the one who has the tiniest hint of faith in his heart, equal to the weight of an atom. Then, Allah will take out of the Fire whoever said "La ilaha illallah," even one day of his entire life, even if he never performed any good deed. After this, no one will remain in the Hellfire, except those it is obligatory upon to remain in the Hellfire forever. This has been reported in many authentic Hadiths from the Messenger of Allah . This is why Allah says,

(Then We shall save those who had Taqwa. And We shall leave the wrongdoers in it, Jithyya.)

Surah: 19 Ayah: 73 & Ayah: 74

وَإِذَا تُتْلَىٰ عَلَيْهِمْ ءَايَٰتُنَا بَيِّنَٰتٍ قَالَ ٱلَّذِينَ كَفَرُواْ لِلَّذِينَ ءَامَنُوٓاْ أَىُّ ٱلْفَرِيقَيْنِ خَيْرٌ مَّقَامًا وَأَحْسَنُ نَدِيًّا ۝

73. And when Our Clear Verses are recited to them, those who disbelieve (the rich and strong among the pagans of Quraish who live a life of luxury) say to those who believe (the weak, poor companions of Prophet Muhammad (peace be upon him) who have a hard life): "Which of the two groups (i.e. believers or disbelievers) is best in (point of) position and as regards station (place of council for consultation)."

Chapter 19: Maryam (Mary), Verses 001-098

وَكَمْ أَهْلَكْنَا قَبْلَهُم مِّن قَرْنٍ هُمْ أَحْسَنُ أَثَاثًا وَرِءْيًا ۝

74. And how many a generation (past nations) have We destroyed before them, who were better in wealth, goods and outward appearance?

Transliteration

73. Wa-itha tutla AAalayhim ayatuna bayyinatin qala allatheena kafaroo lillatheena amanoo ayyu alfareeqayni khayrun maqaman waahsanu nadiyyan 74. Wakam ahlakna qablahum min qarnin hum ahsanu athathan wari/yan

Tafsir Ibn Kathir

The Disbelievers boast over Their good Fortune in the World

Allah, the Exalted, informs that when the clear, evident Ayat of Allah are recited to the disbelievers, they reject them and turn away. They say about those who believe, while boasting to them and arguing that their false religion is correct,

(best dwellings and the finest Nadiyyan.) This means the best houses, with the loftiest levels and the finest Nadiyyan, which are meeting rooms for men to gather and discuss matters. Thus, this means that their meeting rooms are full of more people who come to attend. In this they were saying, "How can we be upon falsehood while we are in this manner of successful living" These people were actually those who were concealed in the house of Al-Arqam bin Abi Al-Arqam and its likes from the other houses. This is as Allah says about them,

(And those who disbelieve say of those who believe: "Had it been a good thing, they (the weak and the poor) would not have preceded us thereto!") (46:11) Nuh's people said,

("Shall we believe in you, when the weakest (of the people) follow you") (26:111) And Allah says,

(Thus We have tried some of them with others, that they might say: "Is it these (poor believers) whom Allah has favored among us" Does not Allah know best those who are grateful) (6:53) This is why Allah refuted their doubts:

(And how many a generations have We destroyed before them) This means, "How many nations and generations did We destroy of those who denied (this message) due to their disbelief"

(who were better in wealth, goods and outward appearance) This means that they were better than these present people in wealth, possessions, looks and appearance. Al-A`mash reported from Abu Zibyan, who reported from Ibn `Abbas that he said concerning the Ayah,

(best dwellings and finest Nadiyyan.) "Position (Maqam) means home, Nadi means place of gathering, wealth refers to material possessions and outward appearance is how they look physically." Al-`Awfi said that Ibn `Abbas said, "Position (Maqam) means dwelling, Nadi means place of gathering and the blessing and happiness that they were living in. This is as Allah says about the people of Fir`awn when He destroyed them and related the story of their situation in the Qur'an,

(How many gardens and springs that they (Fir`awn's people) left behind, and green crops and honored places (Maqam).) (44:25-26) Therefore, position (Maqam) refers to their dwellings and splendid bounties, and Nadi is the places of gathering and meeting where they used to congregate. Allah said while relating the story to His Messenger of what happened with the people of Lut,

(And practice Al-Munkar (evil deeds) in your meeting places (Nadiyakum).) (29:29) The Arabs call a place of gathering a Nadi."

Surah: 19 Ayah: 75

قُلْ مَن كَانَ فِى ٱلضَّلَـٰلَةِ فَلْيَمْدُدْ لَهُ ٱلرَّحْمَـٰنُ مَدًّا ۚ حَتَّىٰ إِذَا رَأَوْا۟ مَا يُوعَدُونَ إِمَّا ٱلْعَذَابَ وَإِمَّا ٱلسَّاعَةَ فَسَيَعْلَمُونَ مَنْ هُوَ شَرٌّ مَّكَانًا وَأَضْعَفُ جُندًا ۝

75. Say (O Muhammad (peace be upon him)) whoever is in error, the Most Gracious (Allâh) will extend (the rope) to him, until, when they see that which they were promised, either the torment or the Hour, they will come to know who is worst in position, and who is weaker in forces. (This is the answer to the question in Verse No.19:73)

Transliteration

75. Qul man kana fee alddalalati falyamdud lahu alrrahmanu maddan hatta itha raaw ma yooAAadoona imma alAAathaba wa-imma alssaAAata fasayaAAlamoona man huwa sharrun makanan waadAAafu jundan

Tafsir Ibn Kathir

The Rebellious Person is given Respite but He is not forgotten

Allah, the Exalted, says,

(Say) This means, "O Muhammad, say to these people who are associating partners with their Lord, while claiming to follow the truth, that they are really following falsehood."

(whoever is in error) This means, `be they from us or from you.'

(the Most Gracious will extend (circumstances) for him.) This means that the Most Beneficent will give him respite in that which he is in, until he meets his Lord and his appointed time will have arrived.

(until, when they see that which they were promised, either the torment) that will strike him,

(or the Hour) that will come suddenly,

(they will come to know) at that time,

(who is worst in position, and who is weaker in forces.) This is in refutation of thier argument about their nice dwellings and splendid places of gathering. This is a challenge against the idolators who claim that they were following guidance in what they were doing. This is similar to the challenge that Allah mentions about the Jews when He says,

(O you Jews! If you pretend that you are friends of Allah, to the exclusion of (all) other people, then long for death if you are truthful.) (62:6) Meaning, `Supplicate for death to come to those who are following falsehood among us if you truly claim to be upon the truth. If you are true, then this supplication will not harm you.' But they refused to do so. An extensive discussion of this has already preceded in Surat Al-Baqarah, and to Allah is the praise. Likewise, Allah mentioned the challenge that was given to the Christians in Surah Al `Imran, when they were persistent in their disbelief and continued in their transgression. They refused to give up their exaggerating claim that `Isa was the son of Allah. Therefore, Allah mentioned His arguments and proofs against the worship of `Isa, and that he was merely a creature like Adam. After this, Allah said,

(Then whoever disputes with you about him after (all this) knowledge that has come to you, say: "Come, let us call our sons and your sons, our women and your women, ourselves and yourselves - then we pray and invoke (sincerely) the curse of Allah upon those who lie.") (3:61) However, they (the Christians) also retreated from this challenge.

Surah: 19 Ayah: 76

وَيَزِيدُ ٱللَّهُ ٱلَّذِينَ ٱهْتَدَوْا۟ هُدًى ۗ وَٱلْبَٰقِيَٰتُ ٱلصَّٰلِحَٰتُ خَيْرٌ عِندَ رَبِّكَ ثَوَابًا وَخَيْرٌ مَّرَدًّا ۝

76. And Allâh increases in guidance those who walk aright. And the righteous good deeds that last, are better with your Lord, for reward and better for resort.

Transliteration

76. Wayazeedu Allahu allatheena ihtadaw hudan waalbaqiyatu alssalihatu khayrun AAinda rabbika thawaban wakhayrun maraddan

Tafsir Ibn Kathir

Increasing Guidance of Those Who are guided

After Allah mentions the extended time and respite that is allowed to those who are in misguidance, increasing them in misguidance, He informs of the increase in guidance of those who are rightly guided. Similarly He says,

(And whenever there comes down a Surah, some of them say: "Which of you has had his faith increased by it") (9:124) And the following Ayah also shows this. Concerning Allah's statement,

(And the righteous good deeds that last) Its explanation has already preceded in Surat Al-Kahf, along with a lengthy discussion concerning it and the related Hadiths.

((they) are better with your Lord for reward.) meaning the recompense and reward.

(and better for resort.) meaning in the final outcome, the result for its doer.

Surah: 19 Ayah: 77, Ayah: 78, Ayah: 79 & Ayah: 80

أَفَرَءَيْتَ ٱلَّذِى كَفَرَ بِـَٔايَٰتِنَا وَقَالَ لَأُوتَيَنَّ مَالًا وَوَلَدًا ۝

77. Have you seen him who disbelieved in Our Ayât (this Qur'ân and Muhammad (peace be upon him)) and said: "I shall certainly be given wealth and children (if I will be alive (again))"

أَطَّلَعَ ٱلْغَيْبَ أَمِ ٱتَّخَذَ عِندَ ٱلرَّحْمَٰنِ عَهْدًا ۝

78. Has he known the Unseen or has he taken a covenant from the Most Gracious (Allâh)?

كَلَّا سَنَكْتُبُ مَا يَقُولُ وَنَمُدُّ لَهُۥ مِنَ ٱلْعَذَابِ مَدًّا ۝

79. Nay! We shall record what he says, and We shall increase his torment (in the Hell);

وَنَرِثُهُۥ مَا يَقُولُ وَيَأْتِينَا فَرْدًا ۝

80. And We shall inherit from him (at his death) all that he talks of (i.e. wealth and children which We have bestowed upon him in this world), and he shall come to Us alone.

Transliteration

77. Afaraayta allathee kafara bi-ayatina waqala laootayanna malan wawaladan 78. AttalaAAa alghayba ami ittakhatha AAinda alrrahmani AAahdan 79. Kalla sanaktubu ma yaqoolu wanamuddu lahu mina alAAathabi maddan 80. Wanarithuhu ma yaqoolu waya/teena fardan

Tafsir Ibn Kathir

Refuting the Disbelievers Who claim that They will be given Wealth and Children in the Hereafter

Imam Ahmad reported from Khabbab bin Al-Aratt that he said, "I was a blacksmith and Al-" ®256ا‎s bin Wa'il owed me a debt. So I went to him to collect my debt from him. He said to me, `No, by Allah, I will not pay my debt to you until you disbelieve in

Muhammad.' I replied to him, `No, by Allah, I will not disbelieve in Muhammad until you die and are resurrected again.' He then said to me, `Verily, if I die and am resurrected, and you come to me, I will also have abundance of wealth and children and I will repay you then.' Then, Allah revealed these Ayat,

(Have you seen him who disbelieved in Our Ayat and said: "I shall certainly be given wealth and children.") until,

(and he shall come to Us alone.) This was also recorded by the two compilers of the Sahihs and other collections as well. In the wording of Al-Bukhari it states that Khabbab said, "I used to be a blacksmith in Makkah and I made a sword for Al-®256ل's bin Wa'il. So I went to him to collect my pay from him..." then he mentioned the rest of the Hadith and he said,

(or has he taken a covenant from the Most Gracious) "This means an agreement. " Concerning Allah's statement,

(Has he known the Unseen) This is a rejection of the person who says,

(I shall certainly be given wealth and children.) Meaning, on the Day of Resurrection. In other words, "Does he know what he will have in the Hereafter, to such an extent that he can swear to it"

(or has he taken a covenant from the Most Gracious) Or has he received a promise from Allah that he will be given these things It has already been stated that in Sahih Al-Bukhari it is mentioned that covenant means an agreement. Concerning Allah's statement,

(Nay,) This is a particle that opposes what came before it and gives emphasis to what follows it.

(We shall record what he says,) what he is seeking, and his idea that he has given himself about what he hopes for, and his disbelief in Allah the Most Great.

(We shall increase his torment.) This is referring to what will happen in the abode of the Hereafter, because of his saying his disbelief in Allah in this life.

(And We shall inherit from him all that he speaks of,) His wealth and children. It means, "We will take all of this from him, in opposition to his claim that he will be given more wealth and children in the Hereafter than he had in this life." To the contrary, in the Hereafter that which he had in this life will be taken from him. This is why Allah says,

(And he shall come to Us alone.) without wealth or children.

Surah: 19 Ayah: 81, Ayah: 82, Ayah: 83 & Ayah: 84

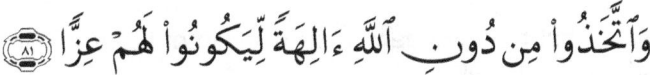

81. And they have taken (for worship) âlihah (gods) besides Allâh, that they might give them honor, power and glory (and also protect them from Allâh's Punishment).

$$كَلَّا ۚ سَيَكْفُرُونَ بِعِبَادَتِهِمْ وَيَكُونُونَ عَلَيْهِمْ ضِدًّا ﴿٨٢﴾$$

82. Nay, but they (the so-called gods) will deny their worship of them, and become opponents to them (on the Day of Resurrection).

$$أَلَمْ تَرَ أَنَّا أَرْسَلْنَا الشَّيَاطِينَ عَلَى الْكَافِرِينَ تَؤُزُّهُمْ أَزًّا ﴿٨٣﴾$$

83. See you not that We have sent the Shayâtîn (devils) against the disbelievers to push them to do evil.

$$فَلَا تَعْجَلْ عَلَيْهِمْ ۖ إِنَّمَا نَعُدُّ لَهُمْ عَدًّا ﴿٨٤﴾$$

84. So make no haste against them; We only count out to them a (limited) number (of the days of the life of this world and delay their term so that they may increase in evil and sins).

Transliteration

81. Waittakhathoo min dooni Allahi alihatan liyakoonoo lahum AAizzan 82. Kalla sayakfuroona biAAibadatihim wayakoonoona AAalayhim diddan 83. Alam tara anna arsalna alshshayateena AAala alkafireena taozzuhum azzan 84. Fala taAAjal AAalayhim innama naAAuddu lahum AAaddan Translation

Tafsir Ibn Kathir

The Idols of the Polytheists will deny Their Worship

Allah, the Exalted, informs about the disbelievers who associate partners with their Lord, that they have taken gods besides Allah, so that these gods may be a source of honor and might for them. They think that these gods give them power and make them victorious. Then, Allah mentions that the matter is not as they claim, and it will not be as they hope. He says,

(Nay, but they will deny their worship of them,) on the Day of Judgement.

(and will become their adversaries.) This means that they will be foes in a state other than what they think about these gods. This is similar to Allah's statement,

(And who is more astray than one who calls upon, besides Allah, such as will not answer him till the Day of Resurrection, and who are (even) unaware of their calls to them And when mankind are gathered, they will become their enemies and will deny their worshipping.) (46:5-6) As-Suddi said,

(Nay, but they will deny their worship of them,) "This means their worshipping of the idols. " Allah said,

Chapter 19: Maryam (Mary), Verses 001-098

(and will become their adversaries) contrary to what they hoped for from these gods. As-Suddi said,

(and will become their adversaries.) "They will be in severe opposition and argument." Ad-Dahhak said,

(and will become their adversaries.) "This means enemies."

The Power of the Devils over the Disbelievers

Concerning Allah's statement,

(See you not that We have sent the Shayatin against the disbelievers to push them to do evil.) `Ali bin Abi Talhah said that Ibn `Abbas said, "They will lead them astray with temptation." Al-`Awfi said that Ibn `Abbas said, "They will incite them against Muhammad and his Companions." Qatadah said, "They will harass them and disturb them until they disobey Allah." `Abdur-Rahman bin Zayd said, "This is similar to Allah's statement,

(And whosoever turns away blindly from the remembrance of the Most Gracious, We appoint for him a Shaytan to be a companion for him.)" (43:36) Concerning Allah's statement,

(So make no haste against them; We only count out to them a (limited) number.) This means, "Do not be hasty with the punishment that is going to befall them, O Muhammad."

(We only count out to them a number.) This means, "We are only delaying them for a fixed appointment whose time is numbered. They are destined for that and there is no escaping the torment of Allah and His exemplary punishment." Allah says,

(And consider not that Allah is unaware of that which the wrongdoers do.) (14:42) And He says,

(So give a respite to the disbelievers; deal gently with them for a while.) (86:17) And Allah says,

(We postpone the punishment only so that they may increase in sinfulness.) (3:178)

(We let them enjoy for a little while, then in the end We shall oblige them to (enter) a great torment.) (31:24)

(Say: "Enjoy! But certainly, your destination is the (Hell) Fire.") (14:30) As-Suddi said,

(We only count out to them a (limited) number.) means years, months, days and hours."

Surah: 19 Ayah: 85, Ayah: 86 & Ayah: 87

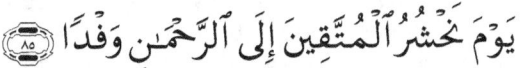

85. The Day We shall gather the Muttaqûn (pious and righteous persons - see V.2:2) unto the Most Gracious (Allâh), like a delegate (presented before a king for honor).

وَنَسُوقُ ٱلْمُجْرِمِينَ إِلَىٰ جَهَنَّمَ وِرْدًا ﴿٨٦﴾

86. And We shall drive the Mujrimûn (polytheists, sinners, criminals, disbelievers in the Oneness of Allâh) to Hell, in a thirsty state (like a thirsty herd driven down to water).

لَّا يَمْلِكُونَ ٱلشَّفَـٰعَةَ إِلَّا مَنِ ٱتَّخَذَ عِندَ ٱلرَّحْمَـٰنِ عَهْدًا ﴿٨٧﴾

87. None shall have the power of intercession, but such a one as has received permission (or promise) from the Most Gracious (Allâh).

Transliteration

85. Yawma nahshuru almuttaqeena ila alrrahmani wafdan 86. Wanasooqu almujrimeena ila jahannama wirdan 87. La yamlikoona alshshafaAAata illa mani ittakhatha AAinda alrrahmani AAahdan

Tafsir Ibn Kathir

The Condition of the Righteous and the Criminals on the Day of Resurrection

Allah, the Exalted, informs about His righteous friends, who feared Him in the life of this world. They followed His Messengers and believed in what the Messengers told them. They obeyed them in what they commanded them and abstained from that which they prohibited. Allah explains that He will gather these people on the Day of Resurrection like a delegation that has come to Him. A Wafd (delegation) is a group that arrives while riding and from it comes the word Wufud (arriving). They will come riding upon noble steeds of light from the riding animals of the Hereafter. They will arrive before the Best Receiver of delegations at the abode of His honor and pleasure. In reference to the criminals, who denied the Messengers and opposed them, they will be driven violently to the Hellfire. Allah says,

(In a thirsty state.) This means parched and thirsting for drink. This was stated by `Ata', Ibn `Abbas, Mujahid, Al-Hasan, Qatadah and many others. Here it will be said,

(Which of the two groups is best in Maqam (position) and the finest Nadiyyan (meeting place).)(19:73) Ibn Abi Hatim reported from `Amr bin Qays Al-Mula'i, who reported from Ibn Marzuq that he said,

(The Day We shall gather those with Taqwa unto the Most Gracious, like a delegation.) "When the believer comes forth from his grave, he will meet the most handsome form he has ever seen and it will have the nicest fragrance. He will say, `Who are you' The being will reply, `You do not know me' The believer will say, `No, but Allah has made you sweet smelling with a handsome face.' The being will say, `I am your righteous deeds. This is how you use to beautify and apply fragrance to your deeds in the worldly life. I was riding upon you in the entire length of your worldly life, so will you not ride upon me now' So the believer will therefore mount the creature. This is the meaning of Allah's statement,

(The Day We shall gather those with Taqwa unto the Most Gracious, like a delegation.)" `Ali bin Abi Talhah reported that Ibn `Abbas said,

(The Day We shall gather those with Taqwa unto the Most Gracious, like a delegation.) "Riding." His saying,

(And We shall drive the criminals to Hell, in a thirsty state.) This means parched and thirsty.

(None shall have the power of intercession,) There will be no one who can intercede for them like the believers who intercede for each other. Allah says about them,

(Now we have no intercessors, nor a close friend.) (26:100-101) Allah said,

(but such a one as has received permission (or promise) from the Most Gracious.) This is a separate exclusion, which means, "But those who have taken a covenant with the Most Beneficent." This covenant is the testimony that none has the right to be worshipped but Allah, and upholding of its rights and implications. `Ali bin Abi Talhah reported that Ibn `Abbas said,

(but such a one as has received permission (or promise) from the Most Gracious.) "The promise is the testimony that none has the right to be worshipped but Allah, that the person accepts that all power and strength belong to Allah and he only places his hope with Allah alone."

Surah: 19 Ayah: 88, Ayah: 89, Ayah: 90, Ayah: 91, Ayah: 92, Ayah: 93, Ayah: 94 & Ayah: 95

وَقَالُوا۟ ٱتَّخَذَ ٱلرَّحْمَٰنُ وَلَدًا ۝

88. And they say: "The Most Gracious (Allâh) has begotten a son (or offspring or children) (as the Jews say: 'Uzair (Ezra) is the son of Allâh, and the Christians say that He has begotten a son ('Iesa (Christ) (peace be upon him)) and the pagan Arabs say that He has begotten daughters (angels and others.))"

لَّقَدْ جِئْتُمْ شَيْئًا إِدًّا ۝

89. Indeed you have brought forth (said) a terrible evil thing.

تَكَادُ ٱلسَّمَٰوَٰتُ يَتَفَطَّرْنَ مِنْهُ وَتَنشَقُّ ٱلْأَرْضُ وَتَخِرُّ ٱلْجِبَالُ هَدًّا ۝

90. Whereby the heavens are almost torn, and the earth is split asunder, and the mountains fall in ruins,

أَن دَعَوْا۟ لِلرَّحْمَـٰنِ وَلَدًا ۝

91. That they ascribe a son (or offspring or children) to the Most Gracious (Allâh).

وَمَا يَنۢبَغِى لِلرَّحْمَـٰنِ أَن يَتَّخِذَ وَلَدًا ۝

92. But it is not suitable for (the Majesty of) the Most Gracious (Allâh) that He should beget a son (or offspring or children).

إِن كُلُّ مَن فِى ٱلسَّمَـٰوَٰتِ وَٱلْأَرْضِ إِلَّآ ءَاتِى ٱلرَّحْمَـٰنِ عَبْدًا ۝

93. There is none in the heavens and the earth but comes unto the Most Gracious (Allâh) as a slave.

لَّقَدْ أَحْصَىٰهُمْ وَعَدَّهُمْ عَدًّا ۝

94. Verily, He knows each one of them, and has counted them a full counting.

وَكُلُّهُمْ ءَاتِيهِ يَوْمَ ٱلْقِيَـٰمَةِ فَرْدًا ۝

95. And everyone of them will come to Him alone on the Day of Resurrection (without any helper, or protector or defender).

Transliteration

88. Waqaloo ittakhatha alrrahmanu waladan 89. Laqad ji/tum shay-an iddan 90. Takadu alssamawatu yatafattarna minhu watanshaqqu al-ardu watakhirru aljibalu haddan 91. An daAAaw lilrrahmani waladan 92. Wama yanbaghee lilrrahmani an yattakhitha waladan 93. In kullu man fee alssamawati waal-ardi illa atee alrrahmani AAabdan 94. Laqad ahsahum waAAaddahum AAaddan 95. Wakulluhum ateehi yawma alqiyamati fardan

Tafsir Ibn Kathir

The Stern Rejection of attributing a Son to Allah

After Allah affirms in this noble Surah that `Isa was a worshipper and servant of Allah and He mentioned his birth from Maryam without a father, He then begins refuting those who claim that He has a son. Holy is He and far Exalted is He above such description. Allah says,

(And they say: "The Most Gracious has begotten a son." Indeed you have brought forth) This means, "In this statement of yours."

(a thing Idda.) Ibn `Abbas, Mujahid, Qatadah and Malik all said, "Terrible." It has been said that it is pronounced Iddan, Addan, and Addan with elongation on the first vowel. All three of these pronunciations are known, but the most popular is the first. Allah said;

Chapter 19: Maryam (Mary), Verses 001-098

(Whereby the heavens are almost torn, and the earth is split asunder, and the mountains Hadda, that they ascribe a son to the Most Gracious.) that is, out of their high esteem for Allah, when they hear this statement of wickedness coming from the Children of Adam. The reason for this is that these are creatures of Allah and they are established upon His Tawhid and the fact that there is no deity worthy of worship except Him. He has no partners, no peer, no child, no mate and no coequal. Rather, He is the One, Self-Sufficient Master, Whom all creatures are in need of. Ibn Jarir reported that Ibn `Abbas said concerning Allah's statement,

(Whereby the heavens are almost torn, and the earth is split asunder, and the mountains Hadda, that they ascribe a son to the Most Gracious.) "Verily, the heavens, the earth, the mountains and all creatures -- except for humans and Jinns -- are frightened by the associating of partners with Allah. Creation will almost cease existing before the association of partners with Allah, due to His Greatness. Just as the idolator does not benefit by his good deeds because of associating partners with Allah, we hope that Allah would forgive the sins of those who believed in His absolute Oneness by worshipping Him alone. The Messenger of Allah said,

«لَقِّنُوا مَوْتَاكُمْ شَهَادَةَ أَنْ لَا إِلَهَ إِلَّا اللهُ، فَمَنْ قَالَهَا عِنْدَ مَوْتِهِ وَجَبَتْ لَهُ الْجَنَّة»

(Encourage your dying people to testify to La ilaha illallah, for whoever says it at the time of their death, they will definitely enter into Paradise.) The people said, "O Messenger of Allah, what about he who says it while in good health" He replied,

«تِلْكَ أَوْجَبُ وَأَوْجَب»

(This will necessitate his entrance into Paradise even more.) Then he said,

«وَالَّذِي نَفْسِي بِيَدِهِ لَوْ جِيءَ بِالسَّموَاتِ وَالْأَرَضِينَ، وَمَا فِيهِنَّ وَمَا بَيْنَهُنَّ وَمَا تَحْتَهُنَّ، فَوُضِعْنَ فِي كِفَّةِ الْمِيزَانِ، وَوُضِعَتْ شَهَادَةُ أَنْ لَا إِلَهَ إِلَّا اللهُ فِي الْكِفَّةِ الْأُخْرَى لَرَجَحَتْ بِهِن»

(I swear by He Whom my soul is in His Hand, if the heavens and the earths, and all that is in them, between them and under them, were brought and placed in a balance of a scale, and the testimony of La ilaha illallah was placed on the other side of the scale, the testimony would outweigh all of it.) This was recorded by Ibn Jarir and it is supported by the Hadith related to the story of the card. And Allah knows best. Ad-Dahhak said,

(Whereby the heavens are almost torn,) "This means to be split apart into pieces due to the fear of the magnificence of Allah." `Abdur-Rahman bin Zayd bin Aslam said, (and the earth is split asunder,) "This is due to its anger on behalf of Allah, the Mighty and Sublime."

(and the mountains Hadda.) Ibn `Abbas said, "This means to be torn down." Sa`id bin Jubayr said, "Haddan means some of it is broken by other parts of it in succession." Imam Ahmad reported from Abu Musa that he said that the Messenger of Allah said,

«لَا أَحَدَ أَصْبَرُ عَلَى أَذًى سَمِعَهُ مِنَ اللهِ إِنَّهُ يُشْرَكُ بِهِ وَيُجْعَلُ لَهُ وَلَدٌ، وَهُوَ يُعَافِيهِمْ وَيَدْفَعُ عَنْهُمْ وَيَرْزُقُهُمْ»

(There is no one more patient than Allah concerning something harmful that he hears. For verily, partners are associated with Him and a son is ascribed to Him, while He is the One Who gives them good health, protects them and sustains them.) This narration is also recorded in the Two Sahihs. In one wording of it he said,

«إِنَّهُمْ يَجْعَلُونَ لَهُ وَلَدًا وَهُوَ يَرْزُقُهُمْ وَيُعَافِيهِم»

(...that they attribute a son to Him, while He is the One Who sustains them and gives them good health.) Allah said;

(But it is not suitable for the Most Gracious that He should beget a son.) Meaning that it is not befitting of Him, nor is it appropriate for His lofty majesty and greatness. There is no coequal for Him in His creation, because all creatures are His slaves. This is why He says,

(There is none in the heavens and the earth but comes unto the Most Gracious as a slave. Verily, He knows each one of them, and has counted them a full counting.) He knows their number from the time He created them, until the Day of Resurrection, male and female, both the small and the large of them.

(And everyone of them will come to Him alone on the Day of Resurrection.) This means that there will be no helper for him and no one to save him, except Allah alone, Who has no partners. He judges His creatures as He wills and He is the Most Just, Who does not do even an atom's weight of injustice. He will not wrong anyone.

Surah: 19 Ayah: 96, Ayah: 97 & Ayah: 98

إِنَّ ٱلَّذِينَ ءَامَنُوا۟ وَعَمِلُوا۟ ٱلصَّٰلِحَٰتِ سَيَجْعَلُ لَهُمُ ٱلرَّحْمَٰنُ وُدًّا ۞

96. Verily, those who believe (in the Oneness of Allâh and in His Messenger (Muhammad (peace be upon him))) and work deeds of righteousness, the Most Gracious (Allâh) will bestow love for them (in the hearts of the believers).

$$\text{فَإِنَّمَا يَسَّرْنَٰهُ بِلِسَانِكَ لِتُبَشِّرَ بِهِ ٱلْمُتَّقِينَ وَتُنذِرَ بِهِۦ قَوْمًا لُّدًّا ﴿٩٧﴾}$$

97. So We have made this (the Qur'ân) easy in your own tongue (O Muhammad (peace be upon him)) only that you may give glad tidings to the Muttaqûn (the pious and righteous persons - See V.2:2), and warn with it the Ludd (most quarrelsome) people.

$$\text{وَكَمْ أَهْلَكْنَا قَبْلَهُم مِّن قَرْنٍ هَلْ تُحِسُّ مِنْهُم مِّنْ أَحَدٍ أَوْ تَسْمَعُ لَهُمْ رِكْزًۢا ﴿٩٨﴾}$$

98. And how many a generation before them have We destroyed! Can you (O Muhammad (peace be upon him)) find a single one of them or hear even a whisper of them?

Transliteration

96. Inna allatheena amanoo waAAamiloo alssalihati sayajAAalu lahumu alrrahmanu wuddan 97. Fa-innama yassarnahu bilisanika litubashshira bihi almuttaqeena watunthira bihi qawman luddan 98. Wakam ahlakna qablahum min qarnin hal tuhissu minhum min ahadin aw tasmaAAu lahum rikzan

Tafsir Ibn Kathir

Allah places Love of the Righteous People in the Hearts

Allah, the Exalted, informs about His believing servants, who work righteous deeds -- deeds that He is pleased with because they are in accordance with the legislation of Muhammad -- that He plants love for them in the hearts of His righteous servants. This is something that is absolutely necessary and there is no avoiding it. This has been reported in authentic Hadiths of the Messenger of Allah in various different ways. Imam Ahmad recorded that Abu Hurayrah said that the Prophet said,

«إِنَّ اللهَ إِذَا أَحَبَّ عَبْدًا دَعَا جِبْرِيلَ، فَقَالَ: يَا جِبْرِيلُ، إِنِّي أُحِبُّ فُلَانًا فَأَحِبَّهُ قَالَ: فَيُحِبُّهُ جِبْرِيلُ، قَالَ: ثُمَّ يُنَادِي فِي أَهْلِ السَّمَاءِ: إِنَّ اللهَ يُحِبُّ فُلَانًا فَأَحِبُّوهُ، قَالَ: فَيُحِبُّهُ أَهْلُ السَّمَاءِ، ثُمَّ يُوضَعُ لَهُ الْقَبُولُ فِي الْأَرْضِ، وَإِنَّ اللهَ إِذَا أَبْغَضَ عَبْدًا دَعَا جِبْرِيلَ فَقَالَ: يَا جِبْرِيلُ إِنِّي أُبْغِضُ فُلَانًا فَأَبْغِضْهُ، قَالَ: فَيُبْغِضُهُ جِبْرِيلُ، ثُمَّ يُنَادِي فِي أَهْلِ السَّمَاءِ: إِنَّ اللهَ يُبْغِضُ فُلَانًا فَأَبْغِضُوهُ، قَالَ: فَيُبْغِضُهُ أَهْلُ السَّمَاءِ، ثُمَّ يُوضَعُ لَهُ الْبَغْضَاءُ فِي الْأَرْضِ»

(Verily, whenever Allah loves a servant of His, He calls Jibril and says, "O Jibril, verily I love so-and-so, so love him." Thus, Jibril will love him. Then, he (Jibril) will call out to the dwellers of the heavens, "Verily, Allah loves so-and-so, so you too must love him."

Then the dwellers of the heavens love him and he will be given acceptance in the earth. Whenever Allah hates a servant of His, He calls Jibril and says, "O Jibril, verily I hate so-and-so, so hate him." Thus, Jibril will hate him. Then, he (Jibril) will call out amongst the dwellers of the heavens, "Verily, Allah hates so-and-so, so you too must hate him." Then the dwellers of the heavens hate him and hatred for him will be placed in the earth.) Al-Bukhari and Muslim reported narrations similar to this. Ibn Abi Hatim recorded that Abu Hurayrah said that the Prophet said,

«إِذَا أَحَبَّ اللهُ عَبْدًا نَادَى جِبْرِيلَ: إِنِّي قَدْ أَحْبَبْتُ فُلَانًا فَأَحِبَّهُ، فَيُنَادِي فِي السَّمَاءِ، ثُمَّ يُنْزِلُ لَهُ الْمَحَبَّةَ فِي أَهْلِ الْأَرْضِ، فَذَلِكَ قَوْلُ اللهِ عَزَّ وَجَلَّ:

(إِنَّ الَّذِينَ ءَامَنُوا وَعَمِلُوا الصَّالِحَاتِ سَيَجْعَلُ لَهُمُ الرَّحْمَنُ وُدًّا)»

(Whenever Allah loves a servant of His, He calls Jibril (saying), "Verily, I love so-and-so, so love him." Then, Jibril calls out into the heavens and love for him descends among the people of the earth. That is the meaning of the statement of Allah, the Mighty and Sublime: (Verily, those who believe and work deeds of righteousness, the Most Gracious will bestow love for them.)) (19:96) This was also reported by Muslim and At-Tirmidhi and At-Tirmidhi said, "Hasan Sahih."

The Qur'an descended to give Glad Tidings and to warn

Allah said;

(So, We have made this easy) meaning the Qur'an.

(in your own tongue,) This is an address to Prophet Muhammad and it means that the Qur'an is in the pure, complete and eloquent Arabic language.

(that you may give glad tidings to those who have Taqwa,) those who respond to Allah and believe in His Messenger,

(and warn with it the people who are Ludda.) meaning, the people who have deviated away from the truth and are inclined towards falsehood. His saying,

(And how many a generation before them have We destroyed!) means from the nations that disbelieved in the signs of Allah and rejected His Messengers.

(Can you find a single one of them or hear even a whisper of them) Meaning, `have you seen any of them or even heard a whisper from them.' Ibn `Abbas, Abu Al-`Aliyah, `Ikrimah, Al-Hasan Al-Basri, Sa`id bin Jubayr, Ad-Dahhak and Ibn Zayd all said, "This means any sound." Al-Hasan and Qatadah both said that this means, "Do you see with your eye, or hear any sound"

This is the end of the Tafsir of Surah Maryam. All praises and thanks are due to Allah.

Following this will be the Tafsir of Surah Ta Ha, Allah willing and all praise is due to Allah.

CHAPTER (SURAH) 20: TA-HA (TA-HA), VERSES 001–135

(بِسْمِ اللَّهِ الرَّحْمَٰنِ الرَّحِيمِ)

In the Name of Allah, the Most Gracious, the Most Merciful.

Surah: 20 Ayah: 1, Ayah: 2, Ayah: 3, Ayah: 4, Ayah: 5, Ayah: 6, Ayah: 7 & Ayah: 8

طه

1. Tâ-Hâ. [These letters are one of the miracles of the Qur'ân, and none but Allâh (Alone) knows their meanings.]

مَا أَنزَلْنَا عَلَيْكَ ٱلْقُرْءَانَ لِتَشْقَىٰ

2. We have not sent down the Qur'ân unto you (O Muhammad (peace be upon him)) to cause you distress,

إِلَّا تَذْكِرَةً لِّمَن يَخْشَىٰ

3. But only as a Reminder to those who fear (Allâh).

تَنزِيلًا مِّمَّنْ خَلَقَ ٱلْأَرْضَ وَٱلسَّمَٰوَٰتِ ٱلْعُلَىٰ

4. A revelation from Him (Allâh) Who has created the earth and high heavens.

ٱلرَّحْمَٰنُ عَلَى ٱلْعَرْشِ ٱسْتَوَىٰ

5. The Most Gracious (Allâh) Istawâ (rose over) the (Mighty) Throne (in a manner that suits His Majesty).

لَهُۥ مَا فِى ٱلسَّمَٰوَٰتِ وَمَا فِى ٱلْأَرْضِ وَمَا بَيْنَهُمَا وَمَا تَحْتَ ٱلثَّرَىٰ

6. To Him belongs all that is in the heavens and all that is on the earth, and all that is between them, and all that is under the soil.

وَإِن تَجْهَرْ بِٱلْقَوْلِ فَإِنَّهُۥ يَعْلَمُ ٱلسِّرَّ وَأَخْفَى

7. And if you (O Muhammad (peace be upon him)) speak (the invocation) aloud, then verily, He knows the secret and that which is yet more hidden.

$$ ٱللَّهُ لَآ إِلَٰهَ إِلَّا هُوَ ۖ لَهُ ٱلْأَسْمَآءُ ٱلْحُسْنَىٰ ﴿٨﴾ $$

8. Allâh! Lâ ilâhla illa Huwa (none has the right to be worshipped but He)! To Him belong the Best Names.

Transliteration

1. Ta-ha 2. Ma anzalna AAalayka alqur-ana litashqa 3. Illa tathkiratan liman yakhsha 4. Tanzeelan mimman khalaqa al-arda waalssamawati alAAula 5. Alrrahmanu AAala alAAarshi istawa 6. Lahu ma fee alssamawati wama fee al-ardi wama baynahuma wama tahta aththara 7. Wa-in tajhar bialqawli fa-innahu yaAAlamu alssirra waakhfa 8. Allahu la ilaha illa huwa lahu al-asmao alhusna

Tafsir Ibn Kathir

The Qur'an is a Reminder and a Revelation from Allah

We have already discussed the separated letters at the beginning of Surah Al-Baqarah, so there is no need to repeat its discussion here. Allah says,

(We have not sent down the Qur'an unto you to cause you distress,) Juwaybir reported that Ad-Dahhak said, "When Allah sent the Qur'an down to His Messenger, he and his Companions adh- ered to it. Thus, the idolators of the Quraysh said, `This Qur'an was only reve- aled to Muhammad to cause him distress.' Therefore, Allah revealed,

(Ta Ha. We have not sent down the Qur'an unto you to cause you distress, but only as a Reminder to those who fear (Allah).) The matter is not like the people of falsehood claim. Rather, whomever Allah gives knowledge to, it is because Allah wants him to have an abundance of good. This like what is confirmed in the Two Sahihs on the authority of Ibn Mas`ud, who said that the Messenger of Allah said,

$$ \langle\langle مَنْ يُرِدِ اللهُ بِهِ خَيْرًا يُفَقِّهْهُ فِي الدِّينِ \rangle\rangle $$

(Whomever Allah wants good for, then He gives him the understanding of the religion.) Mujahid commented on Allah's statement,

(We have not sent down the Qur'an unto you to cause you distress,) "This is like His statement,

(So recite as much of the Qur'an as may be easy (for you).) (73:20) For, the people used to hang ropes at their chests (to hang on to when tired) in the prayer." Qatadah said,

(We have not sent down the Qur'an unto you to cause you distress,) "No, by Allah, He did not make it a thing of distress. Rather, He made it a mercy, a light and a guide to Paradise." Allah said,

(But only as a Reminder to those who fear (Allah).) Allah revealed His Book and sent His Messenger as a mercy for His servants, so that the person who reflects may be reminded. Thus, a man will benefit from what he hears of the Book of Allah, it is a remembrance in which Allah revealed what He permits and prohibits. His saying,

(A Revelation from Him (Allah) Who has created the earth and high heavens.) means, `This Qur'an, which has come to you, O Muhammad, is a revelation from your Lord. He is the Lord of everything and its King. He is Most Able to do whatever He wills. He created the earth with its low depths and dense regions. He created the lofty heavens with their high altitudes and subtleties.' It has been reported in a Hadith, which At-Tirmidhi and others graded as authentic, that the density of each sky of the heavens is the distance of five hundred years travel and the distance between it and the next heaven is also five hundred years. Concerning Allah's statement,

(The Most Gracious Istawa the Throne.) A discussion concerning this has already preceded in Surat Al-A`raf, so there is no need to repeat it here. The safest path to take in understanding this, is the way of the Salaf (predecessors). Their way was to accept that which has been reported concerning this from the Book and the Sunnah without describing it, reinterpreting it, resembling it to creation, rejecting it, or comparing it to attributes of the creatures. Concerning Allah's statement,

(To Him belongs all that is in the heavens and all that is on the earth, and all that is between them, and all that is under the soil.) This means all of this is owned by Him and in His grasp. It is all under His control, will, intent and judgement. He created all of this, He owns it and He is the God of all of it. There is no true God other than He and no Lord other than He. Concerning Allah's statement,

(and all that is under the soil.) Muhammad bin Ka`b said, "This means that which is beneath the seventh earth." Concerning Allah's statement,

(And if you speak aloud, then verily, He knows the secret and that which is yet more hidden.) This means that He Who revealed this Qur'an, has also created the high heavens and the earth and He knows that which is secret and what is even more hidden. As Allah says,

(Say: "It has been sent down by Him Who knows the secret of the heavens and the earth. Truly, He is Oft-Forgiving, Most Merciful.") (25:6) `Ali bin Abi Talhah reported that Ibn `Abbas said,

(He knows the secret and that which is yet more hidden.) "The secret is what the son of Adam hides within himself, and

(that which is yet more hidden.) is the deeds of the son of Adam, which are hidden before he does them. Allah knows all of that. His knowledge encompasses that which has passed and that which is in the future and it is one, complete knowledge. In this regard, all of the creatures are as one soul to Him. That is the meaning of His statement,

(The creation of you all and the resurrection of you all are only as a single person.) (31:28) Concerning Allah's statement,

(Allah! There is no God but Him! To Him belongs the Best Names.) This means, `He Who revealed this Qur'an to you (O Muhammad), He is Allah, there is no God except Him. He is the Owner of the Best Names and the most lofty attributes.'

Surah: 20 Ayah: 9 & Ayah: 10

وَهَلْ أَتَىٰكَ حَدِيثُ مُوسَىٰ ۝

9. And has there come to you the story of Mûsa (Moses)?

إِذْ رَءَا نَارًا فَقَالَ لِأَهْلِهِ ٱمْكُثُوٓا۟ إِنِّىٓ ءَانَسْتُ نَارًا لَّعَلِّىٓ ءَاتِيكُم مِّنْهَا بِقَبَسٍ أَوْ أَجِدُ عَلَى ٱلنَّارِ هُدًى ۝

10. When he saw a fire, he said to his family: "Wait! Verily, I have seen a fire; perhaps I can bring you some burning brand therefrom, or find some guidance at the fire."

Transliteration

9. Wahal ataka hadeethu moosa   10. Ith raa naran faqala li-ahlihi omkuthoo innee anastu naran laAAallee ateekum minha biqabasin aw ajidu AAala alnnari hudan

Tafsir Ibn Kathir

A Discussion of the Message of Musa

From this point, Allah begins to mention the story of Musa, how revelation began to come to Him, and Allah's speaking directly to him. This occurred after Musa had completed the time agreed upon between he and his father-in-law that he would herd sheep. He was traveling with his family, and it has been said that he was headed for the land of Egypt, after having been away from it for more than ten years. He had his wife with him and he became lost on the way during a cold, wintery night. Therefore, he settled down, making a camp between some mountain passes and mountains that were covered with snow, sleet, dense clouds, darkness and fog. He began to try to make a fire with a kindling device he had with him, in order to produce some light, as was customary. However, it would not kindle anything and it even stopped giving off sparks. While he was in this condition, he saw a fire from the side of the mountain. It appeared to him to be a fire glowing from the right side of the mountain from where he was. He then announced the good news to his family saying,

(Verily, I have seen a fire; perhaps I can bring you some burning brand) This means a flame from a fire. In another Ayah he said,

(or a burning firebrand.) (28:29)) This is a coal that has a burning flame.

Chapter 20: Ta-Ha (Ta-Ha), Verses 001-135

(that you may warm yourselves.) (28:29) This proves that it was in fact cold weather at that time. Concerning his statement,

(some burning brand) This proves that it was dark. In reference to his statement,

(or find some guidance at the fire.) This means someone who can guide me to the road. This proves that he lost the road. This is as Ath-Thawri reported from Abu Sa`id Al-A`war, from `Ikrimah, from Ibn `Abbas that he said concerning Allah's statement,

(or find some guidance at the fire.) "This means someone who will guide me to the road. They were cold and had lost their way. Then, when he (Musa) saw the fire he said, `Either I will find someone who can guide us to the road, or at least I can bring you all some fire that you can kindle with.' "

Surah: 20 Ayah: 11, Ayah: 12, Ayah: 13, Ayah: 14, Ayah: 15 & Ayah: 16

فَلَمَّآ أَتَىٰهَا نُودِىَ يَـٰمُوسَىٰٓ ۝

11. And when he came to it (the fire), he was called by name: "O Mûsa (Moses)!

إِنِّىٓ أَنَا۠ رَبُّكَ فَٱخْلَعْ نَعْلَيْكَ إِنَّكَ بِٱلْوَادِ ٱلْمُقَدَّسِ طُوًى ۝

12. "Verily! I am your Lord! So take off your shoes; you are in the sacred valley, Tuwa.

وَأَنَا ٱخْتَرْتُكَ فَٱسْتَمِعْ لِمَا يُوحَىٰٓ ۝

13. "And I have chosen you. So listen to that which will be revealed (to you).

إِنَّنِىٓ أَنَا ٱللَّهُ لَآ إِلَـٰهَ إِلَّآ أَنَا۠ فَٱعْبُدْنِى وَأَقِمِ ٱلصَّلَوٰةَ لِذِكْرِىٓ ۝

14. "Verily! I am Allâh! Lâ ilâha illa Ana (none has the right to be worshipped but I), so worship Me, and perform As-Salât (Iqâmat-as-Salât) for My Remembrance.

إِنَّ ٱلسَّاعَةَ ءَاتِيَةٌ أَكَادُ أُخْفِيهَا لِتُجْزَىٰ كُلُّ نَفْسٍۭ بِمَا تَسْعَىٰ ۝

15. "Verily, the Hour is coming - and I am almost hiding it for Myself - that every person may be rewarded for that which he strives.

فَلَا يَصُدَّنَّكَ عَنْهَا مَن لَّا يُؤْمِنُ بِهَا وَٱتَّبَعَ هَوَىٰهُ فَتَرْدَىٰ ۝

16. "Therefore, let not the one who believes not therein (i.e. in the Day of Resurrection, Reckoning, Paradise and Hell.), but follows his own lusts, divert you therefrom, lest you should perish.

Transliteration

11. Falamma ataha noodiya ya moosa 12. Innee ana rabbuka faikhlaAA naAAlayka innaka bialwadi almuqaddasi tuwan 13. Waana ikhtartuka faistamiAA lima yooha 14. Innanee ana Allahu la ilaha illa ana faoAAbudnee waaqimi alssalata lithikree 15. Inna alssaAAata atiyatun akadu okhfeeha litujza kullu nafsin bima tasAAa 16. Fala yasuddannaka AAanha man la yu/minu biha waittabaAAa hawahu fatarda

Tafsir Ibn Kathir

The First Revelation to Musa

Allah, the Exalted, says,

(And when he came to it,) This is referring to the fire when he approached it.

(He was called by name: "O Musa!") In another Ayah it says,

(He was called from the right side of the valley, in the blessed place, from the tree: "O Musa! Verily, I am Allah.")(28:30) However, here Allah says,

(Verily, I am your Lord!) meaning, `the One Who is talking to you and addressing you,'

(So take off your shoes;) `Ali bin Abi Talib, Abu Dharr, Abu Ayyub and others of the Salaf said, "They (his sandals) were from the skin of a donkey that was not slaughtered." It has also been said that he was only commanded to remove his sandals due to respect for the blessed spot. Concerning Allah's statement,

(Tuwa) `Ali bin Abi Talhah said that Ibn `Abbas said, "It is the name of the valley." Others have said the same. This is merely mentioned as something to give more explanation to the story. It has also been said that it is a figure of speech, which comes from the command to place his feet down. It has also been said that it means `doubly sacred' and that Tuwa is something that has repetitious blessings. However, the first opinion is most correct. It is similar to Allah's statement,

(When his Lord called him in the sacred valley of Tuwa.) (79:16) Allah's statement,

(And I have chosen you.) is similar to His statement,

(I have chosen you above men by My Messages, and by My speaking (to you).) (7:144) This means over all human beings of that time. It has also been said that Allah said, "O Musa, do you know why I chose to speak to you directly out of all of the people" Musa said, "No." Allah then said, "Because I have not made anyone humble himself as much as you have humbled yourself." Concerning Allah's statement,

(So listen to that which will be revealed.) "Now listen to what I say to you and what I reveal to you."

(Verily, I am Allah! There is no God but Me,) This is the first obligation upon all responsible people of age, that they know that there is no God worthy of worship except Allah alone, Who has no partners. Concerning Allah's statement,

(so worship Me,) This means, "Single Me out alone for worship, and establish My worship without associating anything with Me."

(and perform Salah for My remembrance.) It has been said that this means, "Pray in order to remember Me." It has also been said that it means, "And establish the prayer whenever you remember Me." There is a supporting evidence for this second statement in a Hadith recorded by Imam Ahmad from Anas, who said that the Messenger of Allah said,

«إِذَا رَقَدَ أَحَدُكُمْ عَنِ الصَّلَاةِ أَوْ غَفَلَ عَنْهَا، فَلْيُصَلِّهَا إِذَا ذَكَرَهَا، فَإِنَّ اللهَ تَعَالَى قَالَ:

(وَأَقِمِ الصَّلَوةَ لِذِكْرِى)»

(Whenever one of you sleeps past the prayer, or he forgets to pray, then let him pray when he remembers it. For verily, Allah said, (And perform Salah for My remembrance.)) In the Two Sahihs it is reported from Anas that the Messenger of Allah said,

«مَنْ نَامَ عَنْ صَلَاةٍ أَوْ نَسِيَهَا فَكَفَّارَتُهَا أَنْ يُصَلِّيَهَا إِذَا ذَكَرَهَا، لَا كَفَّارَةَ لَهَا إِلَّا ذَلِك»

(Whoever slept past the prayer, or forgot it, then his expiation is that he prays it when he remembers it. There is no expiation for it other than that.) Concerning Allah's statement,

(Verily, the Hour is coming) This means that it is established and there is no avoiding it. It will be and it is inevitable. Concerning Allah's statement,

(I am almost hiding it) Ad-Dahhak related from Ibn `Abbas that he used to recite it as, "I almost kept it hidden -- from myself." Ibn `Abbas then would say, "Because nothing is ever hidden from Allah's Self." `Ali bin Abi Talhah reported from Ibn `Abbas that he said,

(I am almost hiding it.) "This means that no one knows its appointed time except Me (Allah)." Allah also said,

(Heavy is its burden through the heavens and the earth. It shall not come upon you except all of a sudden.) (7:187) This means that its knowledge weighs heavily upon the dwellers of the heavens and the earth. Concerning Allah's statement,

(that every person may be rewarded for that which he strives.) "I will establish it and it is inevitable. I will certainly reward every person who does something, according to what he did."

(So whosoever does good equal to the weight of an atom shall see it. And whosoever does evil equal to the weight of an atom shall see it.) (99:7-8)

(You are only being requited for what you used to do.) (52:16) Allah said,

(Therefore, let not divert you the one who believes not therein,) The address here is directed towards all individuals who are responsible (and capable of taking heed to this message). This means, "Do not follow the way of the person who does not believe in the Hour (Day of Judgement) and he only pursues his desires in this worldly life. He disobeys his Lord and only follows his desires. Whoever behaves like these people, then verily he has failed and lost.

(lest you perish.) This means that you will be destroyed and ruined.

(And what will his wealth avail him when he goes down (in destruction)) (92:11)

Surah: 20 Ayah: 17, Ayah: 18, Ayah: 19, Ayah: 20 & Ayah: 21

وَمَا تِلْكَ بِيَمِينِكَ يَـٰمُوسَىٰ

17. "And what is that in your right hand, O Mûsa (Moses)?"

قَالَ هِىَ عَصَاىَ أَتَوَكَّؤُاْ عَلَيْهَا وَأَهُشُّ بِهَا عَلَىٰ غَنَمِى وَلِىَ فِيهَا مَـَٔارِبُ أُخْرَىٰ

18. He said: "This is my stick, whereon I lean, and wherewith I beat down branches for my sheep, and wherein I find other uses."

قَالَ أَلْقِهَا يَـٰمُوسَىٰ

19. (Allâh) said: "Cast it down, O Mûsa (Moses)!"

فَأَلْقَىٰهَا فَإِذَا هِىَ حَيَّةٌ تَسْعَىٰ

20. He cast it down, and behold! It was a snake, moving quickly.

قَالَ خُذْهَا وَلَا تَخَفْ سَنُعِيدُهَا سِيرَتَهَا ٱلْأُولَىٰ

21. Allâh said: "Grasp it and fear not; We shall return it to its former state,

Chapter 20: Ta-Ha (Ta-Ha), Verses 001-135

Transliteration

17. Wama tilka biyameenika ya moosa 18. Qala hiya AAasaya atawakkao AAalayha waahushshu biha AAala ghanamee waliya feeha maaribu okhra 19. Qala alqiha ya moosa 20. Faalqaha fa-itha hiya hayyatun tasAAa 21. Qala khuthha wala takhaf sanuAAeeduha seerataha al-oola

Tafsir Ibn Kathir

The Stick of Musa turned into a Snake

This was a proof from Allah for Musa and a great miracle. This was something that broke through the boundaries of what is considered normal, thus, it was a brilliant evidence that none but Allah could do. It was also a proof that no one could come with the likes of this (from mankind) except a Prophet who was sent (by Allah). Concerning Allah's statement,

(And what is that in your right hand, O Musa) Some of the scholars of Tafsir have said, "He (Allah) only said this to him in order to draw his attention to it." It has also been said, "He only said this to him in order to affirm for him what was in his hand. In other words, that which is in your right hand is a stick that you are familiar with. You will see what We are about to do to it now."

(And what is that in your right hand, O Musa) This is an interrogative phrase for the purpose of affirmation.

(He said: "This is my stick, whereon I lean...") I lean on it while I am walking.

(and wherewith I beat down branches for my sheep,) This means, `I use it to shake the branches of trees so that the leaves will fall for my sheep to eat them. ' `Abdur-Rahman bin Al-Qasim reported from Imam Malik that he said, "(It is) when a man places his staff into a branch and shakes it so that its leaves and fruit will fall without breaking the stick. It is not the same as striking or beating." Maymun bin Mahran also said the same. Concerning his statement,

(and wherein I find other uses.) This means other benefits, services and needs besides this. Some of the scholars took upon themselves the burden of mentioning many of these obscure uses. Concerning Allah's statement,

((Allah) said: "Cast it down, O Musa!") "Throw down this stick that is in your right hand, O Musa."

(He cast it down, and behold! It was a snake, moving quickly.) This means that the stick changed into a huge snake, like a long python, and it moved with rapid movements. It moved as if it were the fastest type of small snake. Yet, it was in the form of the largest snake, while still having the fastest of movements.

(moving quickly.) moving restlessly. Concerning Allah's statement,

(We shall return it to its former state.) the form that it was in, as you recognized it before.

Surah: 20 Ayah: 22, Ayah: 23, Ayah: 24, Ayah: 25, Ayah: 26, Ayah: 27, Ayah: 28, Ayah: 29, Ayah: 30, Ayah: 31, Ayah: 32, Ayah: 33, Ayah: 34 & Ayah: 35

وَٱضْمُمْ يَدَكَ إِلَىٰ جَنَاحِكَ تَخْرُجْ بَيْضَآءَ مِنْ غَيْرِ سُوٓءٍ ءَايَةً أُخْرَىٰ ۝

22. "And press your (right) hand to your (left) side: it will come forth white (and shining), without any disease as another sign,

لِنُرِيَكَ مِنْ ءَايَـٰتِنَا ٱلْكُبْرَىٰ ۝

23. "That We may show you (some) of Our Greater Signs.

ٱذْهَبْ إِلَىٰ فِرْعَوْنَ إِنَّهُۥ طَغَىٰ ۝

24. "Go to Fir'aun (Pharaoh)! Verily, he has transgressed (all bounds in disbelief and disobedience, and has behaved as an arrogant and as a tyrant)."

قَالَ رَبِّ ٱشْرَحْ لِى صَدْرِى ۝

25. (Mûsa (Moses)) said: "O my Lord! Open for me my chest (grant me self-confidence, contentment, and boldness).

وَيَسِّرْ لِىٓ أَمْرِى ۝

26. "And ease my task for me;

وَٱحْلُلْ عُقْدَةً مِّن لِّسَانِى ۝

27. "And make loose the knot (the defect) from my tongue, (i.e. remove the incorrectness from my speech) (That occurred as a result of a brand of fire which Mûsa (Moses) put in his mouth when he was an infant). (Tafsir At-Tabarî).

يَفْقَهُوا۟ قَوْلِى ۝

28. "That they understand my speech.

وَٱجْعَل لِّى وَزِيرًا مِّنْ أَهْلِى ۝

29. "And appoint for me a helper from my family,

هَـٰرُونَ أَخِى ۝

30. "Hârûn (Aaron), my brother.

ٱشْدُدْ بِهِۦٓ أَزْرِى ۝

31. "Increase my strength with him,

وَأَشْرِكْهُ فِي أَمْرِي ﴿٣٢﴾

32. "And let him share my task (of conveying Allâh's Message and Prophethood),

كَيْ نُسَبِّحَكَ كَثِيرًا ﴿٣٣﴾

33. "That we may glorify You much,

وَنَذْكُرَكَ كَثِيرًا ﴿٣٤﴾

34. "And remember You much,

إِنَّكَ كُنتَ بِنَا بَصِيرًا ﴿٣٥﴾

35. "Verily! You are Ever a Well-Seer of us."

Transliteration

22. Waodmum yadaka ila janahika takhruj baydaa min ghayri soo-in ayatan okhra 23. Linuriyaka min ayatina alkubra 24. Ithhab ila firAAawna innahu tagha 25. Qala rabbi ishrah lee sadree 26. Wayassir lee amree 27. Waohlul AAuqdatan min lisanee 28. Yafqahoo qawlee 29. WaijAAal lee wazeeran min ahlee 30. Haroona akhee 31. Oshdud bihi azree 32. Waashrik-hu fee amree 33. Kay nusabbihaka katheeran 34. Wanathkuraka katheeran 35. Innaka kunta bina baseeran

Tafsir Ibn Kathir

The Hand of Musa turning White without any Disease

This is the second sign of Musa. That is Allah has commanded him to place his hand into the opening of his garment, as is clearly stated in another Ayah. It mentioned here merely as a passing reference, saying:

(And press your hand to your side:) Allah said in another Ayah,

(And draw your hand close to your side to be free from fear. These are two signs from your Lord to Fir`awn and his chiefs.) (28:32) Mujahid said,

(And press your hand to your side:) "This means put your palm under your upper arm." When Musa put his hand into the opening of his garment and brought it out, it came out shining as if it were a half moon. Concerning His statement,

(it will come forth white, without any disease) This means without any leprosy, ailment, or disfigurement. This was stated by Ibn `Abbas, Mujahid, `Ikrimah, Qatadah, Ad-Dahhak, As-Suddi and others. Al-Hasan Al-Basri said, "He brought it out, and by Allah, it was as if it were a lamp. From this Musa knew that he had surely met his Lord, the Mighty and Sublime." This is why Allah says,

(That We may show you (some) of Our greater signs.)

Allah commanded Musa to go to Fir`awn to convey the Message. Allah said,

(Go to Fir`awn! Verily, he has transgressed.) This means, "Go to Fir`awn, the king of Egypt, whom you left Egypt fleeing from, and invite him to the worship of Allah alone, Who has no partners. Command him to treat the Children of Israel well and to not torment them. For verily, he has transgressed, oppressed, preferred the worldly life and forgotten the Most High Lord."

The Supplication of Musa

((Musa) said: "O my Lord! Open for me my chest, and ease my task for me.") Musa requsted his Lord to expand his chest for his mission. For verily, He was commanding him with a great task and a weighty affair. He was sending him to the mightiest king on the face of the earth at that time. He was the most arrogant and severe of all people in his disbelief, and He had the largest army and the most powerful kingdom. He was the most tyrannical and the most obstinate of rulers. His case was such that he claimed not to know Allah at all, and that he knew of no god for his subjects other than himself. Along with this, Musa lived in his home for a period of time as a child. He stayed in Fir`awn's own room and slept on his bed. Then, after this, he killed one of their people and feared that they would retaliate by killing him in return. Thus, he fled from them and remained an outlaw during this entire time. Then, after all of this, His Lord sent him to them as a warner calling them to worship Allah alone, without associating partners with Him. This is why he said,

(O my Lord! Open for me my chest, and ease my task for me.) This means, "I cannot perform this task if You do not help me, aid me and support me."

(And loosen the knot from my tongue, that they understand my speech.) This is referring to the lisp that he had. This lisp was a result of an incident when he was presented a date and a hot coal stone and he placed the coal on his tongue instead of the date. A detailed explanation of this story is forthcoming in the following chapters. However, he did not ask Allah to remove this affliction all together. Rather, he asked for removal of his stammering so the people would understand what he intended in his speech. He was only asking for what was necessary to deliver his message. If he had asked for the removal of his affliction in its entirety, it would have been cured for him. However, the Prophets do not ask for any more than what is required. Therefore, he was left with the remnants of this accident that took place with his tongue. Allah informed of what Fir`awn said concerning him,

(Am I not better than this one who is despicable and can scarcely express himself clearly)(43:52) This means that he is not eloquent in speech. Concerning Allah's statement,

(And appoint for me a helper from my family, Harun, my brother.) This was also a request from Musa concerning something not pertaining to himself. That was his request for the assistance of his brother, Harun. Ath-Thawri reported from Abu Sa`id, from `Ikrimah, who said that Ibn `Abbas said, "Harun was made a Prophet at the same moment that Musa was made a Prophet." Ibn Abi Hatim recorded that `A'ishah went out intending to perform `Umrah and stopped to camp among some bedouins. While she was among them she heard a man say, "Which brother in this life was the most beneficial to his brother" The people said, "We do not know." The man said, "By Allah, I know." `A'ishah said, "I said to myself about his swearing, that he should not swear such an oath, singling himself out as knowing what person was of most benefit to his brother." The man said, "It is Musa, when he asked for prophethood to be bestowed upon his brother." Then `A'ishah said, "By Allah, he has spoken truthfully." This is why Allah commended Musa by saying,

(And he was honorable before Allah.)(33:69) Concerning Musa's statement,

(Increase my strength with him.) Mujahid said, "This means to make my back strong."

(And let him share my task.) make him my consultant in this matter.

(That we may glorify You much, and remember You much.) Mujahid said, "A servant of Allah is not considered of those who remember Allah much until he remembers Allah while standing, sitting and lying down." Concerning his statement,

(Verily, You are ever seeing us.) This means in Your choosing us, giving us the prophethood and sending us to Your enemy, Fir`awn. So unto You is all praise for this.

Surah: 20 Ayah: 36, Ayah: 37, Ayah: 38, Ayah: 39 & Ayah: 40

قَالَ قَدْ أُوتِيتَ سُؤْلَكَ يَٰمُوسَىٰ ۝

36. Allâh said: "You are granted your request, O Mûsa (Moses)!

وَلَقَدْ مَنَنَّا عَلَيْكَ مَرَّةً أُخْرَىٰ ۝

37. "And indeed We conferred a favor on you another time (before).

إِذْ أَوْحَيْنَآ إِلَىٰٓ أُمِّكَ مَا يُوحَىٰٓ ۝

38. "When We inspired your mother with that which We inspired.

أَنِ ٱقْذِفِيهِ فِى ٱلتَّابُوتِ فَٱقْذِفِيهِ فِى ٱلْيَمِّ فَلْيُلْقِهِ ٱلْيَمُّ بِٱلسَّاحِلِ يَأْخُذْهُ عَدُوٌّ لِّى وَعَدُوٌّ لَّهُۥ ۚ وَأَلْقَيْتُ عَلَيْكَ مَحَبَّةً مِّنِّى وَلِتُصْنَعَ عَلَىٰ عَيْنِىٓ ۝

39. "Saying: 'Put him (the child) into the Tabût (a box or a case or a chest) and put it into the river (Nile); then the river shall cast it up on the bank, and there, an enemy of Mine and an enemy of his shall take him.' And I endued you with love from Me, in order that you may be brought up under My Eye.

إِذْ تَمْشِىٓ أُخْتُكَ فَتَقُولُ هَلْ أَدُلُّكُمْ عَلَىٰ مَن يَكْفُلُهُۥ ۖ فَرَجَعْنَـٰكَ إِلَىٰٓ أُمِّكَ كَىْ تَقَرَّ عَيْنُهَا وَلَا تَحْزَنَ ۚ وَقَتَلْتَ نَفْسًا فَنَجَّيْنَـٰكَ مِنَ ٱلْغَمِّ وَفَتَنَّـٰكَ فُتُونًا ۚ فَلَبِثْتَ سِنِينَ فِىٓ أَهْلِ مَدْيَنَ ثُمَّ جِئْتَ عَلَىٰ قَدَرٍ يَـٰمُوسَىٰ ۝

40. "When your sister went and said: 'Shall I show you one who will nurse him?' So We restored you to your mother, that she might cool her eyes and she should not grieve. Then you did kill a man, but We saved you from great distress and tried you with a heavy trial. Then you stayed a number of years with the people of Madyan (Midian). Then you came here according to the fixed term which I ordained (for you), O Mûsa (Moses)!

Transliteration

36. Qala qad ooteeta su/laka ya moosa 37. Walaqad mananna AAalayka marratan okhra 38. Ith awhayna ila ommika ma yooha 39. Ani iqthifeehi fee alttabooti faiqthifeehi fee alyammi falyulqihi alyammu bialssahili ya/khuthhu AAaduwwun lee waAAaduwwun lahu waalqaytu AAalayka mahabbatan minnee walitusnaAAa AAala Aaaynee 40. Ith tamshee okhtuka fataqoolu hal adullukum AAala man yakfuluhu farajaAAnaka ila ommika kay taqarra AAaynuha wala tahzana waqatalta nafsan fanajjaynaka mina alghammi wafatannaka futoonan falabithta sineena fee ahli madyana thumma ji/ta AAala qadarin ya moosa

Tafsir Ibn Kathir

Glad Tidings of the acceptance of Musa's Supplication and the Reminder of the Previous Blessings

This is a response from Allah to His Messenger, Musa, for what he requested from His Lord. It also contains a reminder of Allah's previous favors upon him. The first was inspiring his mother when she was breastfeeding him and she feared that Fir`awn and his chiefs would kill him. Musa was born during a year in which they (Fir`awn's people) were killing all of the male children. So she placed him in a case and cast him into the river. The river carried him away and she became grieved and distressed, as Allah mentioned about her when He said,

(And the heart of the mother of Musa became empty. She was very near to disclose his (case) had We not strengthened her heart.) (28:10) So the river carried him to the home of Fir`awn.

(Then the people of Fir`awn picked him up, that he might become for them an enemy and a (cause of) grief.) (28:8) Means that this was a destined matter, decreed by Allah. They were killing the male children of the Israelites for fear of Musa's arrival. Therefore, with Allah having the great authority and the most perfect power, He determined that Musa would not be raised except upon Fir`awn's own bed. He would be sustained by Fir`awn's food and drink, while receiving the love of Fir`awn and his wife. This is why Allah said,

Chapter 20: Ta-Ha (Ta-Ha), Verses 001-135

(and there, an enemy of Mine and an enemy of his shall take him. And I endued you with love from Me,) This means that I made your enemy love you. Salamah bin Kuhayl said,

(And I endued you with love from Me,) "This means, `I made My creatures love you.'"

(in order that you may be brought up under My Eye.) Abu `Imran Al-Jawni said, "This means, `You will be raised under Allah's Eye.'" Concerning Allah's statement,

(When your sister went and said: `Shall I show you one who will nurse him' So We restored you to your mother, that she might cool her eyes) When he was accepted into the house of Fir`awn, women were brought in attempts to find someone who might be able to nurse him. But he refused to breast feed from any of them. Allah, the Exalted, says,

(And We had already forbidden (other) foster suckling mothers for him) (28:12) Then, his sister came and said, (Shall I direct you to a household who will rear him for you, and look after him in a good manner) (28:12) She meant, "Shall I guide you to someone who can nurse him for you for a fee" So she took him and they went with her to his real mother. When her breast was presented to him, he took it and they (Fir`awn's family) were extremely happy for this. Thus, they hired her to nurse him and she achieved great happiness and comfort because of him, in this life and even more so in the Hereafter. Allah, the Exalted, says here,

(So We restored you to your mother, that she might cool her eyes and she should not grieve.) This means that she should not grieve over you.

(Then you killed man,) This means that he killed a Coptic person (the people of Egypt, Fir`awn's people).

(but We saved you from great distress) This is what he was feeling due to Fir`awn's family intending to kill him. So he fled from them until he came to the water of the people of Madyan. This is when the righteous man said to him, (Fear you not. You have escaped from the people who are wrongdoers.) (28:25)

Surah: 20 Ayah: 40, Ayah: 41, Ayah: 42, Ayah: 43 & Ayah: 44

إِذْ تَمْشِىٓ أُخْتُكَ فَتَقُولُ هَلْ أَدُلُّكُمْ عَلَىٰ مَن يَكْفُلُهُۥ ۖ فَرَجَعْنَٰكَ إِلَىٰٓ أُمِّكَ كَىْ تَقَرَّ عَيْنُهَا وَلَا تَحْزَنَ ۚ وَقَتَلْتَ نَفْسًا فَنَجَّيْنَٰكَ مِنَ ٱلْغَمِّ وَفَتَنَّٰكَ فُتُونًا ۚ فَلَبِثْتَ سِنِينَ فِىٓ أَهْلِ مَدْيَنَ ثُمَّ جِئْتَ عَلَىٰ قَدَرٍ يَٰمُوسَىٰ ۟

40. "When your sister went and said: 'Shall I show you one who will nurse him?' So We restored you to your mother, that she might cool her eyes and she should not grieve. Then you did kill a man, but We saved you from great distress and tried you with a heavy trial. Then you stayed a number of years with the people

of Madyan (Midian). Then you came here according to the fixed term which I ordained (for you), O Mûsa (Moses)!

$$ وَٱصْطَنَعْتُكَ لِنَفْسِى ﴿٤١﴾ $$

41. "And I have chosen you, for Myself.

$$ ٱذْهَبْ أَنتَ وَأَخُوكَ بِـَٔايَـٰتِى وَلَا تَنِيَا فِى ذِكْرِى ﴿٤٢﴾ $$

42. "Go you and your brother with My Ayât (proofs, evidences, verses, lessons, signs, revelations, etc.), and do not, you both, slacken and become weak in My Remembrance.

$$ ٱذْهَبَآ إِلَىٰ فِرْعَوْنَ إِنَّهُۥ طَغَىٰ ﴿٤٣﴾ $$

43. "Go, both of you, to Fir'aun (Pharaoh), verily, he has transgressed (all bounds in disbelief and disobedience and behaved as an arrogant and as a tyrant).

$$ فَقُولَا لَهُۥ قَوْلًا لَّيِّنًا لَّعَلَّهُۥ يَتَذَكَّرُ أَوْ يَخْشَىٰ ﴿٤٤﴾ $$

44. "And speak to him mildly, perhaps he may accept admonition or fear Allâh."

Transliteration

40. Ith tamshee okhtuka fataqoolu hal adullukum AAala man yakfuluhu farajaAAnaka ila ommika kay taqarra AAaynuha wala tahzana waqatalta nafsan fanajjaynaka mina alghammi wafatannaka futoonan falabithta sineena fee ahli madyana thumma ji/ta AAala qadarin ya moosa 41. WaistanaAAtuka linafsee 42. Ithhab anta waakhooka bi-ayatee wala taniya fee thikree 43. Ithhaba ila firAAawna innahu tagha 44. Faqoola lahu qawlan layyinan laAAallahu yatathakkaru aw yakhsha

Tafsir Ibn Kathir

Choosing Musa to go to Fir`awn and to be Soft and Gentle in His Invitation

Allah, the Exalted, says in His address to Musa that he had lived among the people of Madyan, avoiding Fir`awn and his chiefs. He worked as a shepherd for his father-in-law until the appointed time for his work ended. Then he met the decree of Allah and His predetermined will, without him having any set appointment. This entire situation was under the control of Allah, Blessed be He, the Most High. He compels His servants and His creatures to whatever end He wills. This is why Allah says,

(Then You came here according to the fixed term which I ordained (for you), O Musa!) Mujahid said, "For a set appointment." `Abdur-Razzaq recorded that Ma`mar reported from Qatadah that he said,

(Then You came here according to the fixed term which I ordained (for you), O Musa!) "For the decree of messengership and prophethood." Concerning Allah's statement,

(And I have chosen you for Myself.) This means, "I have chosen you and selected you to be a Messenger for Myself. This is as I wish and according to My will." Concerning the Tafsir of this Ayah, Al-Bukhari recorded that Abu Hurayrah said that the Messenger of Allah said,

«الْتَقَى آدَمُ وَمُوسَى فَقَالَ مُوسَى: أَنْتَ الَّذِي أَشْقَيْتَ النَّاسَ وَأَخْرَجْتَهُمْ مِنَ الْجَنَّةِ، فَقَالَ آدَمُ: وَأَنْتَ الَّذِي اصْطَفَاكَ اللهُ بِرِسَالَتِهِ وَاصْطَفَاكَ لِنَفْسِهِ، وَأَنْزَلَ عَلَيْكَ التَّوْرَاةَ؟ قَالَ: نَعَمْ، قَالَ: فَوَجَدْتَهُ مَكْتُوبًا عَلَيَّ قَبْلَ أَنْ يَخْلُقَنِي؟ قَالَ: نَعَمْ، فَحَجَّ آدَمُ مُوسَى»

(Adam and Musa met, and Musa said, "You are the one who made things difficult for mankind and you caused them to be evicted from Paradise." Adam said, "Are you the one whom Allah chose for His Message, and He selected you for Himself and He revealed the Tawrah to you" Musa replied, "Yes." Then Adam said, "Did you find that it was preordained upon me before He (Allah) created me" Musa replied, "Yes." Therefore, Adam defeated Musa's argument.) Both Al-Bukhari and Muslim recorded this narration. Concerning Allah's statement,

(Go you and your brother with My Ayat,) This means with My proofs, evidences and miracles.

(And do not, you both, slacken and become weak in My remembrance.) `Ali bin Abi Talhah related from Ibn `Abbas that he said, "This means do not be slow." Mujahid reported that Ibn `Abbas said, "This means do not be weak." The meaning here is that they should not slacken in the remembrance of Allah. Rather, they both should remember Allah during their meeting with Fir`awn so that the remembrance of Allah can be an aid for them against him. The remembrance of Allah would be their strength and their power that would defeat him. Allah's statement;

(Go both of you to Fir`awn, Verily, he has transgressed.) means that he has rebelled and become haughty and insolent against Allah and he has disobeyed Him.

(And speak to him mildly, perhaps he may accept admonition or fear (Allah).) This Ayah contains a great lesson. Even though Fir`awn was the most insolent and arrogant of people and Musa was the friend of Allah among His creation at that time, Musa was still commanded to speak to Fir`awn with mildness and softness. Therefore, their invitation to him was with gentle, soft and easy speech that is used by one who is a close friend. This is so that the message may have more effect on the souls, and so it would have deeper and more beneficial results. This is as Allah, the Exalted, says,

(Invite (mankind) to the way of your Lord with wisdom and fair preaching, and argue with them in a way that is better.) (16:125) Concerning Allah's statement, (perhaps he may accept admonition or fear (Allah).) This means that perhaps he will recant from that which he is in of misguidance and destruction,

(or he will fear) meaning that he will become obedient due to fear of Allah. This is as Allah says,

(For such who desires to remember or desires to show his gratitude.) (25:62) Thus, to remember means to recant from that which is dangerous, and fear means to attain obedience.

Surah: 20 Ayah: 45, Ayah: 46, Ayah: 47 & Ayah: 48

قَالَا رَبَّنَآ إِنَّنَا نَخَافُ أَن يَفْرُطَ عَلَيْنَآ أَوْ أَن يَطْغَىٰ ﴿٤٥﴾

45. They said: "Our Lord! Verily we fear lest he should hasten to punish us or lest he should transgress (all bounds against us)."

قَالَ لَا تَخَافَآ إِنَّنِي مَعَكُمَآ أَسْمَعُ وَأَرَىٰ ﴿٤٦﴾

46. He (Allâh) said: "Fear not, verily I am with you both, hearing and seeing.

فَأْتِيَاهُ فَقُولَآ إِنَّا رَسُولَا رَبِّكَ فَأَرْسِلْ مَعَنَا بَنِىٓ إِسْرَٰٓءِيلَ وَلَا تُعَذِّبْهُمْ قَدْ جِئْنَٰكَ بِـَٔايَةٍ مِّن رَّبِّكَ وَٱلسَّلَٰمُ عَلَىٰ مَنِ ٱتَّبَعَ ٱلْهُدَىٰٓ ﴿٤٧﴾

47. "So go you both to him, and say: 'Verily, we are Messengers of your Lord, so let the Children of Israel go with us, and torment them not; indeed, we have come with a sign from your Lord! And peace will be upon him who follows the guidance!

إِنَّا قَدْ أُوحِىَ إِلَيْنَآ أَنَّ ٱلْعَذَابَ عَلَىٰ مَن كَذَّبَ وَتَوَلَّىٰ ﴿٤٨﴾

48. 'Truly, it has been revealed to us that the torment will be for him who denies (believes not in the Oneness of Allâh, and in His Messengers.), and turns away (from the truth and obedience of Allâh)"

Transliteration

45. Qala rabbana innana nakhafu an yafruta AAalayna aw an yatgha 46. Qala la takhafa innanee maAAakuma asmaAAu waara 47. Fa/tiyahu faqoola inna rasoola rabbika faarsil maAAana banee isra-eela wala tuAAaththibhum qad ji/naka bi-ayatin min rabbika waalssalamu AAala mani ittabaAAa alhuda 48. Inna qad oohiya ilayna anna alAAathaba AAala man kaththaba watawalla

Tafsir Ibn Kathir

Musa's fear of Fir`awn and Allah's strengthening Him

Allah, the Exalted, informs that Musa and Harun pleaded to Allah, expressing their grievance to him:

(Verily, we fear lest he should hasten to punish us or lest he should transgress.) They meant that Fir`awn might seize them unexpectedly with a punishment, or transgress against them by tormenting them, when they actually did not deserve it. Ad-Dahhak reported from Ibn `Abbas that he said that transgress here means, "To exceed the bounds."

(He (Allah) said: "Fear not, verily, I am with you both, hearing and seeing.") meaning; "Do not fear him (Fir`awn), for verily, I am with you and I hear your speech and his speech as well. I see your place and I see his place as well. Nothing is hidden from Me of your affair. Know that his forehead is in My Hand, and he does not speak, breathe, or use any force, except by My leave and after My command. I am with you by My protection, My help and My support."

(So go you both to him, and say: "Verily, we are both Messengers of your Lord...")

Musa admonishes Fir`awn

Concerning his statement,

(indeed, We have come with a sign from your Lord!) meaning with evidence and a miracle from your Lord.

(And peace will be upon him who follows the guidance!) meaning, `peace be upon you if you follow the guidance.' Because of this, when the Messenger of Allah wrote a letter to Heraclius, the emperor of Rome, beginning with,

«بِسْمِ اللهِ الرَّحْمَنِ الرَّحِيمِ، مِنْ مُحَمَّدٍ رَسُولِ اللهِ إِلَى هِرَقْلَ عَظِيمِ الرُّومِ، سَلَامٌ عَلَى مَنِ اتَّبَعَ الْهُدَى، أَمَّا بَعْدُ، فَإِنِّي أَدْعُوكَ بِدِعَايَةِ الْإِسْلَامِ، فَأَسْلِمْ تَسْلَمْ يُؤْتِكَ اللهُ أَجْرَكَ مَرَّتَيْنِ»

(In the Name of Allah, the Most Gracious, the Most Merciful. From Muhammad, the Messenger of Allah, to Heraclius the emperor of Rome. Peace be upon him who follows the guidance. Thus, to proceed: Verily, I invite you with the invitation of Islam. So accept Islam and you will be safe, and Allah will give you a double reward.) Due to this, Musa and Harun said to Fir`awn,

(And peace will be upon him who follows the guidance! Truly, it has been revealed to us that the torment will be for him who denies, and turns away.) In His flawless revelation, Allah has revealed to us that torment is prepared exclusively for those who reject the signs of Allah and turn away from His obedience. As Allah says,

(Then for him who transgressed all bounds, and preferred the life of this world, Verily, his abode will be Hellfire.) (79:37-39) Allah, the Exalted, also says,

(Therefore I have warned you of a blazing Fire. None shall enter it save the most wretched. Who denies and turns away.) (92:14-16) Allah also says,

(So he neither believed nor prayed! But on the contrary, he belied and turned away.) (75:31-32) This means that he denied with his heart and turned away by his actions.

Surah: 20 Ayah: 49, Ayah: 50, Ayah: 51 & Ayah: 52

$$قَالَ فَمَن رَّبُّكُمَا يَـٰمُوسَىٰ ۝$$

49. Fir'aun (Pharaoh) said: "Who then, O Mûsa (Moses), is the Lord of you two?"

$$قَالَ رَبُّنَا ٱلَّذِىٓ أَعْطَىٰ كُلَّ شَىْءٍ خَلْقَهُ ثُمَّ هَدَىٰ ۝$$

50. (Mûsa (Moses)) said: "Our Lord is He Who gave to each thing its form and nature, then guided it aright."

$$قَالَ فَمَا بَالُ ٱلْقُرُونِ ٱلْأُولَىٰ ۝$$

51. (Fir'aun (Pharaoh)) said: "What about the generations of old?"

$$قَالَ عِلْمُهَا عِندَ رَبِّى فِى كِتَـٰبٍ لَّا يَضِلُّ رَبِّى وَلَا يَنسَى ۝$$

52. (Mûsa (Moses)) said: "The knowledge thereof is with my Lord, in a Record. My Lord neither errs nor He forgets, "

Transliteration

49. Qala faman rabbukuma ya moosa 50. Qala rabbuna allathee aAAta kulla shay-in khalqahu thumma hada 51. Qala fama balu alquroni al-oola 52. Qala AAilmuha AAinda rabbee fee kitabin la yadillu rabbee wala yansa

Tafsir Ibn Kathir

The Conversation between Musa and Fir`awn

Allah, the Exalted, informs about Fir`awn that he said to Musa, in his rejection of the existence of a Supreme Maker and Creator, Who is the God of everything and his own Lord and Owner:

(Who then, O Musa, is the Lord of you two) meaning "Who is the one who called you forth and sent you For verily, I do not know him and I have not given you any god other than myself."

((Musa) said: "Our Lord is He Who gave to each thing its form and nature, then guided it aright.") `Ali bin Abi Talhah related that Ibn `Abbas said, "He is saying that He created a mate for everything." Ad-Dahhak said that Ibn `Abbas said, "He made the man a man, and the donkey a donkey and the sheep a sheep." Layth bin Abi Sulaym reported from Mujahid that he said, "He gave everything its form." Ibn Abi Najih said that Mujahid said, "He fashioned the creation of every moving creature." Sa`id bin Jubayr said concerning His statement,

((Who) gave to each thing its form and nature, then guided it aright.) "He gave each of His creatures what is suitable for its creation." Therefore, He did not give man the form of a wild beast, nor did He give wild beasts the form of the dog. Likewise, the dog's form is not like the sheep's. He also gave creature a suitable spouse, and He influenced everything towards that mate. There is no species of creation that is exactly like another species. They are different in their actions, their forms, their sustenance and their mating. Some of the scholars of Tafsir have said that this statement, "He gave to each thing its form and nature, then guided it aright," is similar to Allah's statement,

(And Who has measured; and then guided.) (87:3) This means He measured out an ordained amount (of sustenance, actions, etc.) and then guided His creatures to it. He wrote the deeds, the appointed times of death and the provisions. Then, the creatures traverse upon that and they are not able to avoid it, nor are they able to abandon it. In this Ayah Musa is saying that our Lord is the One Who created the creation, measured out its ordainment and compelled the creatures to that which He wanted.

((Fir`awn) said: "What about the generations of old"') The most correct opinion concerning the meaning of this, is that when Musa informed Fir`awn that his Lord Who sent him is the One Who creates, sustains, ordains and guides, Fir`awn began to argue, using the previous generations as a proof. He was referring to those people of old who did not worship Allah. In other words, "If the matter is as you say, then what happened to those people They did not worship your Lord. Instead they worshipped other gods besides Him." Musa said to him, in response to this, that if they did not worship Allah, then Allah knows precisely what happened to them and He will give them just recompense for their deeds, as is written in Allah's Book (of decrees). This Book is called Al-Lawh Al-Mahfuz (The Preserved Tablet) and it is the Book of Deeds.

(My Lord neither errs nor forgets.) This means that nothing eludes Him and He does not miss anything, whether it is small or great. He does not forget anything and His Most Exalted knowledge is described as encompassing everything. Blessed be He, the Exalted, the Most Holy and free of any imperfections. The knowledge that creatures have has two deficiencies. The first is that it does not completely encompass anything, and the second is that the creature is prone to forget after knowing. Therefore, Allah has declared Himself above such deficiencies.

Surah: 20 Ayah: 53, Ayah: 54, Ayah: 55 & Ayah: 56

ٱلَّذِى جَعَلَ لَكُمُ ٱلْأَرْضَ مَهْدًا وَسَلَكَ لَكُمْ فِيهَا سُبُلًا وَأَنزَلَ مِنَ ٱلسَّمَآءِ مَآءً فَأَخْرَجْنَا بِهِۦٓ أَزْوَٰجًا مِّن نَّبَاتٍ شَتَّىٰ ۝

53. Who has made earth for you like a bed (spread out); and has opened roads (ways and paths) for you therein, and has sent down water (rain) from the sky. And We have brought forth with it various kinds of vegetation.

كُلُواْ وَٱرْعَوْاْ أَنْعَٰمَكُمْ إِنَّ فِى ذَٰلِكَ لَءَايَٰتٍ لِّأُوْلِى ٱلنُّهَىٰ ۝

54. Eat and pasture your cattle (therein); verily, in this are Ayât (proofs and signs) for men of understanding.

مِنْهَا خَلَقْنَـكُمْ وَفِيهَا نُعِيدُكُمْ وَمِنْهَا نُخْرِجُكُمْ تَارَةً أُخْرَى

55. Thereof (the earth) We created you, and into it We shall return you, and from it We shall bring you out once again.

وَلَقَدْ أَرَيْنَـهُ ءَايَـتِنَا كُلَّهَا فَكَذَّبَ وَأَبَى

56. And indeed We showed him (Fir'aun (Pharaoh)) all Our Ayât (proofs and signs), but he denied and refused.

Transliteration

53. Allathee jaAAala lakumu al-arda mahdan wasalaka lakum feeha subulan waanzala mina alssama-i maan faakhrajna bihi azwajan min nabatin shatta 54. Kuloo wairAAaw anAAamakum inna fee thalika laayatin li-olee alnnuha 55. Minha khalaqnakum wafeeha nuAAeedukum waminha nukhrijukum taratan okhra 56. Walaqad araynahu ayatina kullaha fakaththaba waaba

Tafsir Ibn Kathir

The Completion of Musa's Reply to Fir`awn

This is from the completion of Musa's speech concerning the description of His Lord when Fir`awn asked him about Him. He (Musa) said,

(He Who gave to each thing its form and nature, then guided it aright.) Then, Fir`awn attempted to present some argumentative rebuttal during Musa's reply. Yet, Musa continued by saying, "He is the One Who made the earth as a bed for you." Some recited the word as Mihadan and others recited it as Mahdan, which means `a place of rest that you settle down upon.' It also may mean `that which you stand upon, sleep upon or travel upon its back.'

(and has opened ways for you therein.) This means, `He made roads for you to walk upon their shoulders.' This is just as He, the Exalted, said,

(And placed therein broad highways for them to pass through, that they may be guided.) (21:31)

(and has sent down water from the sky. And We have brought forth with it various kinds of vegetation.) referring to the various species of plants, such as vegetation and fruits. Some are sour, some are sweet, some are bitter and there are other kinds as well.

(Eat and pasture your cattle (therein);) meaning, `something that is food for you and a palatable fruit for you, and something that is for your cattle as fodder for them, both green and dry.'

(Verily, in this are Ayat.) This means proofs, signs and evidences.

(for men of understanding.) meaning those who possess correct and upright intelligence realizing that there is no god worthy of worship except Allah, and there is no true Lord other than Him.

(Thereof We created you, and into it we shall return you, and from it We shall bring you out once again.) meaning, `the earth is your beginning. For your father, Adam, was created with dirt from the surface of the earth. You also will be returned to the earth. This means that you will become dirt when you die and decay.' The statement, "And from it We shall bring you out once again," means,

(On the Day when He will call you, and you will answer with His praise and obedience, and you will think that you have stayed (in this world) but a little while!) (17:52) This Ayah is similar to Allah's statement,

(He said: "Therein you shall live, and therein you shall die, and from it you shall be brought out.") (7:25)

Musa showed Fir`awn all of the Signs but He did not believe Concerning Allah's statement,

(And indeed We showed him (Fir`awn) all Our Ayat, but he denied and refused.) This means that the proofs, signs and evi- dences were establi- shed against Fir`awn and he saw them with his own eyes, but he still denied and rejec- ted them due to his disbelief, abstinence and transgression. This is as Allah, the Exalted, says,

(And they belied them wrongfully and arrogantly, though they themselves were convinced thereof.) (27:14)

Surah: 20 Ayah: 57, Ayah: 58 & Ayah: 59

قَالَ أَجِئْتَنَا لِتُخْرِجَنَا مِنْ أَرْضِنَا بِسِحْرِكَ يَٰمُوسَىٰ ۝

57. He (Fir'aun (Pharaoh)) said: "Have you come to drive us out of our land with your magic, O Mûsa (Moses)?

فَلَنَأْتِيَنَّكَ بِسِحْرٍ مِّثْلِهِ فَاجْعَلْ بَيْنَنَا وَبَيْنَكَ مَوْعِدًا لَّا نُخْلِفُهُ نَحْنُ وَلَا أَنتَ مَكَانًا سُوًى ۝

58. "Then verily, we can produce magic the like thereof; so appoint a meeting between us and you, which neither we nor you shall fail to keep, in an open wide place where both shall have a just and equal chance (and beholders could witness the competition)."

قَالَ مَوْعِدُكُمْ يَوْمُ ٱلزِّينَةِ وَأَن يُحْشَرَ ٱلنَّاسُ ضُحًى ۝

59. (Mûsa (Moses)) said: "Your appointed meeting is the day of the festival, and let the people assemble when the sun has risen (forenoon)."

Transliteration

57. Qala aji/tana litukhrijana min ardina bisihrika ya moosa 58. Falana/tiyannaka bisihrin mithlihi faijAAal baynana wabaynaka mawAAidan la nukhlifuhu nahnu wala anta makanan suwan 59. Qala mawAAidukum yawmu alzzeenati waan yuhshara alnnasu duhan

Tafsir Ibn Kathir

Fir`awn describes Musa's Proofs as being Magic and Their Agreement to hold a Contest

Allah, the Exalted, informs of what Fir`awn said to Musa when he showed him the great proof. This great sign to Fir`awn was Musa casting down his stick which became a huge snake, and his pulling his hand out from under his arm while it was glowing white without any illness. At this, Fir`awn said, "This is magic that you have brought to us to bewitch us and conquer the people, so that they will follow you. Then you will outnumber us." Fir`awn then said, "Your plan will not work. We have magic just like yours, so do not let yourself be deceived by that what you are doing."

(so appoint a meeting between us and you,) Meaning, `a day that we can come together to present some of our magic to confront yours. It will be at a specified place and time.' With this, Musa said to them,

(Your appointed meeting is the day of festival,) That was the day of their celebration and their New Year's festivity. It was a holiday for them when they took vacation from their work and came together for a large gathering. This day was selected so that all of the people could witness the power of Allah to do whatever He wills. They would see the miracles of the prophets and the futility of magic to contest the supernatural prophetic powers. This is why Musa said,

(and let the people assemble) meaning all of them.

(when the sun has risen (forenoon).) meaning in the morning, just before noon. In this way the contest will be most visible, well lit, apparent and obvious in plain view. This is the way of the Prophets. Their work is always clear and apparent. It is never something hidden, or something for sale. This is why he did not say that the meeting should be at night, but rather, it was to be held during the bright part of the day. Ibn `Abbas said, "The day of their festivity was the day of `Ashura'." As-Suddi, Qatadah and Ibn Zayd said, "It was the day of their great celebration." Sa`id bin Jubayr said, "It was the day of their great bazzar." These statements are not contradictory. I say that Allah destroyed Fir`awn and his armies on a day similar to this, just as is confirmed in the Sahih. `Abdur-Rahman bin Zayd bin Aslam said, "It was a flat place where all of the people were on the same level, having an equal view of the event. There was nothing there that would obstruct the view so that some people could see what others did not."

Chapter 20: Ta-Ha (Ta-Ha), Verses 001-135

Surah: 20 Ayah: 60, Ayah: 61, Ayah: 62, Ayah: 63 & Ayah: 64

فَتَوَلَّىٰ فِرْعَوْنُ فَجَمَعَ كَيْدَهُ ثُمَّ أَتَىٰ ۝

60. So Fir'aun (Pharaoh) withdrew, devised his plot and then came back.

قَالَ لَهُم مُّوسَىٰ وَيْلَكُمْ لَا تَفْتَرُوا عَلَى اللَّهِ كَذِبًا فَيُسْحِتَكُم بِعَذَابٍ ۖ وَقَدْ خَابَ مَنِ افْتَرَىٰ ۝

61. Mûsa (Moses) said to them: "Woe unto you! Invent not a lie against Allâh, lest He should destroy you completely by a torment. And surely, he who invents a lie (against Allâh) will fail miserably."

فَتَنَازَعُوا أَمْرَهُم بَيْنَهُمْ وَأَسَرُّوا النَّجْوَىٰ ۝

62. Then they debated one with another what they must do, and they kept their talk secret.

قَالُوا إِنْ هَٰذَانِ لَسَاحِرَانِ يُرِيدَانِ أَن يُخْرِجَاكُم مِّنْ أَرْضِكُم بِسِحْرِهِمَا وَيَذْهَبَا بِطَرِيقَتِكُمُ الْمُثْلَىٰ ۝

63. They said: "Verily! These are two magicians. Their object is to drive you out from your land with magic, and overcome your chiefs and nobles.

فَأَجْمِعُوا كَيْدَكُمْ ثُمَّ ائْتُوا صَفًّا ۚ وَقَدْ أَفْلَحَ الْيَوْمَ مَنِ اسْتَعْلَىٰ ۝

64. "So devise your plot, and then assemble in line. And whoever overcomes this day will be indeed successful."

Transliteration

60. Fatawalla firAAawnu fajamaAAa kaydahu thumma ata 61. Qala lahum moosa waylakum la taftaroo AAala Allahi kathiban fayushitakum biAAathabin waqad khaba mani iftara 62. FatanazaAAoo amrahum baynahum waasarroo alnnajwa 63. Qaloo in hathani lasahirani yureedani an yukhrijakum min ardikum bisihrihima wayathhaba bitareeqatikumu almuthla 64. FaajmiAAoo kaydakum thumma i/too saffan waqad aflaha alyawma mani istaAAla

Tafsir Ibn Kathir

The Meeting of the Two Parties, Musa's Propagation of the Message and the Magicians

Allah, the Exalted informs that when Fir`awn and Musa agreed to an appointed meeting at a specified place and time, Fir`awn began to gather some magicians from the cities of his kingdom. Every person who had any affiliation with magic at that time was summoned, and magic was very widespread and in demand at that time. This is as Allah says,

(And Fir`awn said: "Bring me every well-versed sorcerer.") (10:79) Then, the day came. It was the day when all of the people gathered, which was well-known, being the day of the festival. Fir`awn was there sitting upon his throne surrounded by the elite officials of his kingdom. The subjects were all standing on his right and his left. Then, Musa came forward leaning upon his stick accompanied by his brother Harun. The magicians were standing in front of Fir`awn in rows and he was prodding them, inciting them and encouraging them to do their best on this day. They wanted to please him and he was promising them and inspiring them. They said,

(Will there surely be a reward for us if we are the winners He (Fir`awn) said: "Yes, and you shall then verily be of those brought near (to myself).") (26:41-42)

(Musa said to them: "Woe unto you! Invent not a lie against Allah...") This means, "Do not make an illusion before the people of something that is not real, making it appear as if it were a creature, when it is not really a creature. If you do this, then you would be lying on Allah."

(lest He (Allah) should destroy you completely by a torment.) This means, `He will destroy you with a destructive punishment that will not spare anything, or anyone.'

("...And surely, he who invents a lie will fail miserably." Then they debated one with another what they must do,) It has been said that this means that they argued among themselves. So one of them said, "This is not the speech of a magician, but it is the speech of a Prophet." Another said, "No, he is only a magician." There are other opinions that have been mentioned about what they discussed. And Allah knows best. Allah's statement,

(and they kept their talk secret.) means, they held secret counsel among themselves about this matter.

(They said: "Verily, these are two (Hadhan) magicians...") This is a way of speaking with some of the Arabs and this Ayah has been recited according to the grammar of their dialect. There are also others who recite it as, (إِنَّ هَذَيْنِ لَسَاحِرَانِ) Which carries the same meaning, "Verily, these are two (Hadhayn) magicians." This is the popular style of language in Arabic grammar. The grammarians have extensive discussions in reply to the first recitation and its grammatical explanation, but this is not the place for such a discussion. The main point is that the magicians said among themselves, "You all know that this man and his brother (Musa and Harun) are two knowledgeable magicians who are quite aware of the skill of magic. They want to defeat you and your people today and conquer the people, causing the masses to follow them. They want to fight against Fir`awn and his armies, and they are seeking victory over him. And their ultimate goal is to expel you from your land." Concerning Allah's statement,

(and to take you away from your exemplary way.) This means, `they want to expose this way (of yours) openly, which is magic.' For verily, they were considered great because of their magic. They had wealth and sustenance because of this magic. They were actually saying, "If these two (Musa and Harun) are victorious, they will destroy you and expel you from your land. In doing so, they will be the first individuals to do so, and they will be given great power of leadership without you." Ibn `Abbas mentioned concerning Allah's statement,

(and to take you away from your exemplary way.) "This means their kingdom, which they were in, and their livelihood." `Abdur-Rahman bin Zayd said, "This superior way means that which they were upon."

(So devise your plot, and assemble in line.) This means, "All of you come together in one row, and throw that which is in your hands at one time in order to dazzle the eyes (of the people) and defeat this man and his brother."

(And whoever overcomes this day will be indeed successful.) meaning "Between you and us. As for us (the magicians), we have been promised to be given an abundance of power and sovereignty. And in reference to him (Musa), He will gain great leadership."

Surah: 20 Ayah: 65, Ayah: 66, Ayah: 67, Ayah: 68, Ayah: 69 & Ayah: 70

قَالُوا۟ يَٰمُوسَىٰٓ إِمَّآ أَن تُلْقِىَ وَإِمَّآ أَن نَّكُونَ أَوَّلَ مَنْ أَلْقَىٰ ﴿٦٥﴾

65. They said: "O Mûsa (Moses)! Either you throw first or we be the first to throw?"

قَالَ بَلْ أَلْقُوا۟ ۖ فَإِذَا حِبَالُهُمْ وَعِصِيُّهُمْ يُخَيَّلُ إِلَيْهِ مِن سِحْرِهِمْ أَنَّهَا تَسْعَىٰ ﴿٦٦﴾

66. (Mûsa (Moses)) said: "Nay, throw you (first)!" Then behold, their ropes and their sticks, by their magic, appeared to him as though they moved fast.

فَأَوْجَسَ فِى نَفْسِهِۦ خِيفَةً مُّوسَىٰ ﴿٦٧﴾

67. So Mûsa (Moses) conceived fear in himself.

قُلْنَا لَا تَخَفْ إِنَّكَ أَنتَ ٱلْأَعْلَىٰ ﴿٦٨﴾

68. We (Allâh) said: "Fear not! Surely, you will have the upper hand.

وَأَلْقِ مَا فِى يَمِينِكَ تَلْقَفْ مَا صَنَعُوٓا۟ ۖ إِنَّمَا صَنَعُوا۟ كَيْدُ سَٰحِرٍ ۖ وَلَا يُفْلِحُ ٱلسَّاحِرُ حَيْثُ أَتَىٰ ﴿٦٩﴾

69. "And throw that which is in your right hand! It will swallow up that which they have made. That which they have made is only a magician's trick, and the magician will never be successful, to whatever amount (of skill) he may attain."

فَأُلْقِىَ ٱلسَّحَرَةُ سُجَّدًا قَالُوٓا۟ ءَامَنَّا بِرَبِّ هَٰرُونَ وَمُوسَىٰ ﴿٧٠﴾

70. So the magicians fell down prostrate. They said: "We believe in the Lord of Hârûn (Aaron) and Mûsa (Moses)."

Transliteration

65. Qaloo ya moosa imma an tulqiya wa-imma an nakoona awwala man alqa 66. Qala bal alqoo fa-itha hibaluhum waAAisiyyuhum yukhayyalu ilayhi min sihrihim annaha tasAAa 67. Faawjasa fee nafsihi kheefatan moosa 68. Qulna la takhaf innaka anta al-aAAla 69. Waalqi ma fee yameenika talqaf ma sanaAAoo innama sanaAAoo kaydu sahirin wala yuflihu alssahiru haythu ata 70. Faolqiya alssaharatu sujjadan qaloo amanna birabbi haroona wamoosa

Tafsir Ibn Kathir

The Competition, Musa's Victory, and the Magician's Faith

Allah, the Exalted, informs about the magicians when they met Musa, that they said to Musa,

("Either you throw first...") meaning, "you go first."

("...or we be the first to throw" (Musa) said: "Nay, throw you (first)!") This means, `you magicians should go first so that we can see what magic you are going to perform and so that the true state of their affair will become obvious to the people.'

(Then behold! their ropes and their sticks, by their magic, appeared to him as though they moved fast.) In another Ayah it says that when they threw,

(Then said: "By the might of Fir`awn, it is we who will certainly win!") (26:44) And Allah, the Exalted, says,

(They bewitched the eyes of the people, and struck terror into them, and they displayed a great magic.) (7:116) Here, He says in this Surah,

(Then behold! their ropes and their sticks, by their magic, appeared to him as though they moved fast.) They were a large numbered group and each one of them threw a stick and a rope until the valley became full of snakes piled on top of each other. Concerning Allah's statement,

(So Musa conceived fear in himself.) This means that he feared for the people that they would be tested and deceived by their magic before he could even have a chance to throw what was in his right hand. Thus, Allah revealed to him at the right moment, to throw what was in his right hand, which was the stick. When he did so, it swallowed what they had made. It became a huge, monstrous creature with legs, a neck, a head and fangs. It went after these ropes and sticks until none of them remained, except that it was devoured and swallowed by this beast. At the same time, the magicians and all of the people were watching with their own eyes, seeing this amazing event in broad daylight. Thus, the miracle was performed and the evidence was clear. The truth prevailed and the magic was proven to be falsehood. This is why Allah said, (That which they have made is only a magician's trick, and the magician will never be successful, to whatever amount (of skill) he may attain.) So when the magicians saw the event and witnessed it with their own eyes, while they were knowledgeable of the various tricks and methods in the sciences of magic, they knew with conviction that what Musa had done was not magic or illusionary tricks. They recognized that it was the truth without any doubt. They knew that no one had any power to do this except for One Who says for a thing "Be," and it is. Therefore, when this happened, they fell down into prostration to Allah. They said, "We believe in the Lord of all that exists, the Lord of Musa and Harun!" This is why Ibn `Abbas and `Ubayd bin `Umayr both said, "At the beginning of the day they were magicians and at the end of the day they were outstanding witnesses of faith."

The Number of Magicians

Ibn Abi Hatim recorded that Ibn `Abbas said, "The magicians were seventy men who were magicians in the morning, but witnesses of faith by the time evening came." Ibn Abi Hatim also reported that Al-Awza'i said, "When the magicians fell down in prostration, Paradise was raised up before them until they were looking at it." It is reported from Sa`id bin Jubayr that he said concerning Allah's statement, (So the magicians fell down prostrate.) "They saw their places (in Paradise) made clear before them while they were in their prostration." `Ikrimah and Al-Qasim bin Abi Bizzah both said the same.

Surah: 20 Ayah: 71, Ayah: 72 & Ayah: 73

قَالَ ءَامَنتُمْ لَهُۥ قَبْلَ أَنْ ءَاذَنَ لَكُمْ ۖ إِنَّهُۥ لَكَبِيرُكُمُ ٱلَّذِى عَلَّمَكُمُ ٱلسِّحْرَ فَلَأُقَطِّعَنَّ أَيْدِيَكُمْ وَأَرْجُلَكُم مِّنْ خِلَٰفٍ وَلَأُصَلِّبَنَّكُمْ فِى جُذُوعِ ٱلنَّخْلِ وَلَتَعْلَمُنَّ أَيُّنَآ أَشَدُّ عَذَابًا وَأَبْقَىٰ ﴿٧١﴾

71. (Fir'aun (Pharaoh)) said: "Believe you in him (Mûsa (Moses)) before I give you permission? Verily! He is your chief who has taught you magic. So I will surely cut off your hands and feet on opposite sides, and I will surely crucify you on the trunks of date-palms, and you shall surely know which of us (I (Fir'aun - Pharaoh) or the Lord of Mûsa (Moses) (Allâh)) can give the severe and more lasting torment."

قَالُوا۟ لَن نُّؤْثِرَكَ عَلَىٰ مَا جَآءَنَا مِنَ ٱلْبَيِّنَٰتِ وَٱلَّذِى فَطَرَنَا ۖ فَٱقْضِ مَآ أَنتَ قَاضٍ ۖ إِنَّمَا تَقْضِى هَٰذِهِ ٱلْحَيَوٰةَ ٱلدُّنْيَآ ﴿٧٢﴾

72. They said: "We prefer you not over what have come to us of the clear signs and to Him (Allâh) Who created us. So decree whatever you desire to decree, for you can only decree (regarding) this life of the world.

إِنَّآ ءَامَنَّا بِرَبِّنَا لِيَغْفِرَ لَنَا خَطَٰيَٰنَا وَمَآ أَكْرَهْتَنَا عَلَيْهِ مِنَ ٱلسِّحْرِ ۗ وَٱللَّهُ خَيْرٌ وَأَبْقَىٰ

73. "Verily we have believed in our Lord, that He may forgive us our faults, and the magic to which you did compel us. And Allâh is better as regards reward in comparison to your (Fir'aun's (Pharaoh)) reward, and more lasting (as regards punishment in comparison to your punishment)."

Transliteration

71. Qala amantum lahu qabla an athana lakum innahu lakabeerukumu allathee AAallamakumu alssihra falaoqattiAAanna aydiyakum waarjulakum min khilafin walaosallibannakum fee juthooAAi alnnakhli walataAAlamunna ayyuna ashaddu AAathaban waabqa 72. Qaloo lan nu/thiraka AAala ma jaana mina albayyinati waallathee fatarana faiqdi ma anta qadin innama taqdee hathihi alhayata alddunya 73. Inna amanna birabbina liyaghfira lana khatayana wama akrahtana AAalayhi mina alssihri waAllahu khayrun waabqa

Tafsir Ibn Kathir

Fir`awn's turning against the Magicians, His threatening Them and Their Reply

Allah, the Exalted, informs of Fir`awn's disbelief, obstinance, transgression and haughtiness against the truth in favor of falsehood. When he saw what he saw of the magnificent miracle and the great sign, and he saw those whose help he sought accept faith in the presence of all of the people, and he was absolutely defeated, he began to behave arrogantly and cast accusations. He resorted to using his esteemed honor and might against the magicians. He warned them and threatened them saying,

(Believe you in him (Musa)) This means, "Do you have faith in him"

(before I give you permission) meaning, "I have not commanded you to do so, by which you have rebelled against me." Then he said a statement that he, the magicians and all creatures knew was a forgery and an utter lie.

(Verily, he is your chief who has taught you magic.) meaning "You all only took your magic from Musa and you have made an agreement with him against me and my subjects, that you would help him be victorious." Allah says in another Ayah,

(Surely, this is a plot which you have plotted in the city to drive out its people, but you shall come to know.) (7:123) Then he began threatening them. He said to them,

(So I will surely cut off your hands and feet on opposite sides, and I will surely crucify you on the trunks of date palms,) meaning, "I will certainly make an example of you, I will kill you in a public execution." Ibn `Abbas said, "Thus, he was the first person to ever do this (public execution, crucifixion)." This was reported by Ibn Abi Hatim. Concerning Allah's statement,

(And you shall surely know which of us can give the severe and more lasting torment.) This means, "You say that my people and I are astray and that you (magicians), Musa and his people are following correct guidance, but you will come to know who will be punished and remain punished." So when he attacked with this and threatened them, their souls eased them because of their belief in Allah, the Mighty and Sublime. They exclaimed,

(They said: "We prefer you not over what have come to us of the clear signs...") meaning, "We do not chose you over the guidance and conviction that we have received."

(and to Him (Allah) Who created us.) It could be that they were swearing, "By He Who has created us." It also could be connected in meaning to the clear signs mentioned before it. In this case it would mean, "We do not prefer you over our Originator and Creator, Who produced us from a beginning that was nothing. He created us from clay (or mud). Therefore, He alone deserves worship and humility and you do not (Fir`awn)!"

(So decree whatever you desire to decree,) "Do whatever you wish and whatever your hands are able to achieve."

(for you can only decree (regarding) this life of the world.) meaning, "You only have power in this world and it is a world that will come to an end. Verily, we are hoping in the eternal abode."

(Verily, we have believed in our Lord, that He may forgive us our faults,) "Whatever evils that we did." It specifically means, `which we were forced to do of magic, in order to oppose the sign of Allah and the miracle of His Prophet.' Ibn Abi Hatim recorded that Ibn `Abbas said concerning Allah's statement,

(and the magic to which you compelled us.) "Fir`awn took forty boys from the Children of Israel and commanded that they be taught magic at Al-Farama. He said, `Teach them knowledge that no one in the land knows.'" Ibn `Abbas then said, "They were of those who believed in Musa and they were of those who said,

(We have believed in our Lord, that He may forgive us our faults, and the magic to which you did compel us.)" `Abdur-Rahman bin Zayd bin Aslam said the same. Allah's statement,

(And Allah is better as regards reward in comparison to your reward, and more lasting.) means, "He is better for us than you."

(and more lasting.) More lasting in reward than what you pro- mised us and made us aspire to. It is apparent that Fir`awn (may Allah curse him) was bent upon their punishment, and that what he did to them was a mercy from Allah for them. This is why Ibn `Abbas and others of the Salaf said, "They woke up in that morning as magicians, but they became witnesses of faith by the evening."

Surah: 20 Ayah: 74, Ayah: 75 & Ayah: 76

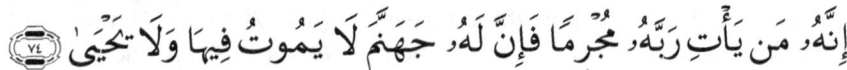

74. Verily whoever comes to his Lord as a Mujrim (criminal, polytheist, sinner, disbeliever in the Oneness of Allâh and His Messengers.), then surely, for him is Hell, wherein he will neither die nor live.

وَمَن يَأْتِهِۦ مُؤْمِنًا قَدْ عَمِلَ ٱلصَّٰلِحَٰتِ فَأُو۟لَٰٓئِكَ لَهُمُ ٱلدَّرَجَٰتُ ٱلْعُلَىٰ ﴿٧٥﴾

75. But whoever comes to Him (Allâh) as a believer (in the Oneness of Allâh), and has done righteous good deeds, for such are the high ranks (in the Hereafter), -

جَنَّٰتُ عَدْنٍ تَجْرِى مِن تَحْتِهَا ٱلْأَنْهَٰرُ خَٰلِدِينَ فِيهَا ۚ وَذَٰلِكَ جَزَآءُ مَن تَزَكَّىٰ ﴿٧٦﴾

76. 'Adn (Eden) Paradise (everlasting Gardens), under which rivers flow, wherein they will abide forever: such is the reward of those who purify themselves (by abstaining from all kinds of sins and evil deeds which Allâh has forbidden and by doing all that Allâh has ordained).

Transliteration

74. Innahu man ya/ti rabbahu mujriman fa-inna lahu jahannama la yamootu feeha wala yahya 75. Waman ya/tihi mu/minan qad AAamila alssalihati faola-ika lahumu alddarajatu alAAula 76. Jannatu AAadnin tajree min tahtiha al-anharu khalideena feeha wathalika jazao man tazakka

Tafsir Ibn Kathir

The Magicians admonish Fir`awn

The clear intent of this is to be a completion of what the magicians admonished Fir`awn with. They warned him of the vengeance of Allah and His eternal and everlasting punishment. They also encouraged him to seek Allah's eternal and endless reward. They said,

(Verily, whoever comes to his Lord as a criminal,) This means, whoever meets Allah on the Day of Judgment while being a criminal.

(then surely, for him is Hell, wherein he will neither die nor live.) This is similar to Allah's statement,

(Neither will it have a complete killing effect on them so that they die, nor shall its torment be lightened for them. Thus do We requite every disbeliever!) (35:36) Allah also said,

(But it will be avoided by the wretched, who will enter the great Fire. There he will neither die nor live.) (87:11-13)

(And they will cry: "O Malik (Keeper of Hell)! Let your Lord made an end of us." He will say: "Verily, you shall abide forever.") (43:77) Imam Ahmad bin Hanbal recorded that Abu Sa`id Al-Khudri said that the Messenger of Allah said,

Chapter 20: Ta-Ha (Ta-Ha), Verses 001-135

«أَمَّا أَهْلُ النَّارِ الَّذِينَ هُمْ أَهْلُهَا، فَإِنَّهُمْ لَا يَمُوتُونَ فِيهَا وَلَا يَحْيَوْنَ، وَلَكِنْ أُنَاسٌ تُصِيبُهُمُ النَّارُ بِذُنُوبِهِمْ فَتُمِيتُهُمْ إِمَاتَةً حَتَّى إِذَا صَارُوا فَحْمًا أُذِنَ فِي الشَّفَاعَةِ فَجِيءَ بِهِمْ ضَبَائِرَ ضَبَائِرَ، فَبُثُّوا عَلَى أَنْهَارِ الْجَنَّةِ، فَيُقَالُ: يَا أَهْلَ الْجَنَّةِ أَفِيضُوا عَلَيْهِمْ، فَيَنْبُتُونَ نَبَاتَ الْحِبَّةِ تَكُونُ فِي حَمِيلِ السَّيْلِ»

(The dwellers of Hellfire, who are those who deserve it, they will not die in it, nor will they be living. Rather, they will be a people who will be punished by the Fire due to their sins. It will be gradually killing them and devouring them until they become burnt coals. Then, intercession will be allowed and they will be brought (out of Hell) group by group and they will be spread on the rivers of Paradise. It will then be said, "O people of Paradise, pour (water) over them." Then, they will start to grow like the growing of a seed on the muddy banks of a flowing river.) A man among the people said, "It is as if the Messenger of Allah lived in the desert." This is how Muslim recorded this narration in his Sahih. Concerning Allah's statement,

(But whoever comes to Him (Allah) as a believer, and has done righteous good deeds,) whoever meets his Lord on the Day of Judgment as a believer in his heart, then verily, his intentions in his heart will be affirmed to be true by his statements and deeds.

(for such are the high ranks,) Paradise, which has the highest levels, the most tranquil rooms and the nicest homes. Imam Ahmad reported from `Ubadah bin As-Samit that the Prophet said,

«الْجَنَّةُ مِائَةُ دَرَجَةٍ مَا بَيْنَ كُلِّ دَرَجَتَيْنِ كَمَا بَيْنَ السَّمَاءِ وَالْأَرْضِ، وَالْفِرْدَوْسُ أَعْلَاهَا دَرَجَةً، وَمِنْهَا تَخْرُجُ الْأَنْهَارُ الْأَرْبَعَةُ، وَالْعَرْشُ فَوْقَهَا، فَإِذَا سَأَلْتُمُ اللهَ فَاسْأَلُوهُ الْفِرْدَوْسَ»

(Paradise has one hundred levels and between each level is a distance like the distance between the sky and the earth. Al-Firdaws is the name of the highest of its levels. From it springs the four rivers and the Throne is above it. Therefore, when you ask Allah, then ask Him for Al-Firdaws.) This narration was also recorded by At-Tirmidhi. In the Two Sahihs it is recorded that the Messenger of Allah said,

«إِنَّ أَهْلَ عِلِّيِّينَ لَيَرَوْنَ مَنْ فَوْقَهُمْ كَمَا تَرَوْنَ الْكَوْكَبَ الْغَابِرَ فِي أُفُقِ السَّمَاءِ لِتَفَاضُلِ مَا بَيْنَهُمْ قَالُوا: يَا رَسُولَ اللهِ تِلْكَ مَنَازِلُ الْأَنْبِيَاءِ قَالَ: بَلَى، وَالَّذِي

«نَفْسِي بِيَدِهِ رِجَالٌ آمَنُوا بِاللهِ وَصَدَّقُوا الْمُرْسَلِينَ»

(Verily, the people of the `Illiyyin will see those who are above them just as you see the fading star in the horizon of the sky, due to the different status of virtue between them.) The people said, "O Messenger of Allah, these are the dwellings of the Prophets." He replied, (Of course. And I swear by the One Whom my soul is in His Hand, (it is for) men who had faith in Allah and they believed the Messengers.) In the Sunan collections this narration is mentioned with the additional wording,

«وَإِنَّ أَبَا بَكْرٍ وَعُمَرَ لَمِنْهُمْ وَأَنْعَمَا»

(And verily Abu Bakr and `Umar are of them and they will be most favored.) His saying,

(Adn Gardens,) meaning established as a residence. It is merely used here in reference to the high ranks mentioned previously.

(under which rivers flow, wherein they will abide forever,) meaning that they will abide in it for eternity.

(and such is the reward of those who purify themselves.) One who purifies himself from dirt, filth and associating partners with Allah. This is the person who worships Allah alone, without ascribing partners to Him, and he follows the Messengers in the good they came with all that they claim.

Surah: 20 Ayah: 77, Ayah: 78 & Ayah: 79

وَلَقَدْ أَوْحَيْنَا إِلَىٰ مُوسَىٰ أَنْ أَسْرِ بِعِبَادِي فَاضْرِبْ لَهُمْ طَرِيقًا فِي ٱلْبَحْرِ يَبَسًا لَّا تَخَافُ دَرَكًا وَلَا تَخْشَىٰ ۝

77. And indeed We revealed to Mûsa (Moses) (saying): "Travel by night with Ibâdi (My slaves) and strike a dry path for them in the sea, fearing neither to be overtaken (by Fir'aun (Pharaoh)) nor being afraid (of drowning in the sea)."

فَأَتْبَعَهُمْ فِرْعَوْنُ بِجُنُودِهِ فَغَشِيَهُم مِّنَ ٱلْيَمِّ مَا غَشِيَهُمْ ۝

78. Then Fir'aun (Pharaoh) pursued them with his hosts, but the sea-water completely overwhelmed them and covered them up.

وَأَضَلَّ فِرْعَوْنُ قَوْمَهُ وَمَا هَدَىٰ ۝

79. And Fir'aun (Pharaoh) led his people astray, and he did not guide them.

Chapter 20: Ta-Ha (Ta-Ha), Verses 001-135   131

Transliteration

77. Walaqad awhayna ila moosa an asri biAAibadee faidrib lahum tareeqan fee albahri yabasan la takhafu darakan wala takhsha 78. FaatbaAAahum firAAawnu bijunoodihi faghashiyahum mina alyammi ma ghashiyahum 79. Waadalla firAAawnu qawmahu wama hada

Tafsir Ibn Kathir

The Children of Israel leave Egypt

Allah, the Exalted, informs that He commanded Musa to journey at night with the Children of Israel, when Fir`awn refused to release them and send them with Musa. He was to take them away from Fir`awn's captivity. Allah expounds upon this in Surahs other than this noble Surah. Musa left with the Children of Israel, and when the people of Egypt awoke in the morning they found that not a single one of them remained in Egypt. Fir`awn became extremely furious. He sent callers into all of the cities to gather together his army from all of his lands and provinces. He said to them,

(Verily, these indeed are but a small band. And verily, they have done what has enraged us.) (26:54-55) Then when he gathered his army and organized his troops, he set out after them and they followed them at dawn when the sun began to rise.

(And when the two hosts saw each other) (26:61) This means that each person of the two parties was looking at the other party.

(The companions of Musa said: "We are sure to be overtaken." (Musa) said: "Nay, verily, with me is my Lord. He will guide me.") (26:61-62) Musa stopped with the Children of Israel and the sea was in front of them and Fir`awn was behind them. Then, at that moment, Allah revealed to Musa,

(And strike a dry path for them in the sea.) So Musa struck the sea with his stick and he said, "Split for me, by the leave of Allah." Thus, it split, and each separate part of the water became like a huge mountain. Then, Allah sent a wind to the land of the sea and it burned the soil until it became dry like the ground that is on land. For this reason Allah said,

(and strike a dry path for them in the sea, fearing neither to be overtaken...) This means being caught by Fir`awn.

(nor being afraid.) meaning, "Do not be afraid of the sea drowning your people." Then, Allah, the Exalted, said,

(Then Fir`awn pursued them with his hosts, but the sea (Al-Yamm) completely overwhelmed them) Al-Yamm means the sea.

(and covered them up.) meaning, covered them up with a thing that was well-familiar to them in such a situa- tion, as Allah states;

(And He destroyed the overthrown cities. So there covered them that which did cover.) (53:53-54) As Fir`awn pursued them into the sea, misled his people and did not lead them to the path of correct guidance, likewise, he will go ahead of his people on the Day of Resurrection, and will lead them in to the Hellfire. And evil indeed is the place to which they are led.

Surah: 20 Ayah: 80, Ayah: 81 & Ayah: 82

يَـٰبَنِىٓ إِسْرَٰٓءِيلَ قَدْ أَنجَيْنَـٰكُم مِّنْ عَدُوِّكُمْ وَوَٰعَدْنَـٰكُمْ جَانِبَ ٱلطُّورِ ٱلْأَيْمَنَ وَنَزَّلْنَا عَلَيْكُمُ ٱلْمَنَّ وَٱلسَّلْوَىٰ ۝

80. O Children of Israel! We delivered you from your enemy, and We made a covenant with you on the right side of the Mount, and We sent down to you Al-Manna and quails,

كُلُوا۟ مِن طَيِّبَـٰتِ مَا رَزَقْنَـٰكُمْ وَلَا تَطْغَوْا۟ فِيهِ فَيَحِلَّ عَلَيْكُمْ غَضَبِى ۖ وَمَن يَحْلِلْ عَلَيْهِ غَضَبِى فَقَدْ هَوَىٰ ۝

81. (Saying) eat of the Tayyibât (good lawful things) wherewith We have provided you, and commit no transgression or oppression therein, lest My Anger should justly descend on you. And he on whom My Anger descends, he is indeed perished. (Tafsir At-Tabari)

وَإِنِّى لَغَفَّارٌ لِّمَن تَابَ وَءَامَنَ وَعَمِلَ صَـٰلِحًا ثُمَّ ٱهْتَدَىٰ ۝

82. And verily, I am indeed forgiving to him who repents, believes (in My Oneness, and associates none in worship with Me) and does righteous good deeds, and then remains constant in doing them, (till his death).

Transliteration

80. Ya banee isra-eela qad anjaynakum min AAaduwwikum wawaAAadnakum janiba alttoori aylmana wanazzalna AAalaykumu almanna waalssalwa 81. Kuloo min tayyibati ma razaqnakum wala tatghaw feehi fayahilla AAalaykum ghadabee waman yahlil AAalayhi ghadabee faqad hawa 82. Wa-innee laghaffarun liman taba waamana waAAamila salihan thumma ihtada

Tafsir Ibn Kathir

A Reminder for the Children of Israel of

Allah's Favors upon Them Allah reminds of His tremendous favors upon the Children of Israel and His numerous blessings. He saved them from their enemy, Fir`awn, and He relieved their eyes by drowning him and his hosts all at one time while they watched. Allah said,

(And We drowned Fir`awn people while you were looking.) (2:50) Al-Bukhari recorded that Ibn `Abbas said, "When the Messenger of Allah came to Al-Madinah, he found

Chapter 20: Ta-Ha (Ta-Ha), Verses 001-135

the Jews fasting the day of `Ashura'. Therefore he asked them about it and they said, `This is the day that Allah gave Musa victory over Fir`awn.' Then, the Prophet said,

«نَحْنُ أَوْلَى بِمُوسَى فَصُومُوه»

(We have more right to Musa (than them), so fast it.) Muslim also recorded this narration in his Sahih. Then, Allah made a covenant with Musa and the Children of Israel on the right side of the Mountain, after the destruction of Fir`awn. This is the Mountain upon which Allah spoke to Musa and He told Musa's people to look at it when they requested to see Allah. It is also the same Mountain upon which Musa was given the Tawrah, while at the same time the Children of Israel began worshipping the (statue of a) calf, as Allah relates in the forth coming Ayat. The manna and quails have previously been discussed in Surah Al-Baqarah and other Surahs. Manna was a sweet substance that descended upon them from the sky and the quail (Salwa) was a type of bird that would fall down to them. They would fill every pot with them as ample provisions until the following day. This was a kindness and a mercy from Allah upon them. It was a manifestation of Allah's good treatment of them. For this reason Allah says,

(Eat of the Tayyibat wherewith We have provided you, and commit no transgression or oppression therein, lest My anger should justly descend on you.) This means, "Eat from this sustenance which I have provided for you, and do not transgress against My sustenance by taking it without necessity or you will be opposing what I have commanded you."

(lest My anger should justly descend on you.) This means, "I will become angry with you."

(And he on whom My anger descends, he is indeed perished.) `Ali bin Abi Talhah related that Ibn `Abbas said, "This means that he will indeed be made miserable." Concerning Allah's statement,

(And verily, I am indeed forgiving to him who repents, believes and does righteous good deeds,) meaning, "Whoever turns to Me in repentance, then I will accept his repentance regardless of whatever sin he did." Allah, the Exalted, even accepts the repentance of the Children of Israel who worshipped the calf. Concerning Allah's statement,

(who repents,) This means to turn away from what one was involved in of disbelief, associating partners with Allah, disobedience of Allah or hypocrisy. Concerning Allah's statement,

(and believes) This means the person's belief in his heart.

(and does righteous deeds,) his action with his bodily limbs. Concerning Allah's statement, (and then Ihtada.) `Ali bin Abi Talhah related that Ibn `Abbas said, "This means that he then does not doubt." Qatadah said,

(and then Ihtada.) "This means he adheres to Islam until he dies." We see here that there is a specific order in which these things are presented. This is similar to Allah's saying,

(Then he became one of those who believed and recommended one another to perseverance and patience and recommended one another to pity and compassion.) (90:17)

Surah: 20 Ayah: 83, Ayah: 84, Ayah: 85, Ayah: 86, Ayah: 87, Ayah: 88 & Ayah: 89

﴿ وَمَآ أَعۡجَلَكَ عَن قَوۡمِكَ يَٰمُوسَىٰ ﴾

83. "And what made you hasten from your people, O Mûsa (Moses)?"

﴿ قَالَ هُمۡ أُوْلَآءِ عَلَىٰٓ أَثَرِى وَعَجِلۡتُ إِلَيۡكَ رَبِّ لِتَرۡضَىٰ ﴾

84. He said: "They are close on my footsteps: and I hastened to You, O my Lord, that You might be pleased."

﴿ قَالَ فَإِنَّا قَدۡ فَتَنَّا قَوۡمَكَ مِنۢ بَعۡدِكَ وَأَضَلَّهُمُ ٱلسَّامِرِىُّ ﴾

85. (Allâh) said: "Verily! We have tried your people in your absence, and As-Sâmiri has led them astray."

﴿ فَرَجَعَ مُوسَىٰٓ إِلَىٰ قَوۡمِهِۦ غَضۡبَٰنَ أَسِفًا قَالَ يَٰقَوۡمِ أَلَمۡ يَعِدۡكُمۡ رَبُّكُمۡ وَعۡدًا حَسَنًا أَفَطَالَ عَلَيۡكُمُ ٱلۡعَهۡدُ أَمۡ أَرَدتُّمۡ أَن يَحِلَّ عَلَيۡكُمۡ غَضَبٌ مِّن رَّبِّكُمۡ فَأَخۡلَفۡتُم مَّوۡعِدِى ﴾

86. Then Mûsa (Moses) returned to his people in a state of anger and sorrow. He said: "O my people! Did not your Lord promise you a fair promise? Did then the promise seem to you long in coming? Or did you desire that wrath should descend from your Lord on you, that you broke your promise to me (i.e. disbelieving in Allâh and worshipping the calf)?"

﴿ قَالُواْ مَآ أَخۡلَفۡنَا مَوۡعِدَكَ بِمَلۡكِنَا وَلَٰكِنَّا حُمِّلۡنَآ أَوۡزَارًا مِّن زِينَةِ ٱلۡقَوۡمِ فَقَذَفۡنَٰهَا فَكَذَٰلِكَ أَلۡقَى ٱلسَّامِرِىُّ ﴾

87. They said: "We broke not the promise to you, of our own will, but we were made to carry the weight of the ornaments of the (Fir'aun's (Pharaoh)) people, then we cast them (into the fire), and that was what As-Sâmirî suggested."

فَأَخْرَجَ لَهُمْ عِجْلًا جَسَدًا لَّهُ خُوَارٌ فَقَالُوا هَٰذَا إِلَٰهُكُمْ وَإِلَٰهُ مُوسَىٰ فَنَسِيَ

88. Then he took out (of the fire) for them (a statue of) a calf which seemed to low. They said: "This is your ilâh (god), and the ilâh (god) of Mûsa (Moses), but he (Mûsa (Moses)) has forgotten (his god).'"

أَفَلَا يَرَوْنَ أَلَّا يَرْجِعُ إِلَيْهِمْ قَوْلًا وَلَا يَمْلِكُ لَهُمْ ضَرًّا وَلَا نَفْعًا

89. Did they not see that it could not return them a word (for answer), and that it had no power either to harm them or to do them good?

Transliteration

83. Wama aAAjalaka AAan qawmika ya moosa 84. Qala hum ola-i AAala atharee waAAajiltu ilayka rabbi litarda 85. Qala fa-inna qad fatanna qawmaka min baAAdika waadallahumu alssamiriyyu 86. FarajaAAa moosa ila qawmihi ghadbana asifan qala ya qawmi alam yaAAidkum rabbukum waAAdan hasanan afatala AAalaykumu alAAahdu am aradtum an yahilla AAalaykum ghadabun min rabbikum faakhlaftum mawAAidee 87. Qaloo ma akhlafna mawAAidaka bimalkina walakinna hummilna awzaran min zeenati alqawmi faqathafnaha fakathalika alqa alssamiriyyu 88. Faakhraja lahum AAijlan jasadan lahu khuwarun faqaloo hatha ilahukum wa-ilahu moosa fanasiya 89. Afala yarawna alla yarjiAAu ilayhim qawlan wala yamliku lahum darran wala nafAAan

Tafsir Ibn Kathir

Musa goes to the Appointment with Allah and the Children of Israel succumb to worship the Calf

Allah relates what happened when Musa traveled with the Children of Israel after Fir`awn's destruction.

(And they came upon a people devoted to some of idols. They said: "O Musa! Make for us god as they have gods." He said: "Verily, you are a people who know not. Verily, these people will be destroyed for that which they are engaged in. And all that they are doing is in vain.") (7:138-139) Then, Allah made a covenant with Musa of thirty nights after which He added to them ten more nights. Thus, they were forty nights in all. The covenant was that he was to fast these number of days, during both the day and night. Thus, Musa made haste to go to the Mountain and he left his brother, Harun, in charge over the Children of Israel. This is why Allah says,

("And what made you hasten from your people, O Musa" He said: "They are close on my footsteps.") These means that they have arrived and are settled near the Mountain.

(and I hastened to You, O my Lord, that You might be pleased.) meaning, "So You will be more pleased with me."

((Allah) said: "Verily, We have tried your people in your absence, and As-Samiri has led them astray.") Allah informs His Prophet, Musa, of what happened to the Children of Israel after he left them, and their deification of the calf that As-Samiri had made for them. During this time period, Allah wrote for Musa the Tablets, which contained the Tawrah. Allah said,

(And We wrote for him on the Tablets the lesson to be drawn from all things and the explanation for all things (and said): "Hold unto these with firmness, and enjoin your people to take the better therein. I shall show you the home of evildoers.") (7:145) This means, "I will show you the final outcome of what will happen to those who abandon My obedience and oppose My command." Concerning Allah's statement,

(Then Musa returned to his people in a state of anger and sorrow (Asif).) This means that after Allah informed him of what they were doing, he became extremely angry and upset with them. He was very worried for them. During this time he received the Tawrah, which contained their Shari`ah (Law), this was a great honor for them. For they were a people who used to worship other than Allah. Every person with sound reason and good sense could see that what they were doing was false and foolish. This is why Allah said that he (Musa) returned to them in a state of anger and sorrow. The word for sorrow used here is Asif, which is used to emphasize to the severity of his anger. Mujahid said, "In a state of anger and sorrow means worried." Qatadah and As-Suddi said, "Asif here means in a state of sadness because of what his people had done after him."

(He (Musa) said: "O my people! Did not your Lord promise you a fair promise...") This means, "Did He not promise you in that which I have spoken to you, every good in this life and in the Hereafter, and the good end in the final outcome of things You have already witnessed how He helped you defeat your enemy (Fir`awn) and He made you victorious over him and He blessed you with other bounties as well through His help."

(Did then the promise seem to you long in coming) meaning, `in waiting for what Allah had promised you and forgetting His previous favors and the covenant that He made with you before.'

(Or did you desire that wrath should descend from your Lord on you,) The word `Or' here means `Nay, but.' It is used here to separate between a previous item and a coming item. It is as if it is saying, "Nay, but you want to make permissible the anger of your Lord upon you by what you have done. Therefore, you have broken your promise to me." The Children of Israel said in reply to Musa's blame and rebuke,

(We broke not our promise to you of our own will,) Meaning by our power and our choice. Then, they began making lame excuses and they told him how they got rid of that which they were carrying of Coptic jewelry that they had borrowed from them (the Egyptian Copts) when they left Egypt. Therefore they cast it, meaning that they threw it away. Thus, it became a calf that made a moaning sound that would gradually rise in pitch. This calf was an ordeal, a hindrance and test. This is why Allah said,

("...that was what As-Samiri suggested." Then he took out (of the fire) for them (a statue of) a calf which was mooing.) Muhammad bin Ishaq reported that Ibn `Abbas said,

(This is your god, and the god of Musa.) "So they became religiously devoted to it (the calf) and they loved it with a love that they had never loved anything else with before." Allah then says,

(but he had forgotten.) This means that he abandoned what he was following of the religion of Islam. This is referring to As-Samiri. Allah says in refuting them and rebuking them, and also explaining to them their folly and foolishness in that which they had done,

(Did they not see that it could not return them a word (for answer), and that it had no power either to harm them or to do them good) This is about the calf. `Do they not see that it does not respond to them when they ask it and when they speak to it'

(and that it had no power either to harm them or to do them good) Meaning in their worldly affairs and matters of the Hereafter. Ibn `Abbas said, "Nay, by Allah, the moaning sound of the calf was nothing but wind that would enter into its behind and come out of its mouth, thus causing it to make a sound." In a Hadith of Al-Fitun recorded from Al-Hasan Al-Basri, it is mentioned that this calf's name was Bahmut. In reference to the excuse of these ignorant people, they claimed that they were merely ridding themselves of the jewelry of the Copts. In the process of doing so, they cast the jewelry (into the pit of fire) and ended up worshipping the calf. Thus, they were seeking to rid themselves of something detestable, but wound up doing something even worse. This is similar to an authentic narration reported from `Abdullah bin `Umar. A man from `Iraq asked him about the ruling of mosquitoes' blood if it get on one's garment. The man wanted to know if it is permissible to pray in such a garment or not. Ibn `Umar replied by saying, "Look at the people of `Iraq. They killed the grandson of the Messenger of Allah , Al-Husayn, and yet they're asking about the blood of the mosquito."

Surah: 20 Ayah: 90 & Ayah: 91

وَلَقَدْ قَالَ لَهُمْ هَٰرُونُ مِن قَبْلُ يَٰقَوْمِ إِنَّمَا فُتِنتُم بِهِۦ ۖ وَإِنَّ رَبَّكُمُ ٱلرَّحْمَٰنُ فَٱتَّبِعُونِى وَأَطِيعُوٓا۟ أَمْرِى ۝

90. And Hârûn (Aaron) indeed had said to them beforehand: "O my people! You are being tried in this, and verily, your Lord is (Allâh) the Most Gracious, so follow me and obey my order."

قَالُوا۟ لَن نَّبْرَحَ عَلَيْهِ عَٰكِفِينَ حَتَّىٰ يَرْجِعَ إِلَيْنَا مُوسَىٰ ۝

91. They said: "We will not stop worshipping it (i.e. the calf), until Mûsa (Moses) returns to us."

Transliteration

90. Walaqad qala lahum haroonu min qablu ya qawmi innama futintum bihi wa-inna rabbakumu alrrahmanu faittabiAAoonee waateeAAoo amree 91. Qaloo lan nabraha AAalayhi AAakifeena hatta yarjiAAa ilayna moosa

Tafsir Ibn Kathir

Harun prohibits them from worship of Calf and the Persistence of the Children of Israel in doing so

Allah, the Exalted, informs of Harun's attempt to prohibit them from worshipping the calf and his telling them that this was only a test for them. He told them that their Lord was the Most Beneficent, Who created everything and decreed for everything its just measure. He is the Owner of the Mighty Throne, the One Who does whatever He wants.

(so follow me and obey my order.) Meaning, "Follow me in that which I am commanding you with and leave that which I forbid you from."

(They said: "We will not stop worshipping it, until Musa returns to us.") meaning, "We will not cease in our worship of this calf until we hear what Musa has to say about it." So they opposed Harun in this matter and they fought against him, nearly killing him.

Surah: 20 Ayah: 92, Ayah: 93 & Ayah: 94

قَالَ يَـٰهَـٰرُونُ مَا مَنَعَكَ إِذْ رَأَيْتَهُمْ ضَلُّوٓا۟ ﴿٩٢﴾

92. (Mûsa (Moses)) said: "O Hârûn (Aaron)! What prevented you when you saw them going astray;

أَلَّا تَتَّبِعَنِ ۖ أَفَعَصَيْتَ أَمْرِى ﴿٩٣﴾

93. "That you followed me not (according to my advice to you)? Have you then disobeyed my order?"

قَالَ يَبْنَؤُمَّ لَا تَأْخُذْ بِلِحْيَتِى وَلَا بِرَأْسِىٓ ۖ إِنِّى خَشِيتُ أَن تَقُولَ فَرَّقْتَ بَيْنَ بَنِىٓ إِسْرَٰٓءِيلَ وَلَمْ تَرْقُبْ قَوْلِى ﴿٩٤﴾

94. He (Hârûn (Aaron)) said: "O son of my mother! Seize (me) not by my beard, nor by my head! Verily, I feared lest you should say: 'You have caused a division among the Children of Israel, and you have not respected my word!'"

Transliteration

92. Qala ya haroonu ma manaAAaka ith raaytahum dalloo 93. Alla tattabiAAani afaAAasayta amree 94. Qala yabnaomma la ta/khuth bilihyatee wala bira/see innee khasheetu an taqoola farraqta bayna banee isra-eela walam tarqub qawlee

Tafsir Ibn Kathir

What happened between Musa and Harun after Musa returned

Allah informs of what happened when Musa returned to his people and saw the great matter that had taken place among them. With this he became filled with anger and he threw down the Divine Tablets that he had in his hand. Then, he grabbed his brother Harun by his head and pulled him towards himself. We expounded upon this previously in Surat Al-A`raf, where we mentioned the Hadith,

«لَيْسَ الْخَبَرُ كَالْمُعَايَنَة»

(Information is not the same as observation.) Then, he began to blame his brother, Harun, by saying,

(What prevented you when you saw them going astray; that you followed me not) meaning, "You should have informed me of this matter as soon as it happened."

(Have you then disobeyed my order) "In that which I entrusted to you," referring to Musa's statement,

(Replace me among my people, act in the right way and follow not the way of the mischief-makers.)(7:142)

(He (Harun) said: "O son of my mother!") This mentioning of the mother was Harun's attempt to soften Musa's anger, because he was Musa's biological brother and they had the same parents. The mentioning of the mother here is more delicate and profound in bringing about gentleness and mildness. This is why he said,

(O son of my mother! Seize (me) not by my beard, nor by my head!) This was Harun's excuse to Musa for being delayed from coming to him and informing him of the great mishap that took place. He said,

(Verily, I feared) meaning, "I was afraid to come after you and inform you of this, because I thought you might accuse me of leaving them alone and causing division between them."

(and you have not respected my word!) This means, "And you did not take care of what I commanded you to do when I left you in charge of them." Ibn `Abbas said, "Harun was respectful and obedient to Musa."

Surah: 20 Ayah: 95, Ayah: 96, Ayah: 97 & Ayah: 98

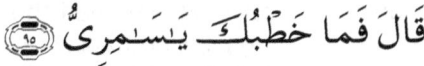

95. (Mûsa (Moses)) said: "And what is the matter with you. O Sâmirî? (i.e. why did you do so?)" Sâmirî

$$قَالَ بَصُرْتُ بِمَا لَمْ يَبْصُرُوا بِهِ فَقَبَضْتُ قَبْضَةً مِّنْ أَثَرِ ٱلرَّسُولِ فَنَبَذْتُهَا وَكَذَٰلِكَ سَوَّلَتْ لِى نَفْسِى ۝$$

96. (Sâmirî) said: "I saw what they saw not, so I took a handful (of dust) from the (hoof) print of the messenger (Jibrîl's (Gabriel) horse) and threw it (into the fire in which were put the ornaments of the Fir'aun's (Pharaoh) people, or into the calf). Thus my inner-self suggested to me."

$$قَالَ فَٱذْهَبْ فَإِنَّ لَكَ فِى ٱلْحَيَوٰةِ أَن تَقُولَ لَا مِسَاسَ وَإِنَّ لَكَ مَوْعِدًا لَّن تُخْلَفَهُ وَٱنظُرْ إِلَىٰ إِلَٰهِكَ ٱلَّذِى ظَلْتَ عَلَيْهِ عَاكِفًا لَّنُحَرِّقَنَّهُ ثُمَّ لَنَنسِفَنَّهُ فِى ٱلْيَمِّ نَسْفًا ۝$$

97. Mûsa (Moses) said: "Then go away! And verily, your (punishment) in this life will be that you will say: "Touch me not (i.e. you will live alone exiled away from mankind); and verily (for a future torment), you have a promise that will not fail. And look at your ilâh (god), to which you have been devoted. We will certainly burn it, and scatter its particles in the sea."

$$إِنَّمَا إِلَٰهُكُمُ ٱللَّهُ ٱلَّذِى لَا إِلَٰهَ إِلَّا هُوَ وَسِعَ كُلَّ شَىْءٍ عِلْمًا ۝$$

98. Your Ilâh (God) is only Allâh, the One (Lâ ilâha illa Huwa) (none has the right to be worshipped but He). He has full knowledge of all things.

Transliteration

95. Qala fama khatbuka ya samiriyyu 96. Qala basurtu bima lam yabsuroo bihi faqabadtu qabdatan min athari alrrasooli fanabathtuha wakathalika sawwalat lee nafsee 97. Qala faithhab fa-inna laka fee alhayati an taqoola la misasa wa-inna laka mawAAidan lan tukhlafahu waonthur ila ilahika allathee thalta AAalayhi AAakifan lanuharriqannahu thumma lanansifannahu fee alyammi nasfan 98. Innama ilahukumu Allahu allathee la ilaha illa huwa wasiAAa kulla shay-in AAilman

Tafsir Ibn Kathir

How As-Samiri made the Calf

Musa said to As-Samiri, "What caused you to do what you did What presented such an idea to you causing you to do this" Muhammad bin Ishaq reported from Ibn `Abbas that he said, "As-Samiri was a man from the people of Bajarma, a people who worshipped cows. He still had the love of cow worshipping in his soul. However, he acted as though he had accepted Islam with the Children of Israel. His name was Musa bin Zafar." Qatadah said, "He was from the village of Samarra."

((Samiri) said: "I saw what they saw not.") This means, "I saw Jibril when he came to destroy Fir`awn."

(so I took a handful (Qabdah) from the print of the messenger) This means from the hoof print of his (Jibril's) horse. This is what is well-known with many of the scholars of Tafsir, rather most of them. Mujahid said,

(so I took a handful (Qabdah) from the print of the messenger) "From under the hoof of Jibril's horse." He also said, "The word Qabdah means a palmful, and it is also that which is grasped by the tips of the fingers." Mujahid said, "As-Samiri threw what was in his hand onto the jewelry of the Children of Israel and it became molded into the body of a calf, which made a light moaning sound. The wind that blew into it was the cause of its sound." Thus, he said,

(and I threw it.) This means, "I threw it along with those who were throwing (jewelry)."

(Thus my inner self suggested to me.) This means that his soul considered it something good and it was pleasing to his self.

The Punishment of As-Samiri and the burning of the Calf Thereupon,

((Musa) said: "Then go away! And verily, your (punishment) in this life will be that you will say: `Touch me not.'") This means, "Just as you took and touched what was not your right to take and touch of the messenger's foot print, such is your punishment in this life, that you will say, `Do not touch (me).'" This means, "You will not touch the people and they will not touch you."

(and verily, you have a promise) This means on the Day of Resurrection.

(that will not fail.) you will have no way to escape it. Qatadah said,

(that you will say: `Touch me not.') "This is referring to a punishment for them and their remnants (i.e. those who have their disease) today still say `Do not touch.'" Concerning Allah's statement,

(and verily, you have a promise that will not fail.) Al-Hasan, Qatadah and Abu Nahik said, "You will not be absent from it."

(And look at your god) that which you worshipped,

(to which you have been devoted.) that which you established worship of, which was the calf.

(Your God is only Allah, there is no God but Him. He has full knowledge of all things.) Musa was saying to them, "This is not your god. Your God is only Allah, the One Whom there is no true God except Him. Worship is not befitting to anyone except Him. For everything is in need of Him and everything is His servant. Concerning the statement,

(He has full knowledge of all things.) The word `Ilm (knowledge) is in the accusative case for distinction. It means that He is the All-Knower of everything.

((Allah) surrounds all things in (His) knowledge.) (65:12) And He says,

(And (He) keeps count of all things.) (72:28) Therefore,

(Not even the weight of a speck of dust escapes His knowledge.) (34:3) He also says,

(Not a leaf falls, but He knows it. There is not a grain in the darkness of the earth nor anything fresh or dry, but is written in a Clear Record.) (6:59) And He says,

(And no moving creature is there on earth but its provision is due from Allah. And He knows its dwelling place and its deposit. All is in a Clear Book.) (11:6) The Ayat that mention this are numerous.

Surah: 20 Ayah: 99, Ayah: 100 & Ayah: 101

كَذَٰلِكَ نَقُصُّ عَلَيْكَ مِنْ أَنۢبَآءِ مَا قَدْ سَبَقَ وَقَدْ ءَاتَيْنَٰكَ مِن لَّدُنَّا ذِكْرًۭا ۝

99. Thus We relate to you (O Muhammad (peace be upon him)) some information of what happened before. And indeed We have given you from Us a Reminder (this Qur'ân).

مَّنْ أَعْرَضَ عَنْهُ فَإِنَّهُۥ يَحْمِلُ يَوْمَ ٱلْقِيَٰمَةِ وِزْرًا ۝

100. Whoever turns away from it (this Qur'ân i.e. does not believe in it, nor acts on its orders), verily, they will bear a heavy burden (of sins) on the Day of Resurrection,

خَٰلِدِينَ فِيهِ وَسَآءَ لَهُمْ يَوْمَ ٱلْقِيَٰمَةِ حِمْلًا ۝

101. They will abide in that (state in the Fire of Hell) - and evil indeed will it be that load for them on the Day of Resurrection;

Transliteration

99. Kathalika naqussu AAalayka min anba-i ma qad sabaqa waqad ataynaka min ladunna thikran 100. Man aAArada AAanhu fa-innahu yahmilu yawma alqiyamati wizran 101. Khalideena feehi wasaa lahum yawma alqiyamati himlan

Tafsir Ibn Kathir

The Entire Qur'an is the Remembrance of Allah and mentioning the Punishment of Those Who turn away from It

Allah, the Exalted, is saying to Prophet Muhammad , `We have told you (O Muhammad) the story of Musa and what happened with him, Fir`awn and his armies, just as it actually happened. Likewise, We relate to you the information of the past just as it happened, without any increase or decrease. We also gave you a remembrance from Us, the Mighty Qur'an, no falsehood comes to it from before it or behind it.' It is a revelation from One Most Wise, Most Praiseworthy. No Prophet was given any Book like it or more complete than it, since the time of the previous Prophets who were sent, until their being sealed off with the coming of Muhammad . No Prophet was given any Book containing as much information than the Qur'an about what has past and what would be. The judgement concerning the distinction between mankind is taken from it. Therefore, Allah says about it,

(Whoever turns away from it,) This means whoever denies it and turns away from following its commands and instructions, while seeking guidance from other than it, then Allah will mislead him and send him on the path to Hell. This is why Allah says,

(Whoever turns away from it, verily, they will bear a heavy burden on the Day of Resurrection.) .Burden here means sin. This is as Allah says,

(But those of the sects that reject it , the Fire will be their promised meeting place.) (11:17) This applies generally to whoever the Qur'an reaches of the Arabs, the non-Arabs, the People of the Book and others. This is as Allah says,

(That I may therewith warn you and whomsoever it may reach.) (6:19) The Qur'an is a final warning for everyone it reaches. Whoever follows it, then he is rightly guided and whoever opposes it and turns away from it, then he is misguided. He will be wretched in this life, and he is promised that on the Day of Resurrection his abode will be the Hellfire. For this reason Allah says,

(Whoever turns away from it, verily, they will bear a heavy burden on the Day of Resurrection. They will abide in that.) (20:100-101) They will not be able to avoid this or escape it.

(And evil indeed will it be that load for them on the Day of Resurrection.)

Surah: 20 Ayah: 102, Ayah: 103 & Ayah: 104

يَوْمَ يُنفَخُ فِى ٱلصُّورِ وَنَحْشُرُ ٱلْمُجْرِمِينَ يَوْمَئِذٍ زُرْقًا ۝

102. The Day when the Trumpet will be blown (the second blowing): that Day, We shall gather the Mujrimûn (criminals, polytheists, sinners, disbelievers in the Oneness of Allâh) blue or blind-eyed with thirst.

يَتَخَفَتُونَ بَيْنَهُمْ إِن لَّبِثْتُمْ إِلَّا عَشْرًا ۝

103. They will speak in a very low voice to each other (saying): "You stayed not longer than ten (days)."

نَحْنُ أَعْلَمُ بِمَا يَقُولُونَ إِذْ يَقُولُ أَمْثَلُهُمْ طَرِيقَةً إِن لَّبِثْتُمْ إِلَّا يَوْمًا ۝

104. We know very well what they will say, when the best among them in knowledge and wisdom will say: "You stayed no longer than a day!"

Transliteration

102. Yawma yunfakhu fee alssoori wanahshuru almujrimeena yawma-ithin zurqan 103. Yatakhafatoona baynahum in labithtum illa Aaashran 104. Nahnu aAAlamu bima yaqooloona ith yaqoolu amthaluhum tareeqatan in labithtum illa yawman

Tafsir Ibn Kathir

The Blowing of the Sur and the Day of Resurrection

It has been confirmed in a Hadith that the Messenger of Allah was asked about the Sur and he replied,

《قَرْنٌ يُنْفَخُ فِيه》

(It is a horn that will be blown into.) It has been related in a Hadith about the Sur, on the authority of Abu Hurayrah that it is a huge horn that has a circumference as large as the heavens and the earth. The angel Israfil will blow into it. Another Hadith has been related which states that the Prophet said,

《كَيْفَ أَنْعَمُ وَصَاحِبُ الْقَرْنِ قَدِ الْتَقَمَ الْقَرْنَ وَحَنَى جَبْهَتَهُ، وَانْتَظَرَ أَنْ يُؤْذَنَ لَه》

(How can I be comfortable when the one with the horn is holding it in his lips and his forehead is leaning forward, waiting to be given permission (to blow it).) The people said, "O Messenger of Allah, what should we say" He said,

《قُولُوا: حَسْبُنَا اللهُ وَنِعْمَ الْوَكِيلُ عَلَى اللهِ تَوَكَّلْنَا》

(Say: Allah is sufficient for us and what a good protector He is. Upon Allah we place our trust.) Concerning His statement,

(And We shall gather the criminals blue-eyed.) It has been said that this means having blue eyes due to the severity of their horrifying situation.

(They will speak in a very low voice to each other.) Ibn `Abbas said, "This means whispering among themselves." This means that some of them will be saying to others,

(You stayed not longer than ten.) meaning in the abode of the worldly life, you only tarried there for a little while. The time was equivalent to ten days or so. Allah, the Exalted, then says,

(We know very well what they will say,) This means in their condition of conversing amongst themselves.

(when the best among them in knowledge and wisdom will say;) the one with perfect intelligence amongst them,

(You stayed no longer than a day!) This is because on the Day of Judgement they will sense the shortness of the worldly life within themselves. For the worldly life, with its repetitious time periods and successive nights, days and hours, is as if it is just one day. For this reason, on the Day of Resurrection the disbelievers will think the worldly life was very short. By this they mean to prevent the establishment of the evidence against them due to the shortness of time that they had. Allah says about this,

(And on the Day that the Hour will be established, the criminals will swear that they stayed not but an hour) until His statement,

(but you knew not.") (30:55-56) Allah also says,

(Did We not give you lives long enough, so that whosoever would receive admonition could receive it And the warner came to you.) (35:37) Allah, the Exalted, also says,

((Allah will say): What number of years did you stay on earth They will say: "We stayed a day or part of a day. Ask of those who keep account." He (Allah) will say: "You stayed not but a little, if you had only known!") (23:112-114) This means that you only remained in it (the earth) a little while. If you only knew, you would have preferred the eternal life over the temporal life. Yet, you conducted yourselves in an evil manner. You gave the present, temporary life precedence over the eternal and everlasting life.

Surah: 20 Ayah: 105, Ayah: 106, Ayah: 107 & Ayah: 108

وَيَسْـَٔلُونَكَ عَنِ ٱلْجِبَالِ فَقُلْ يَنسِفُهَا رَبِّى نَسْفًا ﴿١٠٥﴾

105. And they ask you concerning the mountains: say, "My Lord will blast them and scatter them as particles of dust.

فَيَذَرُهَا قَاعًا صَفْصَفًا ﴿١٠٦﴾

106. "Then He shall leave it as a level smooth plain.

لَّا تَرَىٰ فِيهَا عِوَجًا وَلَآ أَمْتًا ﴿١٠٧﴾

107. "You will see therein nothing crooked or curved."

يَوْمَئِذٍ يَتَّبِعُونَ ٱلدَّاعِىَ لَا عِوَجَ لَهُۥ ۖ وَخَشَعَتِ ٱلْأَصْوَاتُ لِلرَّحْمَٰنِ فَلَا تَسْمَعُ إِلَّا هَمْسًا ﴿١٠٨﴾

108. On that Day mankind will follow strictly (the voice of) Allâh's caller, no crookedness (that is without going to the right or left of that voice) will they show him (Allâh's caller). And all voices will be humbled for the Most Gracious (Allâh), and nothing shall you hear but the low voice of their footsteps.

Transliteration

105. Wayas-aloonaka AAani aljibali faqul yansifuha rabbee nasfan 106. Fayatharuha qaAAan safsafan 107. La tara feeha AAiwajan wala amtan 108. Yawma-ithin

yattabiAAoona alddaAAiya la AAiwaja lahu wakhashaAAati al-aswatu lilrrahmani fala tasmaAAu illa hamsan

Tafsir Ibn Kathir

The destruction of the Mountains, and the Earth becomes a Smooth Plain

Allah says,

(And they ask you concerning the mountains.) This is a question, will they remain on the Day of Resurrection or will they cease to exist

(Say: "My Lord will blast them and scatter them as particles of dust.") This means that He will take them away from their places, wipe them out and remove them completely.

(Then He shall leave it) referring to the earth;

(as a level smooth plain.) This means one expanse spread out. The word Qa` means a piece of land that is level and the word Safsafa is used to place emphasis on this meaning. It has also been said that Safsafa means that which has no vegetation growing in it. The first meaning is preferred, even though the second meaning is also included by necessity. In reference to this, Allah says,

(You will see therein no crookedness nor curve.) meaning, `on that Day you will not see in the earth any valley, hill, or any place, whether low or elevated.' Ibn `Abbas, `Ikrimah, Mujahid, Al-Hasan Al-Basri, Ad-Dahhak, Qatadah and others of the Salaf all said the same.

The People will rush towards the Voice of the Caller

(On that Day mankind will follow strictly Allah's caller, no crookedness will they show him.) On the Day, they see these conditions and these frightening sights, they will hastily respond to the caller. Wherever they are commanded to go, they will rush to it. If they had been like this in the worldly life, it would have been more beneficial for them, but here it does not benefit them. This is as Allah says,

(How clearly will they see and hear, the Day when they will appear before Us!) (19:38) Allah also says,

(hastening towards the caller.) Concerning Allah's statement,

(And all voices will be humbled for the Most Gracious,) Ibn `Abbas said, "This means they will be silent." As-Suddi also said the same.

(And nothing shall you hear except Hamsa.) Sa`id bin Jubayr related that Ibn `Abbas said, "This means the steps of feet." `Ikrimah, Mujahid, Ad-Dahhak, Ar-Rabi` bin Anas, Qatadah, Ibn Zayd and others all said the same. `Ali bin Abi Talhah said that Ibn `Abbas said,

(And nothing shall you hear except Hamsa.) "Hamsa means a hidden voice." This has also been repor- ted from `Ikrimah and Ad-Dahhak. Sa`id bin Jubayr said,

(And nothing shall you hear except Hamsa.) "Hamsa means the secret speech and the steps of feet."

Surah: 20 Ayah: 109, Ayah: 110, Ayah: 111 & Ayah: 112

يَوْمَئِذٍ لَّا تَنفَعُ ٱلشَّفَٰعَةُ إِلَّا مَنْ أَذِنَ لَهُ ٱلرَّحْمَٰنُ وَرَضِىَ لَهُۥ قَوْلًا ﴿١٠٩﴾

109. On that day no intercession shall avail, except the one for whom the Most Gracious (Allâh) has given permission and whose word is acceptable to Him.

يَعْلَمُ مَا بَيْنَ أَيْدِيهِمْ وَمَا خَلْفَهُمْ وَلَا يُحِيطُونَ بِهِۦ عِلْمًا ﴿١١٠﴾

110. He (Allâh) knows what happens to them (His creatures) in this world, and what will happen to them (in the Hereafter), but they will never compass anything of His Knowledge.

۞ وَعَنَتِ ٱلْوُجُوهُ لِلْحَىِّ ٱلْقَيُّومِ وَقَدْ خَابَ مَنْ حَمَلَ ظُلْمًا ﴿١١١﴾

111. And (all) faces shall be humbled before (Allâh), the Ever Living, the One Who sustains and protects all that exists. And he who carried (a burden of) wrongdoing (i.e. he who disbelieved in Allâh, ascribed partners to Him, and did deeds of His disobedience), will be indeed a complete failure (on that Day).

وَمَن يَعْمَلْ مِنَ ٱلصَّٰلِحَٰتِ وَهُوَ مُؤْمِنٌ فَلَا يَخَافُ ظُلْمًا وَلَا هَضْمًا ﴿١١٢﴾

112. And he who works deeds of righteousness, while he is a believer (in Islâmic Monotheism) then he will have no fear of injustice, nor of any curtailment (of his reward).

Transliteration

109. Yawma-ithin la tanfaAAu alshshafaAAatu illa man athina lahu alrrahmanu waradiya lahu qawlan 110. YaAAlamu ma bayna aydeehim wama khalfahum wala yuheetoona bihi Aailman 111. WaAAanati alwujoohu lilhayyi alqayyoomi waqad khaba man hamala thulman 112. Waman yaAAmal mina alssalihati wahuwa mu/minun fala yakhafu thulman wala hadman

Tafsir Ibn Kathir

The Intercession and the Recompense

Allah, the Exalted, says,

(On that day) the Day of Resurrection,

(no intercession shall avail.) meaning with Him (Allah).

(except the one for whom the Most Gracious has given permission and whose word is acceptable to Him.) This is similar to His statement,

(Who is he that can intercede with Him except with His permission) (2:255) It is also similar to His statement,

(And there are many angels in the heavens, whose intercession will avail nothing except after Allah has given leave for whom He wills and is pleased with.) (53:26) He also says,

(And they cannot intercede except for him with whom He is pleased. And they stand in awe for fear of Him.) (21:28) He also says,

(Intercession with Him profits not except for him whom He permits.) (34:23) And He says,

(The Day that Ar-Ruh and the angels will stand forth in rows, they will not speak except him whom the Most Gracious allows, and he will speak what is right.) (78:38) In the Two Sahihs it is reported from the leader of the Children of Adam and the Noblest of all the creatures to Allah, Muhammad :

«آتِي تَحْتَ الْعَرْشِ، وَأَخِرُّ لِلهِ سَاجِدًا، وَيَفْتَحُ عَلَيَّ بِمَحَامِدَ لَا أُحْصِيهَا الْآنَ، فَيَدَعُنِي مَا شَاءَ أَنْ يَدَعَنِي، ثُمَّ يَقُولُ: يَا مُحَمَّدُ، ارْفَعْ رَأْسَكَ وَقُلْ يُسْمَعْ، وَاشْفَعْ تُشَفَّعْ فَيَحُدُّ لِي حَدًّا، فَأُدْخِلُهُمُ الْجَنَّةَ ثُمَّ أَعُودُ»

(I will come under the Throne and I will fall down into prostration. Then, I will be inspired to make praises (of Allah) that I am not able to recall them now. Allah will leave me in this condition as long as He wishes. Then, He will say, "O Muhammad, raise your head. Speak and you will be heard, intercede and your intercession will be accepted." Then, a designated group will be allowed for me (to intercede on their behalf). Allah will then enter them into Paradise and I will return (to repeat the process again).) The Prophet mentioned doing this four times. May Allah's blessings and peace be upon him and the rest of the Prophets as well. In another Hadith it also mentions that he said,

«يَقُولُ تَعَالَى: أَخْرِجُوا مِنَ النَّارِ مَنْ كَانَ فِي قَلْبِهِ مِثْقَالُ حَبَّةٍ مِنْ إِيمَانٍ، فَيُخْرِجُونَ خَلْقًا كَثِيرًا، ثُمَّ يَقُولُ: أَخْرِجُوا مِنَ النَّارِ مَنْ كَانَ فِي قَلْبِهِ نِصْفُ مِثْقَالٍ مِنْ إِيمَانٍ، أَخْرِجُوا مِنَ النَّارِ مَنْ كَانَ فِي قَلْبِهِ مَا يَزِنُ ذَرَّةً، مَنْ كَانَ فِي قَلْبِهِ أَدْنَى أَدْنَى مِثْقَالِ ذَرَّةٍ مِنْ إِيمَانٍ»

(Allah, the Exalted, will say, "Bring out of the Fire whoever has a seed's weight of faith in his heart." So a large number of people will be brought out. Then He will say, "Bring out of the Fire whoever has a half of a seed's weight of faith in his heart. Bring out whoever has the weight of a speck of dust in his heart. Bring out whoever has the weight of the smallest and tiniest particle of dust of faith in his heart.") And the Hadith continues. Concerning Allah's statement,

(He knows what happens to them and what will happen to them,) He encompasses all creation with His knowledge.

(but they will never encompass anything of His knowledge.) This is like His statement,

(And they will never encompass anything of His knowledge except that which He wills.) (2:255) Concerning Allah's statement,

(And (all) faces shall be humbled before the Ever Living, the Sustainer.) Ibn `Abbas and others said, "This means that the creatures will be humbled, submissive and compliant to their Compeller, the Ever Living, Who does not die, the Sustainer of all, Who does not sleep." He is the maintainer of everything. He determines the affairs of everything and preserves everything. He is perfect in His Self. He is the One Whom everything is in need of and whom nothing could survive without. Concerning His statement,

(And he who carried wrongdoing, will be indeed a complete failure.) meaning on the Day of Resurrection. For verily, Allah will give every due right to the one who deserved it. Even the ram who lost its horn will be given revenge against the one who had horns. In the Sahih, it is recorded that the Prophet said,

»إِيَّاكُمْ وَالظُّلْمَ، فَإِنَّ الظُّلْمَ ظُلُمَاتٌ يَوْمَ الْقِيَامَةِ«

(Beware of wrongdoing (or oppression), for verily, wrongdoing will be darknesses on the Day of Resurrection.) And the true failure is for whoever meets Allah while associating partners with Him. Allah the Exalted says,

("Verily, associating partners with Me is the great wrongdoing.") Allah's statement,

(And he who works deeds of righteousness, while he is a believer, then he will have no fear of injustice, nor of any curtailment.) After Allah mentions the wrongdoers and their threat, He then commends the pious people and mentions the judgement they receive. Their judgement is that they will not be wronged nor oppressed. This means that their evils will not be increased and their good deeds will not be decreased. This was stated by Ibn `Abbas, Mujahid, Ad-Dahhak, Al-Hasan, Qatadah and others. Zulm means an increase that comes from the sins of others being placed upon the person, and Hadm means a decrease.

Surah: 20 Ayah: 113 & Ayah: 114

وَكَذَٰلِكَ أَنزَلْنَٰهُ قُرْءَانًا عَرَبِيًّا وَصَرَّفْنَا فِيهِ مِنَ ٱلْوَعِيدِ لَعَلَّهُمْ يَتَّقُونَ أَوْ يُحْدِثُ لَهُمْ ذِكْرًا ۝

113. And thus We have sent it down as a Qur'ân in Arabic, and have explained therein in detail the warnings, in order that they may fear Allâh, or that it may cause them to have a lesson from it (or to have the honor for believing and acting on its teachings).

فَتَعَٰلَى ٱللَّهُ ٱلْمَلِكُ ٱلْحَقُّ ۗ وَلَا تَعْجَلْ بِٱلْقُرْءَانِ مِن قَبْلِ أَن يُقْضَىٰٓ إِلَيْكَ وَحْيُهُۥ ۖ وَقُل رَّبِّ زِدْنِي عِلْمًا ۝

114. Then High above all be Allâh, the True King. And be not in haste (O Muhammad (peace be upon him)) with the Qur'ân before its revelation is completed to you, and say: "My Lord! Increase me in knowledge."

Transliteration

113. Wakathalika anzalnahu qur-anan AAarabiyyan wasarrafna feehi mina alwaAAeedi laAAallahum yattaqoona aw yuhdithu lahum thikran   114. FataAAala Allahu almaliku alhaqqu wala taAAjal bialqur-ani min qabli an yuqda ilayka wahyuhu waqul rabbi zidnee AAilman

Tafsir Ibn Kathir

The Qur'an was revealed so that the People would have Taqwa and reflect

After Allah, the Exalted, mentions that on the Day of Judgement both the good and the evil will be recompensed and there is no avoiding it, He then explains that the Qur'an was revealed as a bringer of glad tidings and a warner in the clear and eloquent Arabic language. There is no confusion or deficiency in it.

(And thus We have sent it down as a Qur'an in Arabic, and have explained therein in detail the warnings, in order that they may have Taqwa of,) This means: so that they will leave off sins, forbidden things and lewd abominations.

(or that it may cause them to have a lesson from it.) This means: to produce acts of obedience and deeds that will bring one closer to Allah.

(Then High above all be Allah, the True King.) This means: Most Holy and Majestic is He, the True King, Who is Himself the Truth and His promise is true. Likewise, His threat is true, His Messengers are true, the Paradise is true, the Hellfire is true and everything from Him is true. His justice is that He does not punish anyone before warning them, sending Messengers to them and granting excuses to His creatures, so that no one will have any argument or doubt (on Judgment Day).

Chapter 20: Ta-Ha (Ta-Ha), Verses 001-135

The Command to the Prophet to listen to the Qur'an when it is revealed without making haste to recite it

Concerning Allah's statement,

(And be not in haste with the Qur'an before its revelation is completed to you,) This is similar to Allah's statement,

(Move not your tongue to make haste therewith. It is for Us to collect it and to give you the ability to recite it. And when We have recited it to you, then follow its recital. Then it is for Us to made it clear (to you).) (75:16-19) It is confirmed in the Sahih on the authority of Ibn `Abbas, who said that the Messenger of Allah used to go through great pains to retain the revelation. In doing so he used to move his tongue rapidly with its recital. Then, Allah revealed this Ayah. This means that whenever Jibril would say an Ayah, the Prophet would say it with him due to his eagerness to memorize it. Then, Allah guided him to that which was easier and lighter in this matter, to relieve him of this difficulty. Allah said,

(Move not your tongue to make haste therewith. It is for Us to collect it and to give you the ability to recite it.) (75:16-17) Meaning, "We will gather it in your chest, then you will recite it to the people without forgetting anything of it."

(And when We have recited it to you, then follow its recital. Then it is for Us to made it clear (to you).) (75:18-19) And He said in this Ayah,

(And be not in haste with the Qur'an before its revelation is completed to you,) This is a command to the Prophet to listen quietly: `Then, when the angel (Jibril) completes reciting to you, you recite it after him.'

(and say: "My Lord! Increase me in knowledge.") meaning, "Give me more knowledge from You." Ibn `Uyaynah said, "The Prophet did not cease increasing (in knowledge) until Allah, the Mighty and Sublime, took him (i.e. he died)."

Surah: 20 Ayah: 115, Ayah: 116, Ayah: 117, Ayah: 118, Ayah: 119, Ayah: 120, Ayah: 121 & Ayah: 122

وَلَقَدْ عَهِدْنَآ إِلَىٰٓ ءَادَمَ مِن قَبْلُ فَنَسِيَ وَلَمْ نَجِدْ لَهُۥ عَزْمًا ۝

115. And indeed We made a covenant with Adam before, but he forgot, and We found on his part no firm will-power.

وَإِذْ قُلْنَا لِلْمَلَـٰٓئِكَةِ ٱسْجُدُوا۟ لِـَٔادَمَ فَسَجَدُوٓا۟ إِلَّآ إِبْلِيسَ أَبَىٰ ۝

116. And (remember) when We said to the angels: "Prostrate yourselves to Adam." They prostrated themselves (all) except Iblîs (Satan), he refused.

فَقُلْنَا يَـٰٓـَٔادَمُ إِنَّ هَـٰذَا عَدُوٌّ لَّكَ وَلِزَوْجِكَ فَلَا يُخْرِجَنَّكُمَا مِنَ ٱلْجَنَّةِ فَتَشْقَىٰٓ ۝

117. Then We said: "O Adam! Verily, this is an enemy to you and to your wife. So let him not get you both out of Paradise, so that you be distressed.

إِنَّ لَكَ أَلَّا تَجُوعَ فِيهَا وَلَا تَعْرَىٰ ۝

118. Verily, you have (a promise from Us) that you will never be hungry therein nor naked.

وَأَنَّكَ لَا تَظْمَؤُاْ فِيهَا وَلَا تَضْحَىٰ ۝

119. And you (will) suffer not from thirst therein nor from the sun's heat.

فَوَسْوَسَ إِلَيْهِ ٱلشَّيْطَٰنُ قَالَ يَٰٓـَٔادَمُ هَلْ أَدُلُّكَ عَلَىٰ شَجَرَةِ ٱلْخُلْدِ وَمُلْكٍ لَّا يَبْلَىٰ ۝

120. Then Shaitân (Satan) whispered to him, saying: "O Adam! Shall I lead you to the Tree of Eternity and to a kingdom that will never waste away?"

فَأَكَلَا مِنْهَا فَبَدَتْ لَهُمَا سَوْءَٰتُهُمَا وَطَفِقَا يَخْصِفَانِ عَلَيْهِمَا مِن وَرَقِ ٱلْجَنَّةِ ۚ وَعَصَىٰٓ ءَادَمُ رَبَّهُۥ فَغَوَىٰ ۝

121. Then they both ate of the tree, and so their private parts became manifest to them, and they began to cover themselves with the leaves of the Paradise for their covering. Thus did Adam disobey his Lord, so he went astray.

ثُمَّ ٱجْتَبَٰهُ رَبُّهُۥ فَتَابَ عَلَيْهِ وَهَدَىٰ ۝

122. Then his Lord chose him, and turned to him with forgiveness, and gave him guidance.

Transliteration

115. Walaqad AAahidna ila adama min qablu fanasiya walam najid lahu Aaazman 116. Wa-ith qulna lilmala-ikati osjudoo li-adama fasajadoo illa ibleesa aba 117. Faqulna ya adamu inna hatha AAaduwwun laka walizawjika fala yukhrijannakuma mina aljannati fatashqa 118. Inna laka alla tajooAAa feeha wala taAAra 119. Waannaka la tathmao feeha wala tadha 120. Fawaswasa ilayhi alshshaytanu qala ya adamu hal adulluka AAala shajarati alkhuldi wamulkin la yabla 121. Faakala minha fabadat lahuma saw-atuhuma watafiqa yakhsifani AAalayhima min waraqi aljannati waAAasa adamu rabbahu faghawa 122. Thumma ijtabahu rabbuhu fataba AAalayhi wahada

Chapter 20: Ta-Ha (Ta-Ha), Verses 001-135

Tafsir Ibn Kathir

The Story of Adam and Iblis

Ibn Abi Hatim recorded that Ibn `Abbas said, "Verily, man was named Insan only because he was given a covenant, but he forgot it (Nasiya)." `Ali bin Abi Talhah reported the same from Ibn `Abbas. Mujahid and Al-Hasan said that he forgot means, "He abandoned it." Concerning Allah's statement,

(And when We said to the angels: "Prostrate yourselves to Adam.") He, Allah mentions how Adam was honored and what respect was given to him. He mentions how He favored him over many of those whom He created. A discussion of this story has already preceded in Surat Al-Baqarah, Surat Al-A`raf, Surat Al-Hijr and Surat Al-Kahf. It will also be mentioned again at the end of Surah Sad. In this story, Allah mentions the creation of Adam and that He commanded the angels to prostrate to Adam as a sign of honor and respect. He also explains the enmity of Iblis for the Children of Adam and for their father, Adam, before them. Due to this Allah says,

(They prostrated themselves (all) except Iblis; he refused.) This means that he refrained from prostrating and became arrogant.

(Then We said: "O Adam! Verily, this is an enemy to you and to your wife...") here wife refers to Hawwa'.

(So let him not get you both out of Paradise, so that you will be distressed.) meaning, `Do not be hasty in doing something that will get you expelled from Paradise, or else you will be fatigued, discomforted and worried, seeking your sustenance. But here, in Paradise, you live a life of ease with no burdens and no difficulties.'

(Verily, you will never be hungry therein nor naked.) The reason that Allah combined hunger and nakedness is because hunger is internal humiliation, while nakedness is external humiliation.

(And you (will) suffer not from thirst therein nor from the sun's heat.) These two characteristics are also opposites. Thirst is the internal heat and being parched from lack of water, while the suns heat is the external heat.

(Then Shaytan whispered to him, saying: "O Adam! Shall I lead you to the Tree of Eternity and to a kingdom that will never waste away") It has already been mentioned that he caused them to fall through deception.

(And he swore by Allah to them both: "Verily, I am one of the sincere well-wishers for you both.") (7:21) It has already preceded in our discussion that Allah took a promise from Adam and his wife that although they could eat from every fruit, they could not come near a specific tree in Paradise. However, Iblis did not cease prodding them until they both had eaten from it. It was the Tree of Eternity (Shajarat Al-Khuld). This meant that anyone who ate from it would live forever and always remain. A Hadith has been narrated which mentions this Tree of Eternity. Abu Dawud At-Tayalisi reported from Abu Hurayrah that the Prophet said,

«إِنَّ فِي الْجَنَّةِ شَجَرَةً يَسِيرُ الرَّاكِبُ فِي ظِلِّهَا مِائَةَ عَامٍ مَا يَقْطَعُهَا، وَهِيَ شَجَرَةُ الْخُلْدِ»

(Verily, in Paradise there is a tree which a rider can travel under its shade for one hundred years and still not have passed it. It is the Tree of Eternity.) Imam Ahmad also recorded this narration. Concerning Allah's statement,

(Then they both ate of the tree, and so their private parts became manifest to them,) Ibn Abi Hatim recorded that Ubayy bin Ka`b said that the Messenger of Allah said,

«إِنَّ اللهَ خَلَقَ آدَمَ رَجُلًا طُوَالًا كَثِيرَ شَعْرِ الرَّأْسِ، كَأَنَّهُ نَخْلَةٌ سَحُوقٌ، فَلَمَّا ذَاقَ الشَّجَرَةَ سَقَطَ عَنْهُ لِبَاسُهُ، فَأَوَّلُ مَا بَدَا مِنْهُ عَوْرَتُهُ، فَلَمَّا نَظَرَ إِلَى عَوْرَتِهِ جَعَلَ يَشْتَدُّ فِي الْجَنَّةِ، فَأَخَذَتْ شَعْرَهُ شَجَرَةٌ فَنَازَعَهَا، فَنَادَاهُ الرَّحْمَنُ: يَا آدَمُ مِنِّي تَفِرُّ، فَلَمَّا سَمِعَ كَلَامَ الرَّحْمَنِ قَالَ: يَا رَبِّ لَا، وَلَكِنِ اسْتِحْيَاءً، أَرَأَيْتَ إِنْ تُبْتُ وَرَجَعْتُ أَعَائِدِي إِلَى الْجَنَّةِ؟ قَالَ: نَعَم»

(Verily, Allah created Adam as a tall man with an abundance of hair on his head. He looked like a clothed palm tree. Then, when he tasted (the fruit of) the tree, his clothes fell off of him. The first thing that became exposed was his private parts. So when he noticed his nakedness, he tried to run back into Paradise. However, in the process a tree caught hold of his hair (i.e. his hair was tangled in a tree), so he ripped his hair out. Then, the Most Beneficent called out to him saying, "O Adam, are you fleeing from me" When he heard the Words of the Most Beneficent, he said, "No my Lord, but I am ashamed. If I repent and recant would You let me return to Paradise" Allah replied, "Yes.") This is the meaning of Allah's statement,

(Then Adam received from his Lord Words. And his Lord pardoned him.) (2:37) However, this narration has a break in the chain of transmission between Al-Hasan and Ubayy bin Ka`b. Al-Hasan did not hear this Hadith from Ubayy. It is questionable as to whether this narration can be correctly attributed to the Prophet . Allah said,

(And they began to cover themselves with the leaves of the Paradise for their covering.) Mujahid said, "They patched the leaves on themselves in the form of a garment." Qatadah and As-Suddi both said the same. Concerning Allah's statement,

(Thus Adam disobeyed his Lord, so he went astray. Then his Lord chose him, and turned to him with forgiveness, and gave him guidance.) Al-Bukhari recorded that Abu Hurayrah said that the Prophet said,

Chapter 20: Ta-Ha (Ta-Ha), Verses 001-135

«حَاجَّ مُوسَى آدَمَ، فَقَالَ لَهُ: أَنْتَ الَّذِي أَخْرَجْتَ النَّاسَ مِنَ الْجَنَّةِ بِذَنْبِكَ وَأَشْقَيْتَهُمْ؟ قَالَ آدَمُ: يَا مُوسَى، أَنْتَ الَّذِي اصْطَفَاكَ اللهُ بِرِسَالَاتِهِ وَبِكَلَامِهِ، أَتَلُومُنِي عَلَى أَمْرٍ كَتَبَهُ اللهُ عَلَيَّ قَبْلَ أَنْ يَخْلُقَنِي أَوْ قَدَّرَهُ اللهُ عَلَيَّ قَبْلَ أَنْ يَخْلُقَنِي؟ قال رسول الله صلى الله عليه وسلّم: فَحَجَّ آدَمُ مُوسَى»

(Musa argued with Adam and he said to him, "Are you the one who got mankind expelled from Paradise because of your sin and you caused them grief!" Adam replied, "Are you the one whom Allah chose for His Divine Messages and His direct Speech. Are you blaming me for a matter that Allah wrote upon me before He created me") Then, the Messenger of Allah said, (Thus, Adam defeated Musa.) This Hadith has various routes of transmission in the Two Sahihs as well as the Musnad collections.

Surah: 20 Ayah: 123, Ayah: 124, Ayah: 125 & Ayah: 126

قَالَ ٱهْبِطَا مِنْهَا جَمِيعًۢا ۖ بَعْضُكُمْ لِبَعْضٍ عَدُوٌّ ۖ فَإِمَّا يَأْتِيَنَّكُم مِّنِّى هُدًى فَمَنِ ٱتَّبَعَ هُدَاىَ فَلَا يَضِلُّ وَلَا يَشْقَىٰ ۝

123. (Allâh) said: "Get you down (from the Paradise to the earth), both of you, together, some of you are an enemy to some others. Then if there comes to you guidance from Me, then whoever follows My Guidance he shall neither go astray, nor shall be distressed.

وَمَنْ أَعْرَضَ عَن ذِكْرِى فَإِنَّ لَهُۥ مَعِيشَةً ضَنكًا وَنَحْشُرُهُۥ يَوْمَ ٱلْقِيَٰمَةِ أَعْمَىٰ

124. "But whosoever turns away from My Reminder (i.e. neither believes in this Qur'ân nor acts on its teachings.) verily, for him is a life of hardship, and We shall raise him up blind on the Day of Resurrection."

$$قَالَ رَبِّ لِمَ حَشَرْتَنِي أَعْمَىٰ وَقَدْ كُنتُ بَصِيرًا ﴿١٢٥﴾$$

125. He will say: "O my Lord! Why have you raised me up blind, while I had sight (before)."

$$قَالَ كَذَٰلِكَ أَتَتْكَ ءَايَٰتُنَا فَنَسِيتَهَا ۖ وَكَذَٰلِكَ ٱلْيَوْمَ تُنسَىٰ ﴿١٢٦﴾$$

126. (Allâh) will say: "Like this: Our Ayât (proofs, evidences, verses, lessons, signs, revelations, etc.) came unto you, but you disregarded them (i.e. you left them, did not think deeply in them, and you turned away from them), and so this Day, you will be neglected (in the Hell-fire, away from Allâh's Mercy)."

Transliteration

123. Qala ihbita minha jameeAAan baAAdukum libaAAdin AAaduwwun fa-imma ya/tiyannakum minnee hudan famani ittabaAAa hudaya fala yadillu wala yashqa 124. Waman aAArada AAan thikree fa-inna lahu maAAeeshatan dankan wanahshuruhu yawma alqiyamati aAAman 125. Qala rabbi lima hashartanee aAAma waqad kuntu baseeran 126. Qala kathalika atatka ayatuna fanaseetaha wakathalika alyawma tunsa

Tafsir Ibn Kathir

The Descent of Adam to the Earth and the Promise of Good for the Guided and Evil for the Transgressors

Allah says to Adam, Hawwa' and Iblis, "Get down from here, all of you." This means each of you should get out of Paradise. We expounded upon this in Surah Al-Baqarah.

(Some of you as enemies to others.) (2:36) He (Allah) was saying this to Adam and his progeny and Iblis and his progeny. Concerning Allah's statement,

(Then if there comes to you guidance from Me,) Abu Al-`Aliyyah said, "This (guidance) means the Prophets, the Messengers and the evidence."

(Then whoever follows My guidance he shall neither go astray nor shall be distressed.) Ibn `Abbas said, "He will not be misguided in this life and he will not be distressed in the Hereafter."

(But whosoever turns away from My Reminder,) This means, "Whoever opposes my command and what I have revealed to My Messenger, then he has turned away from it, neglected it and taken his guidance from other than it."

(verily, for him is a life of hardship,) meaning, his life will be hard in this world. He will have no tranquillity and no expanding of his breast (ease). Rather, his chest will be constrained and in difficulty due to his misguidance. Even if he appears to be in comfort outwardly and he wears whatever he likes, eats whatever he likes and lives wherever he wants, he will not be happy. For verily, his heart will not have pure certainty and guidance. He will be in agitation, bewilderment and doubt. He will always be in confusion and a state of uncertainty. This is from the hardship of life. Concerning His statement,

Chapter 20: Ta-Ha (Ta-Ha), Verses 001-135 — 157

(and We shall raise him up blind on the Day of Resurrection.) Mujahid, Abu Salih and As-Suddi said, "This means he will have no proof." `Ikrimah said, "He will be made blind to everything except Hell." This is as Allah says,

(And We shall gather them together on the Day of Resurrection on their faces, blind, dumb and deaf; their abode will be Hell.) (17:97) This is why Allah says,

(O my Lord! Why have you raised me up blind, while I had sight (before).) This means in the life of this world.

((Allah) will say: "Like this Our Ayat came unto you, but you disregarded them, and so this Day, you will be neglected.) Meaning, "When you turned away from the signs of Allah and dealt with them in the manner of one who does not remember them after they were conveyed to you. You neglected them, turned away from them and were heedless of them. Therefore, today We will treat you in the manner of one who has forgotten you."

(So this Day We shall forget them as they forgot their meeting of this Day.) (7:51) For verily, the punishment will be a retribution that is based upon the type of deed that was done. However, forgetting the words of the Qur'an, while understanding its meaning and acting upon its legislation, is not included in the meaning of this specific threat. Yet, forgetting the words of the Qur'an has been warned against from a different aspect. It has been reported in the Sunnah that it is absolutely forbidden and there is a serious threat against one who forgets Qur'an (that he previously memorized).

Surah: 20 Ayah: 127

وَكَذَٰلِكَ نَجْزِى مَنْ أَسْرَفَ وَلَمْ يُؤْمِنۢ بِـَٔايَـٰتِ رَبِّهِۦ ۚ وَلَعَذَابُ ٱلْءَاخِرَةِ أَشَدُّ وَأَبْقَىٰ

127. And thus do We requite him who transgresses beyond bounds (i.e. commits the great sins and disobeys his Lord (Allâh) and believes not in His Messengers, and His revealed Books, like this Qur'ân), and believes not in the Ayât (proofs, evidences, verses, lessons, signs, revelations, etc.) of his Lord; and the torment of the Hereafter is far more severe and more lasting.

Transliteration

127. Wakathalika najzee man asrafa walam yu/min bi-ayati rabbihi walaAAathabu al-akhirati ashaddu waabqa

Tafsir Ibn Kathir

Severe Torment for Him Who transgresses beyond bounds

Allah says: `Thus We do requite those who transgress beyond bounds and belie the Ayat of Allah in this world and in the Hereafter.'

(For them is a torment in the life of this world, and certainly, harder is the torment of the Hereafter. And they have no defender or protector against Allah.) (13:34) Therefore Allah said,

(and the torment of the Hereafter is far more severe and more lasting.) meaning: a more grievous and more painful penalty than of this world they will remain therein, they will abide forever in such torment. Allah's Messenger said to both husband and wife who took an oath, when the husband accused his wife of committing illegal sexual intercourse:

«إِنَّ عَذَابَ الدُّنْيَا أَهْوَنُ مِنْ عَذَابِ الْآخِرَةِ»

(Verily, the torment of this worldly life is more insignificant, compared to the punishment of the Hereafter.)

Surah: 20 Ayah: 128, Ayah: 129 & Ayah: 130

أَفَلَمْ يَهْدِ لَهُمْ كَمْ أَهْلَكْنَا قَبْلَهُم مِّنَ ٱلْقُرُونِ يَمْشُونَ فِى مَسَٰكِنِهِمْ إِنَّ فِى ذَٰلِكَ لَءَايَٰتٍ لِّأُوْلِى ٱلنُّهَىٰ ۝

128. Is it not a guidance for them (to know) how many generations We have destroyed before them, in whose dwellings they walk? Verily, in this are signs indeed for men of understanding.

وَلَوْلَا كَلِمَةٌ سَبَقَتْ مِن رَّبِّكَ لَكَانَ لِزَامًا وَأَجَلٌ مُّسَمًّى ۝

129. And had it not been for a Word that went forth before from your Lord, and a term determined, (their punishment) must necessarily have come (in this world).

فَٱصْبِرْ عَلَىٰ مَا يَقُولُونَ وَسَبِّحْ بِحَمْدِ رَبِّكَ قَبْلَ طُلُوعِ ٱلشَّمْسِ وَقَبْلَ غُرُوبِهَا وَمِنْ ءَانَآىِٕ ٱلَّيْلِ فَسَبِّحْ وَأَطْرَافَ ٱلنَّهَارِ لَعَلَّكَ تَرْضَىٰ ۝

130. So bear patiently (O Muhammad (peace be upon him)) what they say, and glorify the praises of your Lord before the rising of the sun, and before its setting, and during some of the hours of the night, and at the ends of the day (an indication for the five compulsory congregational prayers), that you may become pleased with the reward which Allâh shall give you.

Transliteration

128. Afalam yahdi lahum kam ahlakna qablahum mina alquroonee yamshoona fee masakinihim inna fee thalika laayatin li-olee alnnuha 129. Walawla kalimatun sabaqat min rabbika lakana lizaman waajalun musamman 130. Faisbir AAala ma yaqooloona wasabbih bihamdi rabbika qabla tulooAAi alshshamsi waqabla ghuroobiha wamin ana-i allayli fasabbih waatrafa alnnahari laAAallaka tarda

Chapter 20: Ta-Ha (Ta-Ha), Verses 001-135 — 159

Tafsir Ibn Kathir

Many Nations were destroyed and in Them is a Lesson

Allah, the Exalted, says,

(Is it not a guidance for them...) This is addressed to those who reject what the Prophet came to them with: `We destroyed those who denied the Messengers from the previous nations before them. They showed open hostility, so now there is not trace of them and none of them are left. This is witnessed by the empty homes that these people left behind, and which others have now inherited, moving about in the dwellings of those of the past.'

(Verily, in this are signs indeed for men of understanding.) This means those who have sound intellect and correct understanding. This is as Allah says,

(Have they not traveled through the land, and have they hearts wherewith to understand and ears wherewith to hear Verily, it is not the eyes that grow blind, but it is the hearts which are in the breasts that grow blind.) (22:46) Allah also said in Surah Alif Lam Mim As-Sajdah,

(Is it not a guidance for them: how many generations We have destroyed before them in whose dwellings they walk about) (32:26) Then, Allah, the Exalted, says,

(And had it not been for a Word that went forth before from your Lord, and a term determined (their punishment), must necessarily have come (in this world).) (20:129) This means that if it were not for the Word that had already preceded from Allah -- that He would not punish anyone until the proof had been established against him and the punishment would take place at an appointed time that He has already determined for these rejecters -- then the punishment would certainly seize them immediately.

The Command to be patient and perform the Five daily Prayers

Allah comforts His Prophet by saying to him,

(So bear patiently what they say,) This means, "Be patient concerning their rejection of you."

(And glorify the praises of your Lord before the rising of the sun,) This is speaking of the Morning (Fajr) prayer.

(and before its setting,) This is speaking of the Mid-afternoon (`Asr) prayer. This has been mentioned in the Two Sahihs on the authority of Jarir bin `Abdullah Al-Bajali, who said, "Once we were sitting with the Messenger of Allah when he looked up at the moon on a night when it was full. He said,

«إِنَّكُمْ سَتَرَوْنَ رَبَّكُمْ كَمَا تَرَوْنَ هَذَا الْقَمَرَ، لَا تُضَامُونَ فِي رُؤْيَتِهِ، فَإِنِ

«اسْتَطَعْتُمْ أَنْ لَا تُغْلَبُوا عَلَى صَلَاةٍ قَبْلَ طُلُوعِ الشَّمْسِ وَقَبْلَ غُرُوبِهَا فَافْعَلُوا»

(Verily, you all will see your Lord (in the Hereafter) just as you see this moon and you will not have to crowd together to see Him. Therefore, if you are able to not miss a prayer before sunrise (Fajr) and before sunset (`Asr), then you should do so.) Then he recited this Ayah." Imam Ahmad recorded that `Umarah bin Ru'aybah that he heard the Messenger of Allah saying,

«لَنْ يَلِجَ النَّارَ أَحَدٌ صَلَّى قَبْلَ طُلُوعِ الشَّمْسِ وَقَبْلَ غُرُوبِهَا»

(Anyone who prays before sunrise and before sunset will never enter the Hellfire.) This was also recorded by Muslim. Concerning Allah's statement,

(and during some hours of the night, glorify the praises.) This means during its hours offer the late night (Tahajjud) prayer. Some of the scholars said it also means the after sunset (Maghrib) and the night (`Isha') prayers.

(and at the ends of the day,) This is the opposite of the hours of the night.

(that you may become pleased) As Allah says,

(And verily, your Lord will give you (all good) so that you shall be well-pleased.) (93:5) In the Sahih, it is recorded that the Messenger of Allah said,

«يَقُولُ اللهُ تَعَالَى يَا أَهْلَ الْجَنَّةِ، فَيَقُولُونَ: لَبَّيْكَ رَبَّنَا وَسَعْدَيْكَ، فَيَقُولُ: هَلْ رَضِيتُمْ؟ فَيَقُولُونَ: رَبَّنَا وَمَا لَنَا لَا نَرْضَى وَقَدْ أَعْطَيْتَنَا مَا لَمْ تُعْطِ أَحَدًا مِنْ خَلْقِكَ، فَيَقُولُ: إِنِّي أُعْطِيكُمْ أَفْضَلَ مِنْ ذَلِكَ، فَيَقُولُونَ: وَأَيُّ شَيْءٍ أَفْضَلُ مِنْ ذَلِكَ؟ فَيَقُولُ: أُحِلُّ عَلَيْكُمْ رِضْوَانِي فَلَا أَسْخَطُ عَلَيْكُمْ بَعْدَهُ أَبَدًا»

(Allah, the Exalted, says, "O people of Paradise." They will reply, "We are here at Your service and Your pleasure our Lord." He will then say, "Are you all pleased" They will reply, "Why should we not be pleased our Lord, when You have given us what You have not given any others of Your creation" Allah will then say, "Verily, I am going to give you something better than that." They will say, "And what thing could be better than that" Allah will say, "I have allowed for you My pleasure, so I will never be angry with you again after this.") In another Hadith, it states that it will be said,

«يَا أَهْلَ الْجَنَّةِ، إِنَّ لَكُمْ عِنْدَ اللهِ مَوْعِدًا يُرِيدُ أَنْ يُنْجِزَكُمُوهُ: فَيَقُولُونَ: وَمَا

هُوَ؟ أَلَمْ يُبَيِّضْ وُجُوهَنَا وَيُثْقِلْ مَوَازِينَنَا وَيُزَحْزِحْنَا عَنِ النَّارِ وَيُدْخِلْنَا الْجَنَّةَ، فَيُكْشَفُ الْحِجَابُ فَيَنْظُرُونَ إِلَيْهِ، فَوَ اللهِ مَا أَعْطَاهُمْ خَيْرًا مِنَ النَّظَرِ إِلَيْهِ، وَهِيَ الزِّيَادَةُ»

("O people of Paradise, verily you all have an appointed promise with Allah that He would like to fulfill for you." They will say, "And what is that Has He not already enlightened our faces, made our Scales (of good deeds) heavy, saved us from the Hellfire and entered us into Paradise" Then, the veil will be lifted and they will gaze upon Him (Allah). By Allah, He has not given them anything better than the opportunity to look upon Him, and that is the increase (extra blessing).)

Surah: 20 Ayah: 131 & Ayah: 132, Ayah: 133, Ayah: 134 & Ayah: 135

وَلَا تَمُدَّنَّ عَيْنَيْكَ إِلَىٰ مَا مَتَّعْنَا بِهِ أَزْوَٰجًا مِّنْهُمْ زَهْرَةَ ٱلْحَيَوٰةِ ٱلدُّنْيَا لِنَفْتِنَهُمْ فِيهِ ۚ وَرِزْقُ رَبِّكَ خَيْرٌ وَأَبْقَىٰ ۝

131. And strain not your eyes in longing for the things We have given for enjoyment to various groups of them (polytheists and disbelievers in the Oneness of Allâh), the splendor of the life of this world, that We may test them thereby. But the provision (good reward in the Hereafter) of your Lord is better and more lasting.

وَأْمُرْ أَهْلَكَ بِٱلصَّلَوٰةِ وَٱصْطَبِرْ عَلَيْهَا ۖ لَا نَسْـَٔلُكَ رِزْقًا ۖ نَّحْنُ نَرْزُقُكَ ۗ وَٱلْعَٰقِبَةُ لِلتَّقْوَىٰ ۝

132. And enjoin As-Salât (the prayer) on your family, and be patient in offering them (i.e. the Salât (prayers)) We ask not of you a provision (i.e. to give Us something: money): We provide for you. And the good end (i.e. Paradise) is for the Muttaqûn (the pious and righteous persons. See V.2:2).

وَقَالُوا۟ لَوْلَا يَأْتِينَا بِـَٔايَةٍ مِّن رَّبِّهِۦٓ ۚ أَوَلَمْ تَأْتِهِم بَيِّنَةُ مَا فِى ٱلصُّحُفِ ٱلْأُولَىٰ ۝

133. They say: "Why does he not bring us a sign (proof) from his Lord?" Has there not come to them the proof of that which is (written) in the former papers (Scriptures, i.e. the Taurât (Torah), and the Injeel (Gospel), etc. about the coming of the Prophet Muhammad (peace be upon him))

وَلَوْ أَنَّآ أَهْلَكْنَٰهُم بِعَذَابٍ مِّن قَبْلِهِۦ لَقَالُوا۟ رَبَّنَا لَوْلَآ أَرْسَلْتَ إِلَيْنَا رَسُولًا فَنَتَّبِعَ ءَايَٰتِكَ مِن قَبْلِ أَن نَّذِلَّ وَنَخْزَىٰ ۝

134. And if We had destroyed them with a torment before this (i.e. Messenger Muhammad (peace be upon him) and the Qur'ân), they would surely have said: "Our Lord! If only You had sent us a Messenger, we should certainly have followed Your Ayât (proofs, evidences, verses, lessons, signs, revelations, etc.), before we were humiliated and disgraced."

قُلْ كُلٌّ مُّتَرَبِّصٌ فَتَرَبَّصُوا۟ ۖ فَسَتَعْلَمُونَ مَنْ أَصْحَـٰبُ ٱلصِّرَٰطِ ٱلسَّوِىِّ وَمَنِ ٱهْتَدَىٰ ﴿١٣٥﴾

135. Say (O Muhammad (peace be upon him)) "Each one (believer and disbeliever.) is waiting, so wait you too; and you shall know who are they that are on the Straight and Even Path (i.e. Allâh's Religion of Islâmic Monotheism), and who are they that have let themselves be guided (on the Right Path).

Transliteration

131. Wala tamuddanna AAaynayka ila ma mattaAAna bihi azwajan minhum zahrata alhayati alddunya linaftinahum feehi warizqu rabbika khayrun waabqa 132. Wa/mur ahlaka bialssalati waistabir AAalayha la nas-aluka rizqan nahnu narzuquka waalAAaqibatu lilttaqwa 133. Waqaloo lawla ya/teena bi-ayatin min rabbihi awa lam ta/tihim bayyinatu ma fee alssuhufi al-oola 134. Walaw anna ahlaknahum biAAathabin min qablihi laqaloo rabbana lawla arsalta ilayna rasoolan fanattabiAAa ayatika min qabli an nathilla wanakhza 135. Qul kullun mutarabbisun fatarabbasoo fasataAAlamoona man as-habu alssirati alssawiyyi wamani ihtada

Tafsir Ibn Kathir

Do not look at the Enjoyment of the Wealthy, be patient in the worship of Allah

Allah, the Exalted, says to His Prophet Muhammad , "Do not look at what these people of luxury and their likes and peers have of nice comforts. For verily, it is only short-lived splendor and a feeble bounty, which We are using to test them with. And very few of My servants are truly thankful." Mujahid said,

(various groups of them,) "This means the wealthy people." This means, "Verily, We have given you (O Muhammad) better than that which We have given them." This is just as Allah says in another Ayah,

(And indeed, We have bestowed upon you seven repeatedly recited verses, and the Grand Qur'an. Look not with your eyes ambitiously.) (15:87-88) Likewise, that which Allah has stored for His Messenger in the Hereafter is something extremely great. It is an unlimited reward that cannot be described. This is as Allah says,

(And verily, your Lord will give you so that you shall be well-pleased.) (93:5) For this reason, Allah says,

(But the provision of your Lord is better and more lasting.) In the Sahih it is recorded that `Umar bin Al-Khattab entered upon the Messenger of Allah while he was in the small room in which he had separated himself from his wives after he had vowed to stay away from them. When he came in, he saw him (the Prophet) lying down upon a sandy straw mat. There was nothing in the house except a pile of sant tree pods and some hanging equipment. `Umar's eyes filled with tears (upon seeing this), so the Messenger of Allah said to him,

«مَا يُبْكِيكَ يَا عُمَرُ؟»

(What makes you cry, O Umar) He replied, "O Messenger of Allah, verily Kisra and Caesar are living in their luxurious conditions, yet you are the chosen Friend of Allah amongst His creation" The Prophet said,

«أَوَ فِي شَكٍّ أَنْتَ يَا ابْنَ الْخَطَّابِ؟ أُولَئِكَ قَوْمٌ عُجِّلَتْ لَهُمْ طَيِّبَاتُهُمْ فِي حَيَاتِهِمُ الدُّنْيَا»

(Do you have doubt, O son of Al-Khattab Those people have had their good hastened for them in the life of this world.) Thus, the Prophet was the most abstinent of people concerning worldly luxuries, even though he had the ability to attain them. If he acquired anything of worldly treasures he would spend it on this and that for the servants of Allah. He would never save anything for himself for the next day. Ibn Abi Hatim reported from Abu Sa`id that the Messenger of Allah said,

«إِنَّ أَخْوَفَ مَا أَخَافُ عَلَيْكُمْ مَا يَفْتَحُ اللهُ لَكُمْ مِنْ زَهْرَةِ الدُّنْيَا»

(Verily, the thing I fear most for you all is what Allah will allow you to acquire of the splendor of this world.) They (the Companions) said, "What is the splendor of this world, O Messenger of Allah" He said,

«بَرَكَاتُ الْأَرْضِ»

(The blessings of the earth.) Qatadah and As-Suddi said, "The splendor of this worldly life means the beautiful adornments of the life of this world." Qatadah said,

(that We may test them thereby.) "So that We may put them to trial." Concerning Allah's statement,

(And enjoin the Salah on your family, and be patient in offering them.) This means to save them from the punishment of Allah by the establishment of the prayer, and you also be patient in performing it. This is as Allah says,

(O you who believe! Ward off yourselves and your families against a Fire (Hell).) (66:6) Ibn Abi Hatim recorded that Zayd bin Aslam reported from his father that he and Yarfa' would sometimes spend the night at `Umar bin Al-Khattab's. `Umar had a certain time of night that he would get up and pray. However, sometimes he would not get up for it. Then, we would say, "He is not going to get up like he usually does." When he would awaken, he would make his family get up as well. He would say,

(And enjoin the Salah on your family, and be patient in offering them.)" Allah said;

(We ask not of you a provision: We provide for you.) This means that if you establish the prayer, your sustenance will come to you from where you did not expect. This is as Allah says,

(And whosoever has Taqwa of Allah, He will make a way for him to get out (from every difficulty). And He will provide him from (sources) he never could imagine.) (65:2-3) Allah also says,

(And I (Allah) created not the Jinn and mankind except that they should worship Me (Alone).) until,

(Verily, Allah is the All-Provider, Owner of Power, the Most Strong.) (51:56-58) Thus, Allah says,

(We ask not of you a provision: We provide for you.) Verily, At-Tirmidhi and Ibn Majah recorded that Abu Hurayrah said that the Messenger of Allah said,

«يَقُولُ اللهُ تَعَالَى: يَا ابْنَ آدَمَ تَفَرَّغْ لِعِبَادَتِي أَمْلَأْ صَدْرَكَ غِنًى وَأَسُدَّ فَقْرَكَ، وَإِنْ لَمْ تَفْعَلْ، مَلَأْتُ صَدْرَكَ شُغْلًا وَلَمْ أَسُدَّ فَقْرَكَ»

(Allah, the Exalted, says, "O son of Adam, perform My worship and I will fill your chest with wealth and fulfill your needs. If you do not do so, then I will fill your chest with toil and I will not fulfill your needs.") It is also reported from Zayd bin Thabit that he heard the Messenger of Allah saying,

«مَنْ كَانَتِ الدُّنْيَا هَمَّهُ فَرَّقَ اللهُ عَلَيْهِ أَمْرَهُ، وَجَعَلَ فَقْرَهُ بَيْنَ عَيْنَيْهِ، وَلَمْ يَأْتِهِ مِنَ الدُّنْيَا إِلَّا مَا كُتِبَ لَهُ، وَمَنْ كَانَتِ الْآخِرَةُ نِيَّتَهُ، جَمَعَ لَهُ أَمْرَهُ وَجَعَلَ غِنَاهُ فِي قَلْبِهِ، وَأَتَتْهُ الدُّنْيَا وَهِيَ رَاغِمَةٌ»

(Whoever makes the worldly life his major concern, then Allah will scatter his situation for him (i.e. make it difficult) and his poverty will be placed between his eyes. He will not get from this world anything except that which has already been written for him. Whoever makes the Hereafter his intention, then his situation will be gathered for him (i.e. made easy) and his wealth will be placed in his heart. The worldly life will come to him anyway (in spite of his not seeking it).) Concerning Allah's statement,

(And the good end is for those who have Taqwa.) This means the good end in this life and in the Hereafter. In the Hereafter the good end will be Paradise for whoever feared Allah. In the Sahih it is reported that the Messenger of Allah said,

The Request of the Polytheists for Proofs while the Qur'an is itself a Proof

Allah, the Exalted, informs about the disbelievers in their statement,

(Why does not) This means, `Why doesn't Muhammad bring us some proof from his Lord' They meant a sign that was proof of his truthfulness in his claim that he was the Messenger of Allah. Allah, the Exalted, said,

(Has there not come to them the proof of that which is in the former papers (Scriptures)) This means the Qur'an which Allah revealed to him while he was an unlettered man who could not write well and who did not study with the People of the Book. Yet, the Qur'an contains information about the people of the past that tells of their events from times long ago and it agrees with the authentic information in the previous Books concerning these matters. The Qur'an is the supervisor of these other Books. It verifies what is correct and explains the mistakes that were falsely placed in these Books and attributed to them. This Ayah is similar to Allah's statement in Surat Al-`Ankabut,

(And they say: "Why are not signs sent down to him from his Lord" Say: "The signs are only with Allah, and I am only a plain warner." It is not sufficient for them that We have sent down to you the Book which is recited to them Verily, herein is mercy and a reminder for a people who believe.) (29:50-51) In the Two Sahihs, it is recorded that the Messenger of Allah said,

«مَا مِنْ نَبِيَ إِلَّا وَقَدْ أُوتِيَ مِنَ الْآيَاتِ مَا آمَنَ عَلَى مِثْلِهِ الْبَشَرُ، وَإِنَّمَا كَانَ الَّذِي أُوتِيتُهُ وَحْيًا أَوْحَاهُ اللهُ إِلَيَّ، فَأَرْجُو أَنْ أَكُونَ أَكْثَرَهُمْ تَابِعًا يَوْمَ الْقِيَامَةِ»

(There was not any Prophet except that he was given signs that caused men to believe. That which I have been given is a revelation that Allah has revealed to me, so I hope that I have the most followers among them (the Prophets) on the Day of Resurrection.) In this Hadith, the Prophet only mentioned the greatest of the signs that he was given, which is the Qur'an. However, he did have other miracles, which were innumerable and limitless. These miracles have all been recorded in the books that discuss them, and they have been affirmed in the places that mention them. Then Allah says,

(And if We had destroyed them with a torment before this, they would surely have said: "Our Lord! If only You had sent us a Messenger...") This means, "If We had destroyed these rejecting people before We sent this Noble Messenger to them and revealed the Mighty Book to them, they would have said,

(Our Lord! If only You had sent us a Messenger,) meaning, `before you destroyed us, so we could have believed in him and followed him.' This is like Allah said,

(we should certainly have followed Your Ayat, before we were humiliated and disgraced.) Allah, the Exalted, explains that these rejecters are stubborn and obstinate and they will not believe.

(Even if every sign should come them, until they see the painful torment.) (10:97) This is as Allah says,

(And this is a blessed Book which We have sent down, so follow it and have Taqwa (of Allah), that you may receive mercy.) Until His statement,

(because of their turning away.) (6:155-157) Allah also says,

(And they swore by Allah their most binding oath that if a warner came to them, they would be more guided than any of the nations (before them).) (35:42)

(And they swear their strongest oaths by Allah, that if there came to them a sign, they would surely believe therein.) (6:109) to the completion of those Ayat. Then, Allah says, (Say) "Say, O Muhammad, to those who deny you, oppose you and continue in their disbelief and obstinance."

(Each one is waiting,) among you and us; (so wait you too;) This is a command to await (anticipate). (and you shall know who are they that are on As-Sirat As-Sawi.) This means the straight road.

(And who are they that have let themselves be guided.) meaning guidance to the truth and the path of right guidance. This is similar to Allah's statement, (And they will know, when they see the torment, who it is that is most astray from the path!) (25:42) And Allah said,

(Tomorrow they will come to know who is liar, the insolent one!) (54:26) This is the end of the Tafsir of Surah Ta Ha, and all praise and gratitude is due to Allah. The Tafsir of Surat Al-Anbiya' will follow this, if Allah wills. And all praise and thanks are due to Allah.

www.ingramcontent.com/pod-product-compliance
Lightning Source LLC
Chambersburg PA
CBHW081110080526
44587CB00021B/3521